IN TWO VOLUMES

History of Ireland

By
Standish James O'Grady

VOLUME I

The Heroic Period

LEMMA PUBLISHING CORPORATION
NEW YORK
1970

HISTORY OF IRELAND

A Lemma Publishing Corporation Reprint Edition

This Lemma Publishing Corporation edition of
Standish James O'Grady's *History of Ireland,*
in two volumes, is an unabridged republication
of the first edition published in London,
1878–80

International Standard Book Number 0-87696-003-4
Library of Congress Catalog Card Number 78-112681

Published by
Lemma Publishing Corporation
509 Fifth Avenue
New York, N.Y. 10017

For Sale and Distribution only in the United States

Printed in U.S.A.

MAP OF IRELAND.
IN THE HEROIC TIMES.

The Moyle

Isle of Towers

from the House of Donn to Isle of Rachlin

Isle of Rachlin

Sea wandered over by the Children of Lear

Aula Mid Forest

Fomorians

Berry Galya

Plain of Ith

Rath Kimbay

Palace of Fergus Mac Roy

Children of Iar & the Clanna Rury

ULLA

The Red Cataract

Iorrus

Rath off Children of Lear

City of Emain Macha

Palace of Grielind

Mohiarna

Fomorians

Fir Bolgs

OLNEMACIA

THE MUIRNICT

Cruachalgan Coraints city

Fore of the Fomorians

also Fore of Pardio

now Ardae

Inver Colpa

The Brug on the Boyne

Four Plains of Ai

Rath Cruahan

Tara

also Bathair

Cro Tara

Emer's birth-place now Lusk

Bal-a-Clia

Palace of Dadarga

scene of Assassination

of Conairey Mor

Descendants of Conmac

Ath Son of Fergus Mac Roy

BREGIA

BORB

COOLAN

Children of Nonae

Friends of Cuchulain

Lake of Dove Oury

Fir Bolgs

Inver Amargin

Limerick

Children of Heber

LERMAN

Slieve Mary Dinn hie

FIR BOLGS

Cahirman

Caiseal

The Osrec

or Ossorians

Inver Slaney

North of Dunn

Slieve Mish

Descendants of Mer

son of Fergus Mac Roy

OON

Tamar na Eri Rien

The Rock of

no Iar Scene

Inver Scene

Harbour of Bera

Oilean Arda Nemed

Boru Lu

Descendants of Lewy Laidher

Son of Ith

Strand of Cliona

HISTORY OF IRELAND:

The Heroic Period.

BY

STANDISH O'GRADY.

"Names, deeds, grey legends, dire events, rebellions,
Majesties, sovran voices, agonies."

KEATS.

VOL. I.

LONDON:

SAMPSON LOW, SEARLE, MARSTON, & RIVINGTON,

CROWN BUILDINGS, FLEET STREET.

DUBLIN: E. PONSONBY, 116 GRAFTON STREET.

1878.

ERRATA.

Page 48, line 2 from bottom, *instead of* "worthy so glorious," *read* "worthy of a theme so glorious."

INTRODUCTION.

I HAD intended at first to let my book explain itself, but as I reflect on the unusualness of its form and character, I feel the advantages which would be derived from some introductory matter. If I appear sometimes to travel over ground covered by the text itself, this must be my excuse.

It is a common-place that the true function of the historian is to give a clear and vivid picture of the past; but, although the principle· is recognised in theory, it is practically set aside, and pure historical composition relegated to the novelist and romancer, whose audience, as they desire merely amusement, make no very stern demands on the veracity and historical faithfulness of the writer. In fact, the province of archæology has so extended its frontiers, as to have swallowed up the dominion of pure history altogether. Nearly every work which one takes up affecting to treat of the past in a rigid and conscientious spirit, is merely archæological. It is an accumulation of names, dates, events, disquisitions, the balancing of probabilities, the

a

testing of statements and traditions, categorical asser-
tions concerning laws and customs. All works of this
character are of the nature of archæology; they are the
material of history, not history itself.

Upon the foundations laid, with the materials provided, by the archæologian the historian builds. When
he has acquainted himself with all that the patient
toil of archæological investigation has amassed, he is
equipped for his work, and not till then. But surely,
no mere accumulation of facts only, no matter how
profound or exhaustive may have been the search whose
results he has laid up in his mind, is by itself to be
dignified by the name of history. Out of the sad leavings of the past, how can even the most cunning
mechanical arrangement evolve a living, adequate, affecting representation of the life of our ancestors.

In history, there must be sympathy, imagination,
creation. The sorry remnants discussed by the antiquarian, do not of themselves supply a picture. All
these the historian will study attentively, after which,
in proportion to his strength and truth of imagination,
a more or less faithful and vivid picture of that life of
which they are the relics, will impress itself on his
mind.

History is the flower of archæology; it justifies,
rewards, and crowns the obscure toil of those patient
and single-minded excavators into the buried past.

In the department of Pre-Norman Irish Archæology,

a generation of workers has passed away. The time has come for an embodiment in a fitting form of the results of their labours. The facts which they have accumulated, the obscurities which they dispelled, the amount of antique Irish literature which they have translated, the pregnant passages which they have collected out of the bardic writings, the number of forgotten heroes, events, characteristics—legal, social, and political—which they have brought to light, furnish such a mass of antiquarian knowledge as can supply the historian with ample materials for the reconstruction by imaginative processes of the life led by our ancestors in this country. Until this mass of information is popularised, and by being popularised, secured and appropriated, it is unlikely that any new surge of antiquarian enthusiasm will again ruffle the tranquil mind of the intellectual classes in Ireland. Until this mound of ore is smelted and converted into current coin of the realm, who will spend a lifetime in adding to those heaps which, as they stand to-day in their gaunt uselessness, almost justify the apathy with which they are regarded.

But how can the historian escape the introduction of elements into the period of which he treats, which it did not really contain, but which are only factors in his own mental and moral temperament, and of the age of which he himself is a part? Will not his own complexion colour all he writes? This is certainly the

case.   The most strenuous efforts will not keep his own
age and his own character altogether out of his work.
Even amongst the historical writers around me, who
affect to aim only at archæological results, and the
lucid arrangement of what has been discovered, I perceive their work dyed deep with the hues of their own
individuality.   There is this danger, indeed, this certainty of misrepresentation; but alas, there has yet
been discovered no photographic agency by which may
be depicted the actual life of our ancestors other than
that fallible and feeble instrument, the human imagination.   Yet this objection will lose some of its force by
a consideration of the nature of that period, which will
be represented in the present and succeeding volumes.

The forefront of Irish History we find filled with
great heroic personages of a dignity and power more
than human.   The age in which these heroes lived was
that which almost alone absorbed the attention of the
Irish bards.   Century after century the mind of the
country was inflamed by the contemplation of those
mighty beings whom, too, men believed to be their own
ancestors.   All the imaginative literature of the country
revolved round this period, was devoted to the glorifi-
cation of the gigantic figures with whom it was filled.

Naturally then, this heroic age was as it were a huge
bright mirror, in which were reflected the magnified
images of the bards themselves, and of the contemporary kings and heroes for whom they sang.   The value

of any, even the slightest characteristic of the heroic age, is, therefore, of the highest historic importance. The vastness and populousness of this age, which have been employed for the purpose of pointing derision at this country are really the best proof of the value of Irish antiquarian research; they indicate the enormous fecundity and force of the imagination of a people whose Pantheon was so great.

Now, it is not to be supposed that the heroes and events of this wonderful period are to be lightly passed over—a period which, like the visible firmament, was bowed with all its glory above the spirit of a whole nation. Those heroes and heroines were the ideals of our ancestors, their conduct and character were to them a religion, the bardic literature was their Bible. It was a poor substitute, one may say, for that which found its way into the island in the fifth century. That is so, yet such as it was under its nurture, the imagination and spiritual susceptibilities of our ancestors were made capable of that tremendous outburst of religious fervour and exaltation which characterised the centuries that succeeded the fifth, and whose effect was felt throughout a great portion of Europe. It was the Irish bards and that heroic age of theirs which nourished the imagination, intellect, and idealism of the country to such an issue. Patrick did not create these qualities. They may not be created. He found them, and directed them into a new channel.

The heroic period demands treatment, the very best and fullest that can be accorded to it. There is one mode in which it has been treated, and that I think the worst. All the names, dates, battles, events, births, deaths, genealogies, &c., have been set down in due order. In this treatment there is absolutely no advantage. One name is as good as another. Abracadabra is as good as Owen Mōr, if we are told naught concerning him than that he had a certain father and mother, fought certain battles, and died. Moreover, the archæological and scientific objections would apply to such a treatment with full force, namely, the unprovability of the statements so made.

The manner of Keating is different from this, and better, but not to my mind the best. Keating, following the old rationalistic compilers of the Irish chronicles, sets down in regular order the kings and heroes of ancient Eiré, and related concerning many of them, one or two of what seemed to him the most important anecdotes. Now, Keating believed that all this ancient bardic lore represented pure historic fact, which caused him to commit many grave errors, artistic and archæological, by which the value of his beautiful treatise is much impaired. Even his anecdotes lose their importance by being deprived of their substance, colour, and life, so that each under his handling has become the mere *residuum* and anatomy of the old bardic tale, whose essential elements he desired to represent.

Treating these tales as history, he attached no importance to those qualities which have alone value to me,
viz., the epic and dramatic.

But even pursued in this direction, a fuller and more
artistic treatment would not be satisfactory. No single
tale, however well adapted to the modern literary taste,
would form a complete and perfect representation of
any of the more important heroic personages or events.
Round each of the heroes revolves a whole cycle of
literature in prose and verse, and no treatment would
be adequate which did not take in this cycle in its completeness.

I now come to that treatment which has been sug-
gested by O'Curry, but the effect of which he did not
fully realise, viz., the narration of all the bardic tales
and fragments in connection with each hero and
heroine. Such a work is physically impossible, or if it
were effected, the result would not be satisfactory. The
bardic literature of ancient Erin would fill, perhaps, a
hundred volumes such as the present, When completed, the piled up mass would be without harmony,
meaning, or order. The valuable and the valueless
would be mingled together. It would be utterly incon-
dite, inorganic, and, I think, unreadable, except to
archæologians and the philosophical. A passage illus-
trating the character of a hero might be imbedded in a
tale concerning another, or in a note to a Christian
hymn, or in the life of a saint, or in some ancient

chronicle, dictionary, or legal treatise. Moreover, the genesis of these tales must be ascribed to peoples separated from one another by wide tracts of country and distances of time, so that contradiction and confusion are inevitable. The result would be a huge literary chaos, not a work of art, and this would be true even if the tales were reduced each to its pure epic elements. For instance, Tierna, the Abbot of Clonmacnoise, and a man thoroughly conversant, I think, with the heroic history, tells us that the greatest of the Irish heroes died young, yet there is extant a celebrated tale in which he is represented as contending in single combat with his own son.

The treatment which I have myself adopted consists in the reduction to its artistic elements of the whole of that heroic history taken together, viewing it always in the light shed by the discoveries of modern archæologians, frequently using the actual language of the bards, and as much as possible their style and general character of expression. The death of Conäirey Mōr is almost a literal transcript from the tale. Through the loose chaotic mass of bardic story and monkish chronicle, I have endeavoured to trace the mental and physical personality of the heroes and heroines in their essential elements, and to discover that order of events which best harmonises with the records and traditions of the poets, and the characters of the heroic personages. Hence it follows, that in order to be faithful

to the generic conception, one must disregard often the
literal statement of the bard. That the whole should be
fairly represented, one must do violence to the parts
upon which, indeed, no more violence can be wrought
than they inflict upon one another, perpetually diverg-
ing in detail, though in unison generally as to the main
idea of characters and events.

But there is another element than the merely epic
one in this volume, and which represents a great portion of our literary remains with an almost verbal
exactitude and precision.

The bardic mind affected a certain fastidiousness in
its mode of treating the heroic period. A conventional
set of ideas were deemed poetic, and all outside that
was unpoetic. We can see how some such traditions
clung around the mind of Homer. For instance, he
obstinately refuses to allude to writing of any sort, or to
horsemen other than drivers of chariots. The same
limitations, to a great extent, pervade the heroic literature of Ireland. There are many allusions to
Oghams, and inscribed tablets of wood, but the bards
would have us imagine that they never heard of a book
or a parchment. In the more ancient literature also
they do not allude to the riding of horses, nor to horses
at all in connection with Mac Cool and his Fenians.
From the bardic literature too, we would imagine that
there was not a wolf to be seen in ancient Ireland.

Now, in relating the heroic history, I have departed

wholly from the limited range of ideas permitted to themselves by the bards, and have introduced boldly the ancient civilisation of the country. In this part of my work I have preserved the closest adherence to the authorities. In all that relates to the material, social, political condition of the country, I believe that in this and the succeeding volumes will be found an accurate and faithful representation of the civilisation of ancient Ireland. In these volumes the heroic period reflects the actualities of the early historic times. I remember some remark of Horace to this effect, "Hence it happens that we see, as in a picture, all the life of the old man." This has been my object to represent, as in a picture, the state of society which obtained in this country in ancient times, which, though distant in one sense, are near in many others. It is the same sky that bent over them, which shines or darkens over us. The same human heart beat in their breasts as beats amongst us to-day. All the great permanent relations of life are the same. Therefore, I think I am also justified in treating that old heroic history in connection with the enduring facts of nature and of humanity. I do not like to contemplate that heroic age as vague, shadowy, and remote, and have not so contemplated it. Upon the realisation of the bards I have superadded a realisation more intense, working closer to those noble forms, whose outlines are more or less wavering and uncertain in the literature of the bards.

Nevertheless, the outlines are there, and in many an instance a flash of genius disperses altogether the mist for a moment, and lets us see the real hero. From these outlines I do not depart, where they appear with any consistency and definiteness. Yet when a whole nation is busy realising its heroes, it must follow that many an ignoble thought and tale will find its way into the preserved literature. The tales that are canonical and that are not must be determined. For instance, the tales told on pages 256 and 257 concerning both Cuculain and Emer strike down deep into the bardic conception of the characters of both. Nothing that interferes with these can be tolerated by the historian of the heroic period. We feel instinctively that they are essential, while we feel that others are not essential or wholly to be rejected. The nobler conception of any character, is, of course, to be preferred to the ignoble.

One of the most interesting features of early Irish civilisation, the religious feature, is also unfortunately the most obscure. In the absence of clear philosophical statements by the monks, we are obliged to fall back upon the tales and poems. The only monkish allusion to the Irish gods with which I have met, excepting another by St. Fiech, is one in Cormac's Glossary, where Ana is called the mother of the Irish gods, *mater deorum Hibernensium.* Now, if we had a sufficient quantity of pre-Christian Irish literature, there would be no loss sustained by the unfortunate reticence of the ecclesiastics; but this is not so. The bards were but the abstracts and brief chronicles of their own time, and in their hands the ancient tales and traditions varied from century to century, acquiring more and more a new complexion as the ages ran on. The consequence has been that, although all the Irish bardic tales revolve round the Pagan and heroic period, yet under the stress of the new faith the old distinction between gods and heroes was lost, and it is only here and there that we can see the differences that formerly obtained. For instance, in the battle of Moy Tura, Mac Erc, King of the Fir-bolgs, figures only as a mighty warrior, yet in the following ancient rann, discovered by Professor Sullivan, in what a different character does he appear :

> " Twice during the Treena of Tailteen,
> Each day at sunrise I invoked Mac Erc
> To remove from me the pestilence."

The chronicles follow the later tales, and the Fir-bolgs, as well as the Tuatha De Danan, are set down with circumstantial births and deaths; yet this single verse shows clearly the true character of Mac Erc as a great and powerful deity.

That the Tuatha De Danan were deities, is perfectly apparent to one who reads carefully the old tales and poems. In the tale called the Sick Bed of Cuculain, the Tuatha De Danan are also termed the Shee; and in St. Fiech's hymn, in honour of St. Patrick, St.

Fiech distinctly states, that in the old times the people *used to worship* the Shee. The term Fir-bolg has, however, acquired a very definite meaning, which we cannot forego, in the received accounts of early Irish history. It is applied generally to nations not of Milesian descent. The word itself means no more than giant.

When a complete collection and translation of all the bardic literature has been effected, I should not be surprised if we should be in a position to give a clear and intelligible description of all the occupants of the Irish Olympus.

The old heroic history is overlain and concealed, but much of it is still there. In the bardic account of the Milesian invasion, we find a multitude of ancient tales reduced to their essence, or rather their anatomies, and then poured pell-mell together. By looking closely into these relics, we see that the real history was something very different from that which the last redactor desired to represent. The materials which he employs tell a different tale.

There seems to have been a bardic golden age, as well as one of brass, or even earth. The advent of Christianity ruined the bards. The missionaries felt instinctively that the bards were their enemies. The praise of gods and demi-gods, and of heroes who were favoured and helped by these, was the theme of the bards. The

degradation of the bardic class was therefore essential
to the success of the missionaries. Both could not live
in the same country. On the two occasions on which
St. Columba refers to the bards, he speaks of them as
homunculi, and on one of these he alludes disrespect-
fully to their art. On a third occasion, he is represented as snubbing the chief poet of Ulster, when he
addressed to him a laudatory poem. In fact, St.
Columba silenced him after the first line.

The consequence was that as the missionaries grew
powerful, the bards declined, descending in every generation lower and lower in the social scale. The relations at first subsisting between them are reversed.
St. Patrick, and his compeers and fellow-missionaries,
seem to have been rude, uneducated men. Their Latin
is rude, clumsy, and ungrammatical. His own compo-
sitions are so bad, that they have been considered
forgeries; but his pupil, St. Sechnall, was quite as
illiterate. In the same age, Duvac Mac Ua Luhair,
the chief poet of the King of Leinster, composed two
magnificent Irish poems—bold, glowing, energetic, and
even sublime. On the other hand, in the time of
Adamnan, three centuries later, the monks had per-
fected a splendid Latin style, enriched with contribu-
tions from the Greek and Hebrew, and giving the
reader the ᶴimpression that they were the intellectual
lords of the land. In the bardic literature of this

period, we look in vain for anything which might be considered in profane literature the equivalent of " The Life of St. Columba."

In fact, the positions of the contending parties had been reversed. The bards now amused only farmers and tradesmen, while the monks crowned kings, and trained the minds of princes. The consequence was, that secular literature did not flourish, or flourished only in the monasteries, where it was not the chief thing, but an ornament of the monastic mind. The generous tribute paid to the chief hero of the Red Branch by the Abbot of Clonmacnoise, proves not only the growth of a scientific and secular spirit in the monasteries, but also, I think, the complete collapse and prostration of the bardic class. Otherwise, it is unlikely that the monks would have affected to perceive the grandeur of the heroic period. We perceive, also, traces of an union between the two modes of thought in the statement of St. Fiech, that the Tuatha of Erin, *i.e.,* the gods, used to prophesy the reign of a new faith, and certain stories of favourite personages of the heroic period announcing the approach of Christianity, or in other ways brought into connection with the Christian idea. Cuculain, borne in his fairy. chariot over the City of Emain Macha, with his steeds trampling the winds, announces from on high to the weeping people the coming of the Talkend. Concobar Mac Nessa is informed of the death of Christ by one Altus, a Roman centurion, and loses his life in the fit of wrath which the account produces.

As we examine closely the bardic tales, we will see traces of the same transformation. There are clearly marked vestiges of a golden age of bardic composition in the existing tales. In the midst of flat wordy prose, vulgar in tone, and barbarous in construction, are embedded perfect gems of bardic verse, clear, noble, and pathetic. To work back into the elder vein of thought and feeling as much as possible, has been my object in the composition of the history. I have in the present volume no more than adumbrated the hierarchy of the Irish gods. In a future volume I shall pursue this subject more in detail.

If it be asked whether the principal characters of the heroic age really existed, I would myself answer that they certainly did. I have the strongest belief in the incapacity of the uncivilised mind to create imaginary characters, or to discover a personality in the various beautiful or sublime aspects of nature. The Wordsworthian notion of the genesis of the gods and fairies, I think quite incorrect. I believe that all the characters in the present volume really existed, and had more or less the general attributes with which they are invested. Hardly was the mighty barrow piled above the charred relics of the hero, than he started forth to run a new career of glory in the imagination of his people; a career whose goal was a serene god-hood; but the first impressions left upon their minds by his actual life, though heightened, were not destroyed. I cannot help thinking that whether the local hero became a national hero, or advanced to the dignity of a god, depended very much on the size of the barrow that concealed his bones. But, indeed, such a notion one ought to be ashamed of entertaining; yet, too, the mound of Achilles is the highest of those that cluster upon that ancient cemetery called Ilium.

I desire to qualify considerably those passages in which I speak of the old bardic tales as romances. They are by no means correctly so designated. Romance is a product of civilisation, and belongs to a luxurious and leisured age. The bardic tales were to our ancestors genuine history, and implicitly believed in. In their genesis there was never anything like conscious creation.

As I have excluded from my book all traces of investigation and inquiry, I must leave to others the task of justifying me, or undertake it myself in a separate volume. I had some thought of doing this in foot-notes, but to do so adequately, would need considerable space, and a greater amount of printed matter than is comprised in the text itself.

A considerable number of strange words will be

A

found whose meaning, I think, will be generally discovered by the context.

I have taken the great liberty of spelling proper names in the way in which an ordinary reader would best arrive at the correct pronunciation.

STANDISH O'GRADY.

CONTENTS.

xxii   *Contents.*

HISTORY OF IRELAND.

CHAPTER I.

THE PRIME.

" Worlds on worlds are rolling ever,
From creation to decay,
Like the foam-flakes on the river,
Bubbling, bursting, borne away."

SHELLEY.

OF planetary epochs, the Eocene and Meiocene have slowly receded into the past, their huge cycles having been accomplished, and the Pleistocene, with new tribes of animals, and amongst them one destined to the mastery of the rest, is advancing over North-Western Europe. The uncouth monsters to whom Cuvier and others have affixed names as uncouth as themselves, have disappeared. The hipparion, a delicate equine creature, will not dart through the woods any more. The mastodon, both that which made its den in the woods, and that which housed itself in caves, will not shake the earth again. The stag of Polignac, the early field-bear, the megatherium, the trogotherium, are all gone. The pleisiosauros, king of the lizard tribe, will not enjoy the heat of the sun any more. His horrid length he has committed to the safe-keeping of the mud, that will one day be marble. In due time he will be disinterred, and assigned an honourable place in the museum. The two first cycles of the modern geological era have passed away. Time, the old scene-shifter, alters the world's stage, a new act begins, and new actors appear.

Pleistocene Europe was not what it is at the present day. There was then no Mediterranean inlet from the Atlantic. There were then no British isles. Between Africa and Europe there was communication at two points : Algiers met Spain at Gibraltar, and where there is now a strait, there was then an isthmus ; from the toe of Italy to Sicily, and from that to Morocco, ran a broad belt of land, dividing the Mediterranean into two great lakes. In the Pleistocene epoch, the Thames, the Rhine, and the Elbe were but tributaries of a mighty river that flowed northward, draining the great plain between England and Scandinavia, over which roll now the waves of the German Ocean. This mighty stream, receiving the Humber and the Forth in its course, emptied itself into the Arctic Ocean hundreds of miles to the north of Scotland. Then the Suir, the Nore, and the Barrow, uniting their waters with the Bandon and the Lee, flowed southwards till they met the Seine, by whom they were borne on to the Atlantic, into which they poured their giant waters many miles to the south-west of what we now term Cape Clear. Then the Liffey, running eastward, met the Mersey from England and the Clyde from Scotland, and uniting, ran northward, till their combined current met the Arctic waters many miles beyond the remotest of the Isles of Orc.

Such was North-Western Europe when it was first occupied by man, such the region out of which Ireland was carved.

As the mastadon and his brood of earth-shaking and reptile brethren disappeared, new tribes of living creatures began to swarm up from the south and down from the north. With the varying temperature altered too the kinds of animals that took possession of these countries. Sometimes the thick-skinned rhinoceros would wander up this way from his African haunts; at others his woolly cousin would wander down from Siberia or Scandinavia, and with him the musk-sheep and the deer of the northern latitudes. In the hyena caves lie mingled pell-mell the bones of animals native to the torrid and to the frozen zones.

And now, too, came the Irish elk, whose raised antlers stood twenty feet from the ground—came the mammoth, with long curving tusks and flowing mane that swept the ground—came the cave-bear, the fox, and the wolf— the bison still wild in America, the urus still preserved in Germany—came the primitive horse with his enormous head, the lion, and tiger, and hyenas in their troops hunting down both lion and tiger, when no grass-eating animals were to be had—new varieties of deer and of elephants, the wild boar, and a strange brute half lion half tiger, with broad flat tusks notched like a saw along the edges, his name machœrodus or sabre-tooth. And now, too, came another animal not yet extinct nor like to be until the planet itself becomes uninhabitable. Sabre-tooth did not slay him; he escaped the banded hyenas; and to-day he examines the serrated edges of sabre-tooth's great tusks, and carries the hyena from village to village as a curiosity.

CHAPTER II.

GLACIALIS IERNE.

" The crawling glaciers pierce me with the spears
Of their moon-freezing crystals, the bright chains
Eat with their burning cold into my bones."

SHELLEY.

DURING the Pleistocene epoch, and prior to the arrival of
man in this portion of the world, owing, as is supposed,
to a violent eccentricity of the earth's orbit, the ice
and snow of the Arctic regions invaded Europe. The
cold was still further intensified by the contemporaneous divergence of the course of the Gulf Stream.
The severe heat of ensuing summers, which was one of
the consequences of that eccentricity, was powerless to
melt to any great extent the ice and snow which had so
far transcended their normal bounds. The raised mists
stood thick and dense above the ice, down to which the
struggling sunbeams could not penetrate. Year by year
the ice frontier crept steadily downward. Rain-clouds
from the south wafted northwards, deposited their
humid burthens, in the form of snow and hail, in those
cold latitudes, upon the gradually extending Arctic do-
mains.

The warm atmosphere which had produced the rich
vegetation of the earlier Pleistocene epoch was now growing every year more cold. The tropical animals disappeared altogether from North-Western Europe, and
creatures of Arctic origin began to occupy these regions

as their natural habitation. The mammoth, the woolly rhinoceros, and the reindeer became more and more frequent, and each winter stayed a longer season, as the highlands became more and more capped with perpetual snow. It was now, too, that man made his appearance in this portion of the world. The rough stone arrow-heads and knives which are discovered in the deeper strata of the caves were dropped there by a people which came into Europe with the great and permanent invasion of the Arctic animals, who stayed here as long as they, and who retreated at the same time. This people descended into Europe because the growing cold had driven them southwards, and because the animals upon whom they lived were moving southwards too, and they retreated from Europe, either because the growing heat drove them northwards, together with the animals which formed their subsistence, or because they were expelled by the advent of new races of man, who, as the frost powers retreated to the north, took gradual possession of the whole of Europe.

As the climate of these countries grew colder, the forms of vegetation native to warm and temperate climates died away, and their places were taken by the hardy lichens of the north. Year by year the winter snow upon the hill-tops lasted longer into the spring, until at last upon our highlands there was no thaw, and the mountains were capped with perpetual snow.

And now, as century succeeded century, and the ice increased in mass and stretched down into the plains, great glaciers, huge rivers of slow-moving ice, began to push down into the valleys, making for the low-lands and the sea. Glaciers, moving slowly over the whole face of the country for many thousands of years, have left behind universal and indelible traces. Plains were scooped and hollowed out, and the substance borne onward by the ice was deposited far away at the point at which the thaw had dissolved the ice and strewn the boulder clay and stones over the ground. The tops of the mountains were worn away and polished as with fine sand-paper, their bases grooved and chiselled by the abrading power of the ice. What happens to-day in Switzerland happened then over Ireland and all North-Western Europe—in summer mighty torrents, the solution of snow and ice, and in winter long, crawling glaciers, planing down the country, polishing the mountains. At last the ice became too vast and the climate too cold to admit any thaw, the hardiest of the Arctic animals and plants were obliged to disappear; the seal-hunters passed southwards into France and Spain, and the whole of this country, which we now call Ireland, was buried under a dense and impenetrable incubus of ice. The ignorant epithet of the Roman writer was then ndeed deserved, when even the Eskimo and the reindee had to flee from her icy coasts. She was then indeed Glacialis Ierne.

CHAPTER III.

MEN OF THE ICE-PERIOD.

" Who believe that in all ages
    Every human heart is human,
    That in even savage bosoms
    There are longings, yearnings, strivings,
    For the good they comprehend not,
    That the feeble hands and helpless
    Groping blindly in the darkness
    Touch God's right hand in the darkness."

                    LONGFELLOW.

THE man of the ice-period was the antique representative of the modern Eskimo, if not actually his progenitor. He was short, flat-faced, and prognathous. He was filthy, brutish, and a cannibal. Fishing and hunting formed his occupation. The divine command to till the earth and to eat of the fruits thereof had not been enjoined upon his ancestors, or had not been obeyed, nor yet did he drive about flocks and herds, leading a nomadic and pastoral life, and subsisting on the milk of cows or mares. No gentle domestic animals roamed around his house. The wolf was still untamed. No watch-dog's honest bark greeted him as he drew near home.

Ignorant, filthy, and brutish as was this ancient man, yet him, too, the gods had visited. Prometheus and Apollo had taught him many arts by which he might mitigate the cruelty of the frost powers. The divine theft had brought a blessing upon him too. He knew how to kindle a fire, and supply himself with the warmth which the climate denied.

To the potter's art he had not attained. When he desired to boil his food, a deer-skin was his pot, into which, filled with melted snow, he dropped red hot stones until the flesh was cooked.

He had his needles of bone and thread of gut, and made raiment for himself out of skins.

When he desired to build, he sought a ravine where the snow lay deep. Removing the surface out of the compact snow beneath, he, with his stone hatchet, hewed bricks or slabs out of the solid snow. With these he built his habitation, shaped like a beehive, with door, and a window of transparent ice. Inside, all along the white walls, ran banks of snow, upon which were thrown skins, and upon these the family lay and slept.

In a French cave, in the strata of the Pleistocene era, has been found the shoulder-blade of an animal, upon which is graved with some pointed instrument a fine representation of the mammoth, and also another of the primitive horse. There, too, has been found a piece of horn, carved into the shape of a deer's head, with branching antlers, executed with faithfulness and spirit.

Deep in the recesses of the caves we learn the history and life of this ancient people. The excavation of a few feet reveal articles manufactured under the sway and genius of Rome. Below these we find the iron and bronze implements of the half-civilized predecessors of the Romans. Another descent brings to light the flint tools of the Neolithic and Palæolithic times. Then come the marks of the great submergence, and below them the tools of this people who, more than two hundred thousand years ago, lived and died upon the plains of Ireland. Below these again, and upon the basement of this strange house—this eternal refuge of the homeless—lie the pulverized or demi-pulverized relics of the vast cycles, huge and obscure, that preceded the advent of man. They are the annals of the world, tome above tome, in that strange library.

CHAPTER IV.

IERNE REDIVIVA.

"So sinks the day-star in the ocean-bed,
And yet anon repairs his drooping head,
And tricks his beams, and with new-spangled ore
Flames in the forehead of the morning sky."
MILTON.

IRELAND lies now buried beneath a load of impenetrable ice. Man, animals, and plants have been gradually driven southwards into France and Spain before the steady and insupportable advance of the frost-powers. But now another huge alteration began to take place. North-Western Europe descended gradually into the sea. As with a vast millennial suspiration, the earth's bosom fell. Steadily as the land sank the sea rose. Thus, as Great Britain and Ireland are but the highlands of a great plateau, a time arrived at which the rest of the plateau being submerged, the British Isles appeared on the breast of the Atlantic in the same form that they present to-day. But the huge suspiration had not yet ceased. Still deeper the earth sank, still higher the waters rose, till at last only the tops of the mountains showed here and there, and all Ireland was rolled over by the waves of the Atlantic.

But the end was not yet. Ireland, tenanted only by shell-fish and sea-weeds, above which the whale wallowed

and the frequent iceberg sailed, was destined to ascend
from her watery grave into the light of the sun, to be a
a joyful home of men and animals, and to play her part
in the great drama of the world. That vast planetary
suspiration ceased, an inspiration as vast commenced,
and North-Western Europe rose again slowly, millennium
after millennium, inch by inch, through the centuries,
rose even to the height of the early Pleistocene epoch,
and then subsided once more to the point at which the
historic period found her.

All this time the frost-powers still reigned. Ireland
but emerged from the water to be buried under a still
more barren incubus of ice. But at last their cruel
grasp began to grow faint ; genial influences from the
south penetrated northwards ; the solid and irrefragable
ice yielded to glaciers and summer torrents ; vegetation
re-appeared and animals ; the reindeer returned and the
Eskimo ; milder and milder still grew the climate, till
the glaciers and Arctic animals in their turn became
things of the past, till the plains were clothed with grass,
and great forests roughened the face of the country.
Glacialis Ierne had passed away, and Inis na Veeva appeared upon the liquid surface of the sea, bearing a soil
fit for the dent of spade and ploughshare. A new and
nobler race of men were now advancing from the south
and east. It was not Nemeth and his tribe, or the lady
Kasār, or Partholanus, the ill-starred. Civilization and
the means of recording their history they did not bring
with them. The annals of the cave do not tally with
those of the Four Masters. The Book of Invasions is
contradicted by silent witnesses out of the earth. The
Lowr Gawla must be re-written, and the time-honoured
traditions of the bards interpreted after a new method.

It was no branch of Scythic stock, no Aryan-speaking people, who now swarmed over these countries, but a dark, small, oval-faced race, between whom and the tall, fierce, blue-eyed Celt there was neither kinship nor resemblance.

CHAPTER V.

THE DISPERSION.

" A multitude, like which the populous north
　Poured never from her frozen loins to pass
　Rhene or the Danaw, when her barbarous sons
　Came like a deluge from the north, and spread
　Beneath Gibraltar to the Lybian sands."

MILTON.

THE earth is inhabited by eight distinct races of man— the Australian, the Negrito, the Maorie, the Red Indian, the Eskimo, and the African, the Mongol, the Scythian, and the Turanian. The Australian, with fine dark wavy hair and chocolate-coloured skin; the Negrito, of like complexion, but with woolly hair; the Red Indian, broad-headed, olive-skinned, with black eyes and coarse black hair; the Eskimo (perhaps a variety of the Indian), short-headed and stunted; the Mongol, round-headed, flat-nosed, slant-eyed, low of stature, broad faced, with black eyes and straight black hair; the Scythian, tall, fair-haired, blue-eyed, round-headed; the Turanian,* well-proportioned, long-headed, brown-skinned, oval-

---

* The reader will remember that the names used in this chapter are employed in a broad physical signification, having no reference to the linguistic distribution of mankind. The needed terminology not having been yet invented, necessitates the employment of a questionable name-system.

faced, with large dark eyes and soft wavy hair. With these two last lies the future of the world.

Russia was the vast nest of the fair-haired races, the heart from which, as in strong pulsations, were jetted forth those great Celtic and other migrations to desolate the world. It was that frozen north which, throughout early historic periods, and through the darkness that preceded the known birth of letters, poured forth her multitudes under their sea-kings and shepherd-kings, their Vikings and their Hyksos, to submerge for a season all that the thought and toil of nobler nations had produced.

From Southern Asia, perhaps from that classic plain eastward in Eden, the Turanian emerged upon the world, thence he spread eastward till he met the Mongol, and southward till stopped by the Malayan coming up from the isles of the Indian Sea; westward along the shores of the Mediterranean, over all Egypt and Barbary, over Phœnicia and Greece and Italy, over Spain, France, Belgium, and the British Isles. Here the Turanian stream, pouring from the south, ship-borne perhaps, and curving round to overflow Northern Europe, was met by the Scythian flood pouring through Germany into France, and through Scandinavia and the Baltic into the British Isles.

From the Scythian stock shot forth branches—over Europe, the Cymri, the Gael, and the Teuton, the Norseman, and the Sclave, with their many families; and over Asia the terrible name of the Tartar, that ever-impending deluge, banked in by the Caspian, the Balkan, and the Steppes, around the Sea of Aral, but ever and anon bursting its barriers, and under some Timour or Ghengiz Khan, flooding all Southern Asia, and obliterating for a season every vestige of civilization.

From the Turanian stock shot forth branches, not barren. In Asia, the Hindoo, the Arabian, and the Zend, the Assyrian, the Phœnician, and the Jew. Further west, the Pelasgian of Greece, the Etruscan of Italy, and in a less pure form the Hellene and the Roman, the Carthaginian, the forgotten Berber, and the Basque.

Of these two mighty divisions of the human race it seems to have been the special task of the latter to found civilizations, and of the former to crush them. They founded the splendid civilizations of Babel, Nineveh, and Babylon, and the Scythians crushed them ; of the Pelasgian Greeks and Italians, and the Scythians crushed them. Slowly and laboriously they built up the splendid and pacific empire of the Romans, in which, as in a field ploughed and watered, the seeds of all that was noble and lovely were quietly germinating towards a new spring. It too was broken into fragments, and trampled beneath the hoofs of a brutish multitude from the north. For a thousand years the silt and slime of that huge deluge overlay the budding germs of civilization, and the naked horror of sensuality, ignorance, and martial law was laid bare. Good things of day began to droop and drowse, and night's black bird made wing for the leafy woods. To this day the wrecks and fragments of that noble empire are hurled against each other upon a restless and barren ocean of war or preparation of war. The gripe of the Vandal is still in the throat of Europe.

It is one of the colossal misapprehensions of history, and one which owes its origin to the uncandid egotism of our northern writers, that the exhausted populations of the south were refreshed and invigorated by the young warlike blood of the north. The Cimmerian regions, until they were touched by the quickening contact of the south, bred nought but ignorance, slow melancholy, and war. The peoples whom the father of history beheld upon their knees worshipping the naked sword, seem to have been absolutely incapable of raising themselves without assistance out of the primæval welter. The renaissance and modern civilization made their way through the silt and mire of that northern deluge, in spite of Cimmerian influences, and not through their help. Else how comes it that through the length and breadth of that vast Aryan land, from the Isles of Britain to the Great Wall of China and the extremities of Kamschatka, we light nowhere upon any trace of the civilization which, upon the theory of chances, their young warlike blood must at least somewhere have succeeded in establishing, somewhere the birth of a noble piety, somewhere the invention of letters, somewhere the existence of beautiful manners and a true theory of life. We do not ask for any sublime ruins upon the Baltic comparable to those which fill men's eyes with tears as they travel through Southern Italy and along the shores of the Levant. We ask for no Republican Tartary, with multitudinous free states pouring their light like stars upon the dark turmoil of the mediæval night, with some pile-built Venice on the Sea of Aral, bright Lucifer of the glittering flock; we crave but some slight proof of some slight indigenous civilization, some echo of a strain sweeter to the ear than the howl of the wolf and the war-cry of the Sclave. We look and listen in vain. There is none. Whatever may have been the capacities of the northern peoples and their latent aptitudes, it was with the Mediterranean and Semitic peoples that civilizations have had their origin.

CHAPTER VI.

BASQUE AND CELT.

" Dark blue eyes that glanced,
Drooped o'er by lashes chaffer-black."

ANCIENT BARD.

THE Irish are a mixed race, the Basque and the Celt
went to their formation. The original inhabitants of
the country were Basque, but successive Celtic invasions
obliterated the ancient Basque language, and altered the
physical appearance of the people. In this respect the
history of Ireland, and indeed of all North-Western
Europe, resembles that of Greece. In the times of
which Homer sang, the Greek nobles had yellow hair and
blue eyes. At the time when the heroic literature of
Ireland was composed, the Irish nobles had yellow hair
and blue eyes. Athene seized Achilles by the yellow
locks, while she herself was a blue-eyed goddess. Crimthann, who held in check the rebellious sons of Cathair
More for Conn of the Hundred Battles, was surnamed
Culboy, because the smelted gold was not yellower than
his hair; while the locks of Cuculain, the great Ultonian
hero, were yellower than the blossom of the sovarchy.
On the other hand, the historic Greeks resembled physically the Italians, and were equally with them surprised
at the tall stature and fierce blue eyes of the northern
warriors, while in Irish bardic literature the lower orders
are represented as dark. The history of both countries
was the same. The aborigines, a dark Turanian

people, were conquered and submerged by successive
Celtic invasions, until their language was lost in that of
their conquerors. The purest type of Irish beauty has
been produced by this blending of races. We often see
in Ireland, and not elsewhere, blue eyes fringed with
lashes as black as jet, a pure clear skin through which
glows the warmth of southern blood.

Herodotus found lingering in the heart of the Pelo-
ponnesus a people speaking a tongue which he could not
comprehend. The modern philologist finds in one portion of Europe a people speaking a tongue which he
cannot connect with any of the Aryan dialects of Europe.
The language of the Basque Provinces of Spain shows
like the solitary peak of a world long since submerged.
More than half of Europe is Turanian, yet the ancient
language is now spoken only in that small district.
Whether any and what words of Basque origin linger
still in the Gælic speech is a question whose solution
has not been yet accomplished.

The ancient Basque was of small stature, but appears
to have amply atoned for his deficiency in size. His
head was long, or what is termed boat-shaped, his countenance oval, features regular, and teeth small, his eyes
dark and soft, and his skin brown. The Celts, on the
other hand were tall and large-limbed, with fierce gray
and blue eyes, high cheek bones, and large teeth. The
Celt was the foremost wave of the Scythic tide of European invasion. The Basques played the same part in
the Turanian.

The received theory of the colonization of Europe is
evidently untrue. According to this theory a single race
styled the Indo-European, having its cradle in Armenia,
issued forth from thence upon all sides, and overspread

every portion of Europe and Asia, in which are spoken
any of those languages which can be connected with the
Sanskrit. Of late, however, it struck some minds not
so simple as the rest, that if this theory were correct, it
would prove that the Negroes of the United States were
Englishmen.

At what time the Basques took possession of Ireland
cannot be determined with accuracy. It is, however,
certain that they were in France three thousand years
before the birth of Christ. Unlike their predecessors,
they were an agricultural and pastoral people. From
Asia they brought with them the sheep, the horse, the
dog, the donkey, the goat, and the cow which is known
in Ireland as the Kerry, and among savants as the
Celtic shorthorn.

They buried their dead in caves and sepulchral
chambers. Over their great people they raised a high
tumulus, not round like those of the Celt, but oblong.
Unacquainted with iron or bronze, they yet knew how to
smelt gold. Their tools and weapons were made of flint
which they ground sharp, and polished to a remarkable
smoothness and lustre.

It is an error to term either the Basque or the earlier
Eskimo Troglodytes, *i.e.*, cave-dwellers. We would,
with as much reason, term the Romanized Britons
cave-dwellers, because Roman arms and implements are
discovered in the English caves. That they *sometimes*
used them as dwelling-places is all that can be inferred.
The perpetual damp, the fewness of natural caves, the
difficulty of digging or quarrying artificial ones, and, on
the other hand, the abundance of timber and the ease
with which booths and timber-houses might be constructed by a people so intelligent and advanced, neces-

c

sitate the conclusion that their houses were made of this material, and that they did not live from choice in earth-holes like vermin.

Among minor characteristics of this race it may be mentioned that the length of the head was caused by the development of the occiput, the forehead being vertical, that the shin-bone exhibits a peculiar flattened form, termed platycnemic, and which is supposed to have been caused by the habit of walking bare-footed during many generations. Also a peculiar osseous ridge ran along the thigh bone from the hip down to the knee, not found in other races.

CHAPTER VII.

DAWN.

" Apparelled in celestial light,
The glory and the freshness of a dream."

WORDSWORTH.

THERE is not, perhaps, in existence a product of the human mind so extraordinary as the Irish annals. From a time dating more than two thousand years before the birth of Christ, the stream of Milesian history flows down uninterrupted, copious and abounding, between accurately defined banks, with here and there picturesque meanderings, here and there flowers lolling upon those delusive waters, but never concealed in mists, or lost in a marsh. As the centuries wend their way, king succeeds king with a regularity most gratifying, and fights no battle, marries no wife, begets no children, does no doughty deed of which a contemporaneous note was not taken, and which has not been incorporated in the annals of his country. To think that this mighty fabric of recorded events, so stupendous in its dimensions, so clean and accurate in its details, so symmetrical and elegant, should be after all a mirage and delusion, a gorgeous bubble, whose glowing rotundity, whose rich hues, azure, purple, amethyst and gold, vanish at a touch and are gone, leaving a sorry remnant over which the patriot disillusionized may grieve.

Early Irish history is the creation mainly of the bards. Romances and poems supplied the great blocks with which the fabric was reared. These the chroniclers fitted into their places, into the interstices pouring shot, rubbish, and grouting. The bardic intellect, revolving round certain ideas for centuries, and round certain material facts, namely, the mighty barrows of their ancestors, produced gradually a vast body of definite historic lore, life-like kings and heroes, real-seeming queens. The mechanical intellect followed with perspicuous arrangement, with a thirst for accuracy, minuteness, and verisimilitude. With such quarrymen and such builders the work went on apace, and anon a fabric huge rose like an exhalation, and like an exhalation its towers and pinnacles of empurpled mist are blown asunder and dislimn.

Doubtless the legendary blends at some point with the historic narrative. The cloud and mist somewhere condense into the clear stream of indubitable fact. But how to discern under the rich and teeming mythus of the bards, the course of that slender and doubtful rivulet, or beneath the piled rubbish and dust of the chroniclers, discover the tiny track which elsewhere broadens into the highway of a nation's history. In this minute, circumstantial, and most imposing body of history, where the certain legend exhibits the form of plain and probable narrative, and the certain fact displays itself with a mythical flourish, how there to fix upon any one point and say here is the first truth. It is a task perilous and perplexing.

Des Cartes commenced his investigations into the nature of the soul by assuming the certainty of his own existence. Standing upon this adamantine foot-hold, he sought around him for ground equally firm, which should support his first step in the quagmire of metaphysics. But in the early Irish history, what one solid and irrefutable fact appears upon which we can put foot or hand and say, " This, at all events, is certain ; this that I hold is not mist ; this that I stand on is neither water nor mire" ? Running down the long list of Milesian kings, chiefs, brehons, and bards, where first shall we pause, arrested by some substantial form in this procession of empty ghosts—how distinguish the man from the shadow, where over all is diffused the same concealing mist, and the eyes of the living and the dead look with the same pale glare ? Yeoha of the heavy sighs, how shall we certify or how deny the existence of that melancholy man, or of Tiernmas, who introduced the worship of fire ? Lara of the ships, did he really cross the sea to Gaul, and return thence to give her name to Leinster, and beget Leinster kings ? Ugainey More, did he rule to the Torrian sea, holding sea-coast towns in fee, or was he a pre-historic shadow thrown into the past from the stalwart figure of Nial of the Hostages ? Was Morann a real brehon, or fabulous as the collar that threatened to strangle him in the utterance of unjust judgments ? Was Ferkeirtney a poet, having flesh and bones and blood, and did Bricrind, the satirist, really compose those bitter ranns for the Ultonians ? or were both as ghostly as the prime druid, Amergin, who came into the island with the sons of Milesius, and in a manner beyond all praise, collected the histories of the conquered peoples ? Or do we wrong that venerable man whose high-sounding name clung for ages around the estuary of the Oboka.

One thing at all events we cannot deny—that the national record is at least lively. Clear, noble shapes of kings and queens, chieftains, brehons, and bards gleam in the large rich light shed abroad over the triumphant progress of the legendary tale. We see Dúns snow-white with roofs striped crimson and blue, chariots, cushioned with noble skins, with bright bronze wheels and silver poles and yokes. The lively-hearted, resolute steeds gallop past, bearing the warrior and his charioteer with the loud clangour of rattling spears and darts. As in some bright young dawn, over the dewy grass, and in the light of the rising sun, superhuman in size and beauty, their long, yellow hair curling on their shoulders, bound around the temples with torcs of gold, clad in white linen tunics, and loose brattas of crimson silk fastened on the breast with huge wheel-brooches of gold, their long spears musical with running rings ; with naked knees and bare crown, they cluster round their kings, the chieftains and knights of the heroic age of Ireland.

The dawn of history is like the dawn of the day. The night of the pre-historic epoch grows rare, its dense weight is relaxed ; flakes of fleeting and uncertain light wander and vanish ; vague shapes of floating mist reveal themselves, gradually assuming form and colour ; faint hues of crimson, silver, and gold strike here and there, and the legendary dawn grows on. But the glory of morn, though splendid, is unsubstantial; the glory of changing and empurpled mist—vapours that conceal the solid face of nature, the hills, trees, streams, and the horizon, holding between us and the landscape a concealing veil, through whose close woof the eye cannot penetrate, and over all a weird strange light.

In the dawn of the history of all nations we see this deceptive light, these glorious and unearthly shapes; before Grecian history, the gods and demigods who fought around Ilium; before Roman, the strong legends of Virginius and Brutus : in the dawn of Irish history the Knights of the Red Branch, and all the glory that surrounded the Court of Concobar Mac Nessa, High King of the Ultonians.

But of what use these concealing glories, these cloudy warriors, and air-built palaces ? Why not pass on at once to credible history ?

A nation's history is made for it by circumstances, and the irresistible progress of events ; but their legends, they make for themselves. In that dim twilight region, where day meets night, the intellect of man, tired by contact with the vulgarity of actual things, goes back for rest and recuperation, and there sleeping, projects its dreams against the waning light and before the rising of the sun.

The legends represent the imagination of the country; they are that kind of history which a nation desires to possess. They betray the ambition and ideals of the people, and, in this respect, have a value far beyond the tale of actual events and duly recorded deeds, which are no more history than a skeleton is a man. Nay, too, they have their own reality. They fill the mind with an adequate and satisfying pleasure. They present a

rhymthic completeness and a beauty not to be found in
the fragmentary and ragged succession of events in time.
Achilles and Troy appear somehow more real than
Histiœus and Miletus; Cuculain and Emain Macha
than Brian Boromh and Kincoráh.

CHAPTER VIII.

SUPREMACY.

" Me quoque vicinis pereuntem gentibus, inquit,
Munivit Stilichon totam cum Scotus Iernen
Movit et infesto spumavit remige Tethys. "

CLAUDIAN.

THE mechanical intellect does not appear to depend upon
circumstances for its vigour and effectiveness, but the
imagination is never strong unless under conditions
most favourable, for hope and joy are essential to its free
and daring exercise. The inspired history of the Penta-
teuch will be found to be the creation of the Hebrew
mind, wrought upon by the conquests of David, the glory
of Solomon, and the consolidation of the scattered tribes.
The Iliad was the creation of the Greek mind during or
after a great military career. The Hellenes had conquered Greece and the Ægean Islands, and filled their
home with Asiatic plunder. Then came Homer and the
Cyclic poets, and Achilles was revealed. In Ireland, too,
the Heroic age was the creation of the Irish mind, at a
time when Scotic influence was felt over North-Western
Europe, when an Irish king holding the Picts in fee devastated England, and filled his country with the plunder
of the Continent. The warlike spirit of the people was

high, the imagination aflame, the national idea had laid hold upon the Irish mind. It was a single nation that inhabited all Ireland and the west of Scotland, and tributary to a single chief. This was the age in which were created the national heroes of ancient Eiré—the Knights of the Red Branch, the Monarchs of Tara, and behind them, looming over all, the Fianna Eireen, the Tuatha De Danan, and the Titanic Firbolgs.

The pictures drawn, the ideals conceived, the history elaborated in a great age, are not lightly departed from in one which is not great. The period at which ancient Eiré reached her height of national prosperity and national elation was that which intervened between the fourth and the eighth centuries. The ideal worlds and their inhabitants, which were then created, constituted a κτῆμα εἰς ἀεὶ for all succeeding ages. But before Eiré became the *Insula Sanctorum* and School of the West, she had for centuries maintained her freedom, and that of her ally, the Picts, in the face of Rome. She had conquered Alba and West Britain, had occupied London, and twice, if not oftener, invaded and plundered Gaul. The spiritual pre-eminence of the island had been preceded by success in arms; an exodus of Irish conquerors, an influx of captives and booty, had preceded the exodus of missionaries and the influx of students and artists.

It was in this second and scholastic period that the genealogies and annals of the bards, their poems and romances, were elaborated into that luxurious and abounding history which we find in the pages of Keating and the Lowr Gawla. Succeeding centuries were satisfied to accept the history which the sixth and seventh delighted to construct.

CHAPTER IX.

THE FIRST FACT.

> "A dismal conflict
> Till that *Bellona's bridegroom* lapped in proof,
> Confronted him with self-comparisons,
> Point against point rebellious, arm against arm,
> Curbing his lavish spirit."
>
> SHAKESPEARE.

IN modern Ireland the men of Ulster have out-distanced all the other provinces in wealth and prosperity. The superior energy of the north, which is incontestible, has been attributed to the introduction, in the seventeenth century, of a large English and Scotch element; but that energy which is the modern characteristic of the North of Ireland did not then commence. From the dawn of history those northern regions were inhabited by a tougher and more masterful breed. As far back as the eye can reach into the remote past, and on into the mythic twilight of the morn of history, the political and military predominence of the north is apparent. Ulster seems to have been ever what in wealth and material success she is to-day, the Queen of the Provinces.

Ulster was the old Ultonia, the patrimony of the Red Branch Knights, whose glory fills the pre-historic world of the bards. It was Ulster that gave monarchs to Ireland down to the extinction of the Ard-Rieship; it was Ulster that, unaided or opposed by the other provinces, all but wrested the whole island from the greatest of the English princes.

On the other hand, that physical and mental type which is more distinctively termed Irish, has had its home in the south both in ancient and modern times. To the warlike predominence of the north in ancient times, to her material predominence now, the south has been always able to oppose imagination, sprightliness, and art.

The north first made history, and the south first wrote it. It is with the north Irish history begins, yet a signal proof of the extent to which the pre-historic record has been affected by southern genius is to be seen in the fact, that although hardly a single southern chief ever arrived at the dignity of Ard-Rie, yet in the pre-historic times, southern Ard-Ries appear with great frequency. The point at which, according to Tierna, credible Irish history begins is that at which the southern Ard-Ries begin to disappear—a remarkable confirmation of the extraordinary sagacity of this re-markable man, who, born in the heart of the dark ages in the eleventh century, exhibited an elevation and pene-tration of mind to which no parallel is afforded in the annals of the world. *Omnia monumenta Scotorum usque* Cıombᴀoᴄ *incerta sunt*, forms one of the most memorable and pregnant sentences that the pen of wise man ever committed to the keeping of paper or parchment. Tierna drew his pen across and cancelled the greater portion of the recorded history of his country—a history which had been committed to writing many centuries before his time, which was consecrated in the imagination of the people, and which combined the splendour of romance with the minuteness and exactitude of the most accurately finished chronicle. Seven hundred years have passed away since Tierna died, and at last a ray of glory smites across that obscured and ancient brow, revolving thoughts that belonged not to his times. The age that has welcomed Niebhur must honour the memory of Tierna.

According to that chronicler, Irish history commences neither with Adam nor Partholan, but with the foundation, in the third century, B.C., of the Royal Palace and intrenched seat of Emain Macha, and the establishment in the North of Ireland of a powerful confederacy, under the presidency of one of the chiefs of the nation, which was styled the Children of Iar. This was Kimbay, whose centre and capital was Emain Macha, the sacred heights of Macha, the War Goddess of the Gæil, and according to a favourite bardic image, wife of the triumphant Kimbay.

CHAPTER X.

STILL PERPLEXED.

" Forms that no man can discover
For the dews that drip all over."
POE.

WITH Kimbay, Irish history perhaps commences, yet even thenceforward the historic track is doubtful and elusive in the extreme. Spite its splendid appearance in the annals, it is thin, legendary, evasive. Looked at with the severe eyes of criticism, the broad-walled highway of the old historians, on which pass many noble figures of kings and queens, brehons, bards, kerds and warriors, legislators and druids, real-seeming antique shapes of men and women, marked by many a carn, piled above heroes illustrious with battles, elections, conventions, melts away into thin air. The glare of bardic light flees away; the broad, firm highway is torn asunder and dispersed; even the narrow, doubtful track is not seen; we seem to foot it hesitatingly, anxiously, from stepping-stone to stepping-stone set at long distances in some quaking Cimmerian waste. But all around, in surging, tumultuous motion, come and go the gorgeous, unearthly beings that long ago emanated from bardic minds, a most weird and mocking world. Faces rush out of the darkness, and as swiftly retreat again. Heroes expand into giants, and dwindle into goblins, or fling aside the heroic form and gambol as buffoons; gorgeous palaces are blown asunder like a smoke-wreath; kings, with wand of silver and ard-rōth of gold, move with all their state from century to century; puissant heroes, whose fame reverberates through and sheds a glory over epochs, approach and coalesce; battles are shifted from place to place and century to century; buried monarchs re-appear, and run a new career of glory. The explorer visits an enchanted land where he is mocked and deluded. Everything seems blown loose from its fastenings. All that should be most stable is whirled round and borne away like foam or dead leaves in a storm.

But behind all this, behind Tierna's point of departure, his *fons et origo* of Irish history, lies a vast silent land, a land of the dead, a vast continent of the dead, lit with pale phosphoric radiance. That weird light that surges round us now has passed away from that land. The phantasmal energy has ceased there—the transmutation scenes that mock, the chaos, and the whirlwind. There, too, at one time the same phantasmagoria pre-

vailed, real seeming warriors thundered, kings glittered,
kerds wrought, harpers harped, chariots rolled.   But all
that has passed away.   Reverent hands, to whom that
phantasmal world was real, decently composed and laid
aside in due order the relics and anatomies of those airy
nations, building over each hero his tomb, and setting up
his grave-stone, piously graving the year of his death
and birth, and his battles.   There they repose in their
multitudes in ordered and exact numbers and relation,
reaching away into the dim past to the edge of the great
deluge, and beyond it; there the Lady Kasār and her
comrades, pre-Noachian wanderers; there Fintann, who
lived on both sides of the great flood, and roamed the
depths when the world was submerged; there Partholanus and his ill-starred race—the chroniclers know
them all; there the children of Nemeth in their own
Golgotha, their stones all carefully lettered, these not
so ancient as the rest, only three thousand years before
the birth of Christ; there the Clan Fomor, a giant race,
and the Firbolgs with their correlatives, Fir-Domnan
and Fir-Gaileen—the Tuatha De Danan, whom the
prudent annalist condemns to a place amongst the dead
—a divine race they will not die—they flee afar, pre-
ferring their phantasmal life; even the advent of the
Talkend will not slay them, though their glory suffers
eclipse before the new faith.   The children of Milith
are there with their long ancestry reaching to Egypt
and Holy Land.   Heber, Heremon, Ith, and Iar, with
all their descendants, each beneath his lettered stone;
Tiernmas and Moh Corb, Ollav Fohla, their lines descending through many centuries; all put away and
decently composed for ever.   No confusion now, no dis-
solving scenes or aught that shocks and disturbs, no

conflicting events and incredible re-appearances.   Chronology is respected.   The critical and historical intellect
has provided that all things shall be done rightly and in
order, that the obits and births and battles should be
natural and imposing, and worthy of the annals of an
ancient people.

The bardic intellect and imagination never slept.
The creative energy of the Irish mind tallied that of
Nature herself, bringing into existence generation after
generation of heroic persons.   In the spiritual world the
glorified semblance of the real, king succeeded king,
hero begot hero, the untired imagination of the country
passing from father to son, from son to grandson.   In
the later phases of the Ossianic literature we distinctly
see Fionn Mac Cool falling into disrepute and senility,
and Oiseen's son Oscar, the prime hero of the Fianna.

Thus behind each hero, still lusty with imagined
valour and beauty, extends a long line of heroes, from
whom has been withdrawn the aliment which was their
life, even the reverence and interest of the bards.   But
for the genius of Homer, who seized the ephemeral heroes
who then interested the Greek world, and breathed into
them the breath of immortality and lusty life to all
eternity, Achilles' and Hector would now be only names.

There is one heroic cycle which, as it lasted longest,
was also, perhaps, the most ancient, otherwise it is unlikely that it should be a common possession of Erin
and Alba, and that in Scotia Minor its heroes should be
located as if in their original home.

CHAPTER XI.

THE FIANNA EIREEN.

" Long, long ago, beyond the misty space
Of twice a thousand years,
In Erin old there lived a mighty race,
Taller than Roman spears."

M'GEE.

LOOMING in the misty-dark night, just relieved from
complete darkness by the approach of the still distant
dawn, huge forms are seen moving, scarce yet distinguishable from the shadows. Anon, a Babel of many
voices such as that had traveller heard in the realms of
Nox and Chaos—not like the small pipe of human
organs, but as if from throats tuned to the voices of the
elements—of the winds and waters. We hear the
names of their mighty men, Iregreen and Morna, Downa
and Corc, Trenmore and Cool, gigantic figures in the
dusky air. Ireland is their play-ground. They set up
their goals in the north and the south in Titanic hurl-
ing-matches, they drive their balls through the length
and breadth of it, storming through the provinces.

Battles there, half seen through intervening shadows,
flashes from smitten bronze, crash of shattering shields,
hiss of swift javelins, the war of giants, thunder-blasts
of the Baarr-Boh. The powers of heaven they laugh at
and defy. To be less than gods fits them not. They
set themselves in array against the Eternal.

" Highly they rage
Against the highest, and fierce with graspéd arms,
Clash on their sounding shields the din of war,
Hurling defiance 'gainst the vault of heaven."

" Where dwelt God," cries Ossian, " when we were in our prime ? Surely we would have shattered his Dûn, and bound and imprisoned him. Oh ! that my son and he were hand to hand on Knock-na-Fian."

Hark, the baying of many hounds held in the leash, Braan and Sgeolan, Mac an Smole, Yeolla and Ceola and Gawr, unearthly yelling of hounds worthy of that mammoth brood. Hark, the Dord Fian sounding in the misty dawn, the giant crew summoning to the chase.

Feasts then in the darkness. From the doors of huge booths, on hill-side and forest, glares the red light, laughter that shakes the trembling stars, clang of great goblets drained, anon melody, and passionate voices singing, the stricken tympan and the harp.

They are the Fianna of ancient Erin ; cold hell received them in the end. They perished here as elsewhere. In Greece they piled Pelion on Ossa, scaling the heavens, and sank at last into Tartarus before the shafts of Jove. In Asia they were swept away by the great deluge. " There were giants in the earth in those days ; the same were mighty men which were of yore, men of renown."

At last the mighty brood emerge into clearer light. The Ossianic cycle rolls on, bringing before us the last generation of the Fianna. There is their captain and ruler Fionn, the son of Cool. His hair is white and lustrous, but not with age. It falls down over his wide shoulders. His countenance expresses more than the warrior and the hunter. For the delight of the noble-faced son of Cool was to sleep by the cataract of Assaroe, to hear the scream of the seagulls over Eyerus, to listen to the black-bird of Derry Carn, and to see ships tossing in the brine. He was nursed by the Shee of Slieve Blahma, and tutored by poets in the forests of the Galtees, where he, too, practised the art of the bards, not without success :—

"Spring, delightful time ! How welcome is the noble
Brilliance of the season ever ! On the margin of the
    branchy woods
The summer swallows skim the streams,
The swift horses seek the pools, the weak fair bog-
    down grows.
The heath spreads out her long hair.
Sudden consternation attacks the signs.
The planets as they run exert an influence.
The sea is lulled' to rest ;
Flowers cover the earth."

Over Fionn floats the banner of the Fianna Eireen, the likeness of the rising sun half seen above the horizon.

Like the sun-rise, before which evil things of darkness flee away, Fionn, like Apollo Sauroktonos, had slain and exterminated all the savage reptiles of Erin, the two dragons of Glen Inny and the dragon of Loch Cuan, which is Strangford, the Piasta of the Shannon, and the great serpent of Ben Edar, which is Howth.

By his side are two hounds, Braan, the darling of all the Fianna, and Sgeolan. All the poets grow tender at the name of Braan. They caress her in their verses ; they have made a picture of her in words. " Yellow legs had Braan and red ears; the rest of her jet black, save a white spot on her breast and sprinkled white over the loins." " If thou curse Braan," cried Fionn, " my active, intelligent dog, I will not leave of thy house one

D

stone standing upon another." When Braan died, Fionn wept. Save then, and for the death of Oscar, he never shed a tear.

Oscar, the son of Ossian, a giant among giants, without fear, without malice, gentle in peace, irresistible in war, a mountain of placid strength, dear to all, the Hector of the Fianna, and like the great Trojan, melancholy and tender. At the battle of Gowra was he slain. *Sic cecinit Oiseen :—*

"I wandered over the battle-field. Many a broken shield and helmet lay scattered there, many a mailed warrior. I wandered wildly searching for my own son.

"I found my own son leaning on his left arm; his shield by his side, his hand still grasping the hilt of his broken sword, and the blood pouring through his mail.

"I flung my spear on the ground and cried aloud. Oscar looked up. Oh, what a face! He held out his arms to meet me.

"I sat down beside him. It was night. I forgot all else. 'I thank heaven that you are safe,' said Oscar. I was speechless. I could not speak.

"Then came Kaylta and his tribe. They, too, sought for Oscar. He knelt down quickly beside him; he passed his arm up to the elbow in Oscar's body, searching for the bitter spear-head.

"'Remember the battle of Shee Drum,' said Kaylta, pleasantly. 'I could count armies through the holes in your body that night.'

"But vain were the words of Kaylta. He, too, raised the cry of the dead. He cast his own pure body on the ground, and tore his yellow hair.

"We raised Oscar aloft upon our spears; we bore him

to a green mound. There we took off his armour and garments, and washed all his white body, from head to foot full of open wounds, but his face had got no hurt.

" We sat there through the night watching his white body. The morning dawned frosty and grey. We saw the silken banners waving in the dim air. We saw Oscar's banner, the slender roan-tree with scarlet fruit.

" At last Fionn approached. They went to him and spoke, but he answered not. He advanced swiftly in silence.

" He turned from us and wept. There we all raised together the cry of lamentation over Oscar. The Fianna wept over the great Oscar.

" We buried Oscar on the north side of the hill of Gowra, and we buried no one in that cairn save Oscar only. We made his cairn great and high like a king's."

Conan, the foul-mouthed, must not be forgotten; Ajax, with the tongue of Thersites, bald, corpulent, the standing jest of the Fianna; nor Diarmait of the women, the ruddy-faced Paris of the throng, renowned for success in love and daring in battle; nor Diaring, the companion and attendant of the chief, Phelan, MacLewy, Fergus, and many more well known to the bards.

But what shall we say of Oiseen, better known by his North British appellation, the poet and historian of the Fianna, the reviler of Patrick, the sorrowful mourner, the last of all the giant brood, withering away a white-haired shadow in scholastic cells, in mind and body the mere ghost of the once mighty Ossian, ever wondering whither had departed his comrades, and how any power was able to smite them with decay.

CHAPTER XII.

THE BURDEN OF OISEEN.

" ἦ γὰρ σοί γε σιδήρεος ἔνδοθι θυμος
Φράζεο νῦν μήτοι τι θεῶν μήνιμα γένωμαι
Ημ ατι τῷ ὅτε κέν σε Πάρις καὶ Φοῖβος Απόλλων
'Εσθλὸν ἐόντ' ὀλέσωσιν ἐνὶ Σκαιῆσι πύλησιν."

HOMER.

" O son of Calpurn of the crosses, hateful to me is the
sound of thy bells and the howling of thy lean clerics.
There is no joy in your strait cells; there are no women
among you, no cheerful music.

"You have practised magic against the Fianna. At
the sound of your bells they grew pale. At the howling
of your clerics they became like ghosts; they melted
into the air. When we marched against our enemies
every step that we took could be heard through the firmament. Now all are silent; they have melted into the
air. I, too, linger for a while, a shadow; I shall soon
depart.

"I took no farewell of Fionn nor of any of the Fenians;
they perished far away from me. Out of the west, out
of the sea, riding on a fairy steed, shod with gold, came
a lady seeking a champion. Brighter than gold was her
hair, like lime her fair body, and her voice was sweeter
than the angled harp.

"I set her before me on the steed. The sea divided
before us, and arched above us. We descended into the
depths. A fawn flew past me, whom two hounds pursued; a fair girl ran by with an apple of gold; a youth

with drawn sword pressed behind. I knew not their import.

"Three hundred years I lived in the Tiernanōg, in the land of the ever young, the isles of the blest ; but, far away I heard the hateful clanging of thy bells (the thought of my comrades come over me like a flood), and I returned to fade away beneath thy spells, O son of Calpurn.

"How stood the planets when power was given you, that we should grow pale before your advent. Withered trees are ye, blasted by the red wind. Your hair, the glory of manhood, is shaven away ; your eyes are leaden with much study ; your flesh wasted with fasting and self-torture ; your countenances sad. I hear no gleeful laughter ; I see no eyes bright and glad ; and ever the dismal bells keep ringing, and sorrowful psalmody sounds.

"Life is a burden to you, not a pleasure. It is the journey of one travelling through desolate places hastening homeward.

"Not such, not such, was our life, O cleric ; not such the pleasures of Fionn and the Fianna. The music that Fionn loved was that which filled the heart with joy and gave light to the countenance, the song of the black-bird of Letter Lee, and the melody of the Dord Fian, the sound of the wind in Droum-derg, the thunders of Assaroe, the cry of the hounds let loose through Glen Rah, with their faces outward from the Suir, the Tonn Rury lashing the shore, the wash of water against the sides of ships, the cry of Braan at Knock-an-awr, the murmur of streams at Slieve Mish, and oh, the black-bird of Derry Carn. I never heard, by my soul, sound sweeter than that. Were I only beneath his nest !

" We did not weep and make mournful music. When we let our hounds loose at Locha Lein, and the chase resounded through Slieve Crot, there was no doleful sound, nor when we mustered for battle, and the pure, cold wind whistled in the flying banners of the Fianna of Erin; nor yet, in our gentle intercourse with women, alas, O Diarmait; nor in the banqueting hall with lights, feasting and drinking, while we hearkened to the chanting of noble tales and the sound of the harp and the voice.

"How, then, hast thou conquered, O son of Calpurn."

CHAPTER XIII.

ARD-RIE ERENN UILI.

" The bright morning star, day's harbinger,
   Comes dancing from the east, and leads with her
   The flowery May, that from her green lap throws
   The yellow cowslip and the pale primrose. "

THERE is a pleasure in watching the reclamation of desert land—the choking moisture drained away, the sour peat mingled with sand, the stones collected into heaps, the making of roads and the building of fences, and, in the end, the sight of corn-fields where the snipe shrieked, and herds of kine where the morass quaked.

There is a pleasure in watching the dispersion of darkness before the rising sun, the gloom changing slowly into the silver twilight, the twilight ripening gradually into the golden day.

There is a pleasure in watching with the scientist the subsidence of some vast and horrible chaos into a shape of celestial beauty, fulfilling its part in some sidereal system, rolling through space around its sun, clear and determinate, a world and a star.

But there is a pleasure more certain, more human, more sublime, felt by one who contemplates out of the seething welter of warring tribes the slow growth of a noble people, the reclamation of a vast human wilderness, the stormful gloom of ignorance and hate growing less and less dense, shot through by the rays of imagination, knowledge, and love—the chaos of confusion and aimless strugglings concentre gradually into the wise and determined action of a nation fulfilling its part in the great national confraternity of the world.

To trace from small beginnings the gradual growth of the Ard-Rieship of Erin, with accuracy and critical hesitation, with the balancing of reasons, and the slow deduction of doubtful conclusions, with marshalled names and dates, the collation of manuscripts and inscriptions, the determination of the exact age of each separate composition, with a preceding inquiry into the changing phases of the language, and of the modes of thought of the ancient Gæil, would be a noble work indeed, but one which would necessitate the consenting labours of many minds. The golden ore of historic inquiry is usually only obtained by patient toil in the dark under-world of the past. Yet in Irish history the whole surface of the ground is strewn with the glittering metal, unnoticed and ungathered, from the very gleanings of which less fortunate peoples might trick out their past with a barbaric splendour. For myself, I lay no claim to the discovery of subterranean treasures, nor are the times ripe for that co-operation of thought and study of associated and ardent inquirers from whom alone such results may be expected. Till men recognize the greatness of the heroic period of their history, the labours of the patient brood of scholars will be feebly conducted and inadequately rewarded. Enthusiasm itself must chill in the presence of a hard and enduring apathy. Irish archæology is now, and has been hitherto, a flickering flame, whose intermittent flashes only serve to reveal its own sad state.

The task which I have set before myself is different; it is to recast in a literary form that old heroic history, taking typical characters from each period, infusing into the tale, with a freedom unknown to the bards, the civilization of their own times, which, now at least, is sufficiently poetical, using for a foundation that chronology which the bards and monks agreed upon, and which has not been yet overthrown. But before commencing, I desire to write a few words concerning one strong fact that looms for ever through the wild bardic traditions, a fact still, whether true of the times concerning which the bards wrote, or whether the reflection of one of the prime elements of their own civilization.

In ancient Erin we find at Tara, a spot for ever sacred, the locus of the plastic and formative principle, the centre upon which the chaos of the septal struggles was destined to subside, a palace, a strength, a city, a place of rude parliaments and conventions of the justest law and the wisest brehons, the most frequented fair-green, best place for the jeweller to sell his rings and brooches, the armourer his weapons, where the harper found his art best judged and best rewarded, where the chronicler could best display and best correct his dry antiquities, the bard find the most liberal and appreciative audience. Who can tell the number of brave men whose blood has reddened those green plains, warring to keep or gain for their own chief those sacred and king-making Raths.

The social functions, which in modern times are discharged by cities and parliaments, were in ancient times discharged by great periodical gatherings at stated intervals and places. Primarily and essentially, the Isthmian and Olympian gatherings were not held for purposes of sport, but for commerce and the adjustment of inter-tribal relations. But the more sensational and exhilarating character of any event tends to absorb in popular estimation all its other and more intimate characteristics. Thus the great Olympian and Isthmian gatherings are remembered as games, and not as fairs.

In Ireland, in addition to the local and provincial fairs which took place more frequently, there was held every third year, on the plains of Meath, one great fair, which surpassed all the rest in public importance.

To the great triennial fair of Tara, held midway between north and south, the chiefs gathered from the most remote parts of the country. To violate this fair was the highest public offence known to our ancestors. The use of a weapon was punished by instant death, for which no Eric was or could be accepted. It was the jubilee season of the Irish; ancient prestige and reverence protected those who journeyed to and from that fair, and wars were suspended during its celebration.

From a small beginning the great Feis of Tara advanced in public importance, until it became for Ireland what the Olympian festival was to Greece. Eventually, with the growing traffic, the increasing numbers of those who flocked to the fair, the gathering complexity and multitude of the relations and requirements of the event, the necessity of control and regulation began to be felt, and a chieftain was elected who should fulfil this duty.

To the great customary Feis of Tara, more than to actual conquest and downright superiority in arms, is to be attributed the power and dignity of the Irish Ard-Rie. Yet there was action and counter-action. The power of the chieftain enhanced the dignity and authority of the fair, and the importance of the fair extended the influence and renown of the chieftain. Accordingly, it is with the strife of contending factions, eager to secure for their own candidate the possession of this coveted honour, that Irish history begins. Through the gilt and embellished curtain of myth and legend the first thing of which we are made aware is the crash of contending armies struggling for the possession of Temair.

In Grecian history we know the importance attached to the right of celebrating the great games, and the civil wars which occasionally took place between tribes contending for the honour. But in Greece the office was not open to election. The prescriptive right of the Eleans to the celebration of the Olympian festival was universally acknowledged ; but their slender political and military power rendered them unable to make use of the position in order to extend their authority and compel their neighbours to yield them tribute and allegiance. They were simply trustees and agents acting on behalf and under the sanction of the remaining Greek tribes, many of whom were infinitely more powerful than themselves, and would not permit the festival to be turned to any political purpose for the aggrandisement of the Eleans. If, instead of being vested by prescription in a single tribe, this honour had been the subject of election, and the perpetual appanage of

military and political predominance, how eagerly would
every powerful state have put forward her pretensions,
and how many bloody battles would have been fought in
the territory of the Eleans, who, as an independent
sept, would speedily have disappeared from the map of
Greece in the contentions of their great neighbours.
In ancient Ireland, unlike Greece, this noble privilege,
the right of celebrating the great Temairian festival and
fair, was not vested in any particular tribe, but was left
open to the ambition, energy, and power of individual
kings, and of the coalitions which they were able to
form. Thus the Irish did work out for themselves
unity, which the Greeks did not; for out of these contentions for the possession of Tara sprang the Ard-Rie
Erenn Uili.

CHAPTER XIV.

TARA.

" With rosy fingers soon to grasp
And wrestle with the giant gloom."

EDMUND ARMSTRONG.

THE name of the tribe was the name of its founder.
The great Norman-Irish sept of the Geraldines was
founded by the sons of Gerald, the son of Raymond.
The great Scotic-Irish nation of the Hee Neill was
founded by Neill of the Nine Hostages, Neill Nae-yeela.
From time to time the progress of events broke up old
organizations and created new; the ancient tribe-names
passed away, and others took their places; social con-
vulsions brought into prominence new and powerful
chieftains whose names became impressed upon the

organizations which they created. To the chieftaincy of
these organizations their posterity alone were eligible.
The Clan Carty of Desmond were preceded by the
Owenacts, who were themselves preceded by the Corca
Lewy ; that is, the descendants of Cartha succeeded the
posterity of Owen, who were preceded by the children of
Lewy.

Perhaps the earliest trustworthy fact in Irish history
is that of the contemporary existence in Ireland of four
powerful septs, impressed with the names of Heber,
Herēmon, Ith, and Iar. Who were these chieftains,
when they lived, and whether contemporary or separated
by centuries, who shall tell ? I myself follow the ancient
tradition, which assuredly contains more truth than my
own speculations. Yet, as there are many persons who
like a theory, I crave permission to suggest one.

The national unity which, in the days of Neill
Nae-yeela was an accomplished fact, produced on the one
hand political expression in the institution of Ard-Rie,
and on the other, bardic expression in the romance of
the Milesian invasion of Ireland by the sons and kindred
of Milesius.

Had the advent of letters and civilization been delayed in Ireland down to the Tudor era, and no memory
of the Norman settlement survived, we may be certain
that some such myth as the Milesian would have been
invented to account for the origin of the then great Irish
septs. Neill, De Burgo, Gerald, Brian, and Cartha
would naturally present themselves to the imagination
as the sons of some powerful warrior who had subdued
and divided the land amongst his children, and the prior
history of this conqueror would have been gradually
elaborated through a series of bardic tales, finally to

be crystallized into history and incorporated with the annals.

Royalty is a strange growth. A halo of sovereignty and legitimate authority gradually settles upon and deepens round one family, whose pre-eminence is recognized and acquiesced in by the rest. The divinity that doth hedge a king is more the work of imagination than the result of mere pre-eminence in actual force and power. The Earl of Warwick possessed more land, castles, and dependants than the king; yet he never dared to put forward any pretension to the Crown.

When the curtain is raised, and, on the stage of Irish history, the septs are seen contending for the Ard-Rieship, the four Milesian families alone enjoyed a prescriptive title to the regulation of the great Feis of Temair. It is not to be supposed that the clans of Heber, Heremon, Ith, and Iar were even then the only strong and numerous septs in the island. There were many tribes non-Milesian, but the prescriptive right to the dignity and tributes of this office had gradually come to be vested in these four tribes alone. The non-Milesian tribes occupied territories in different parts of Ireland, particularly in the west. At last the growing importance of the office induced them to make common cause against the families of the Blood. All the non-Milesian septs throughout the island conspired to break the prescriptive title of the royal tribes, and to elect a ruler of the great Feis who should not belong to any of the four Bloods. The revolution, which was aided by a massacre, succeeded, and the excluded families established one of their own number in the sovereignty of Tara. This was the celebrated revolution of the Aithech Tuatha—*gentes plebcianæ*—and took place in the first century of our era.

The royal tribes now united, and electing their own
Ard-Rie, succeeded in driving the usurper from Tara,
and established indefeasably the exclusive royal privileges of the four Milesian tribes.

The revolution of the Aithech Tuatha had European
results. The counter-revolution produced the expulsion
from Eiré of many non-Milesian tribes. Passing over
to the Continent, their fighting-men became incorporated in the Roman army, and, under the name of Atti-
cotti, are frequently mentioned by Latin writers, not
always to their credit.

Time and fate have revenged these expatriated tribes.
Sixteen hundred years later, the descendants of the four
conquering septs, themselves subdued by an alien race,
were forced to fly from their country, and in foreign
lands to fight the battles of strange peoples.

There is no reason to suppose that the royal septs
differed in blood and race from the rest of the inhabitants of the island. In an unsettled state of society
some clans must come to the front, and exert a pre-
eminence over the less fortunate or the less brave ; and
in Ireland it so happened, that these four families
emerged victorious out of the septal struggles.

The power and pride of the royal septs, and their
contempt for the tribute-paying classes, produced the
conception of a diversity of race. In the rich soil of
the bardic mind the idea took root and flourished.
Eventually, the royal tribes were regarded universally
as a race of Spanish origin, ruling in the midst of a
people whom their ancestors had subdued, and the history of Milesian was distinguished from that of Fir-
bolgic Erin. Yet the fact that in historic times there
was no connection between Ireland and Spain renders it

exceedingly probable that, at least in its main features, the ancient and universal tradition represents what really took place.

By degrees the Fir-bolgic tribes melted away utterly before the dominant families and their spreading branches. In the commencement of the historic era, we find them in a position of inferiority, indeed, but possessing a considerable amount of territory. In the end they held none. The Milesian septs extended themselves over the whole island, until every petty king and chieftain traced his pedigree to one of the four Spanish conquerors.

But through all the turmoil and confusion of these antique, obscure times, clear and distinct only when the wonderful mirror of the bards is held up against them, through all displacements and expansions of beaten or triumphant tribes and tribal confederacies, that one spot upon the plains of Meath gleams brighter and brighter as day advances, and mighty Rome, the sun of our northern regions, rolls up from the under-world. In the waning night it glitters like the morning star before the eye of the historian. That group of green mounds, palisaded and dyked, surmounted with painted wicker-houses, is the central harmonizing point of the wild chaos which surges and bellows in the darkness and the haze. Starlike now, it will itself be one day a sun. All the tribes shall look to it for light and heat, for justice and order. All Eiré, from sea to sea, shall be convulsed for its possession. From Innishowen, from the House of Donn, from Eyerus, from Cahirman, warriors shall come together in battle, warring to secure for their own captain that centre of the assemblages of Erin.

CHAPTER XV.

THE KINGS OF DINN RIE.

"The raven himself is hoarse
That croaks the fatal entrance of Duncan
Under my battlements."

SHAKESPEARE.

"ANTIGONUS rex Asiæ Minoris occisus est.—An. Rom. 453."

"Eodem tempore initiatus est regnare in Emania, *i.e.*, ᴀɴ Emᴀɪɴ Eochᴀ ᴆuᴀᴠᴀċ ᴀċᴀɪꝝ Uᴈᴀɪne ab aliis fertur (nos vero perscripsimus olim ab ipso Uᴈᴀɪne), tunc ibi imperatum esse."

"Omnia monumenta Scotorum ante Cꝛombᴀoċ incerta sunt."

Thus the sober-minded Tierna, Abbot of Clonmacnoise, commences his celebrated book of synchronisms.

Not *falsa* or *fabulosa* but *incerta*. Nevertheless I, too, propose to start from the same point, and to describe the heroes of ancient Eiré as I find them reflected in the magic mirror of the bards, only setting up against the whole the glass which they applied severally to the parts. Therein mirrored, the confusion and dislocation caused by a fragmentary treatment yields to a more lucid and tranquil arrangement—the heroic tale tones down to epic proportion and reasonableness. Spirits of the ancient bards, my ancestors, and ye sacred influences that haunt for ever the soil and air of my country, nameless now and unworshipped, but strong and eternal, be with me and befriend, that in circles worthy so glorious singing their praise upon whom nations looked back as upon their first and best, with a flight unfailing I may rise to regions where no wing of laborious ollav or chanting shanachie ever yet fanned that thinner air.

Out of the west came Macha seeking a new home, deserting her ancient habitation where the Red Cataract pours the waters of the Erne into the sea.

Now about this time all the princes of Ulla had assembled to a great hunt that was given by the eldest of the sons of Dithorba, and amongst those who were invited was Kimbay Mac Fiontann, a young and very brave warrior, whose patrimony lay along the Dalriadic coast facing the Muirnict, and he was king of his tuath, and conspicuous both in peace and war. Now it so happened that Kimbay Mac Fiontann and the other kings who were most eminent and powerful found themselves alone as the night fell, for they had advanced beyond the others. Therefore, choosing a dry place in the forest, they kindled a fire, and, being weary from running, they lay down and slept. Then amongst them appeared the great war-queen, Macha the Red-maned, stern-browed and minatory, no tender damsel, and red as if she had bathed in blood, but with lustrous eyes, having strange power over the soul, and a voice, to hear which, tears not of sorrow sprang into men's eyes, and through that stern countenance there struck a beauty unfelt by the vile, but all-powerful with noble hearts, and she was armed like a warrior equipped for battle. Then, with her lance she touched one of the sleeping kings, and he awoke and sat up, and when he saw her he stood upon his feet, and his whole soul went out towards her, and he proffered homage and love. Then she bade him follow her, and she went through the forest, and he pursued, but when, as they were alone

E

conversing, he offered to embrace her. Then she arose against him, and bound him with her strong hands easily, as a shepherd binds a lamb, having stripped from a willow tree the pliant saplings. There then, having bound him with these green wyths, she left the warrior in bonds, and returning, did likewise to the second and to the third and the rest; but at last she came to Kimbay, and when she laid hands upon him, he arose against her, and seized her in his mighty arms, and bore her to the earth; but in his arms she changed into a blooming and beautiful maiden, and she responded to his love, and became his bride.

 Then Kimbay builded a city there, and he cleared the forest all round, making a smooth plain, and the kings whom his wife had bound he set at liberty, when they had sworn to become tributary to him and to serve him; and these kings, with their peoples, laboured at the great Dûn which he erected at this place, and he called his city after the name of his wife, Emain Macha, the sacred height of Macha, and it was the capital of his realm.

Thereafter then Mac Fiontann, having fortified Emain Macha, extended his authority southwards to Tailteen, and westwards to the Muirnict, where, that he might have a sure outlet for the produce of his realm, he restored the ancient Dûn of Nemeth, where the Dalriadic coast, stretching an arm northwards into the sea, encloses with the land a safe haven for ships. There, on the site of the old Nemedian Strength, Kimbay raised a great Dûn, and called it after his own name.

Now, while Kimbay reigned in Emain Macha, a strong king rose up southwards, beyond the Boyne, and he, having seized Tara, extended his authority far and wide, so that his power was felt beyond the borders of Eiré, and his war-fleets went out from Cahirmān and Inver Colpa. Moreover, he caused all the kings of the isle to swear for themselves and their children that they would suffer none who was not of his race to hold the sovereignty of Fail ; and Kimbay Mac Fiontann sware likewise that oath, though he was the foster-father of Ugainey.

But when Ugainey More died, he was buried at the Brugh upon the Boyne, where the ground swelled with many a huge barrow of the giants, and the raths and prison-houses of the men of old. There the Tuatha of Erin had their fairy palaces, looking over the Boyne, and all the ground was sacred to Yeoha the Ollav, who was also called the Dàda Mor, and to his wife Moreega, but especially to his son Angus the Beautiful, he who was once seen in the halls of Tara by Art's son—for the Ard-Rio pondered alone in his chamber after the Saba of his kings was broken up ; but when Cormac raised his head, lo, the son of the Dàda stood before him in the gloaming with a shining tiompan in his hands.

Moreover, there too was interred the marvellous steed of Macha. In the ancient wars which the Tuatha had waged against the giants, she had borne the war-goddess to battle, and when she died they had piled above her a great ferta, as above a hero slain. But a second time the Lia Macha was seen upon the plains of Eiré, bearing to battle once more her armed mistress, the warlike spouse of Kimbay. And yet once again was she seen of the Gæil in the service of the heroic Cuculain, the son of Sualtam ; but after that the Lia Macha was no more seen till the coming of the Talkend, when

the incantations of the son of Calpurn drew Cuculain
out of Fairy-land, and, in his war-car, with Læg by his
side, he flashed past the raths of Tara, bending fierce
brows against the shaven cleric, and, hurling his javelin,
vanished into the west. There also was the cromlech
on which men said the Dâda, having first bound and
haled him thither, had slain the hundred-armed, four-
headed monster which oppressed the inhabitants of the
isle, and many mighty barrows and cairns, raths, pillar-
stones and muirs were strewn all around, and there men
were accustomed to invoke the succour of the Shee.

There, then, they interred Ugainey beside the river,
and after that there was held a great convention of the
kings at Temair, and they invested Lorc, the son of
Ugainey, with the Ard-Rieship of Erin, for he had been
named Tanist by Ugainey. But when Lorc had set his
foot upon the Lia Fail, receiving the wand of the Ard-
Rieship, then the sacred stone roared beneath him, even
as a war-steed neighs beneath his rider mounting for the
battle, and the sound was heard over all Bregia.

But after this the kings separated each to his own
tuath and his own Dûn, and Lorc returned to Dinn
Rie, upon the Barrow, and he ruled over the people of
Lahan, the descendants of Milith and of the Fir-bolgs,
and he was good to all his people, but especially to his
brethren, the sons of Ugainey More. For he preserved
the precepts of his father, and kept in check the warlike
tribes, and advanced the dignity of the ollavs, and dis-
couraged border warfare and lawlessness between tuath
and tuath.

Now there was an elder brother than Lorc, who was
pale-faced and lean. He had been fostered in Bregia,
wherefore men called him Cœl-Bray, but his own name

was Covac. He was enraged that his brother should be preferred before him, and, marking the discontent of the warriors, he conspired against his brother, and drew to his faction all the mutinous and dissatisfied chiefs. Nevertheless, he kept himself serene and silent in assemblies, though by nature fierce. He transgressed also the laws and forced illegal tributes from his vassals, and with a strong hand defied the ollavs of his tuath, and collected about his Dùn many mercenaries, and numerous were the complaints which were brought up before the Cùl-Airecta of the High King. But Lorc reasoned with his brother, and forbore to put into execution the laws for the protection of vassals.

Now Cœl-Bray and the kings of his faction had resolved to slay the Ard-Rie ; but this they were not able to compass, for the guards of Lorc were very vigilant, being aware of a plot ; but the generous king believed nothing.

Then to Covac and his associates plotting, this plan seemed the best, to send a messenger to his brother announcing his sudden illness and death ; which thing accordingly was done. But when Lorc heard that his brother was dead, he wept and lamented, and set out straightway. Now, it was evening when the news came, and he travelled all night with a small retinue, and in the morning he came to the borders of the Oun Liffey, where was the tuath over which his brother was king, and he came to the Dùn, and hastened beyond his ambus, and went into his brother's chamber, which was darkened, and kneeled by the bed-side, weeping ; but as he leant above him, Covac drew unperceived from beneath the clothes a brazen colg which he had hid there, and thrust it into the side of the other, and he, springing forward with a shriek, fell upon the bed, and Covac withdrew the red brass, and the blood of his brother spurted out over his face and breast.

Then, starting from the chamber, he gave the signal, blowing a sudden blast upon the winding stocca, and his warriors and the conspirators ran in, and cut down the ambus of the High King.

Thereafter, collecting all his force, he marched southwards upon Dinn Rie, and there poured into him upon the way all the kings and nobles that were of his faction—for the warlike class adhered to him—and he stormed the city of Dinn Rie, and slew all the sons and grandsons of Læry Lorc, save one only, and broke down all opposition, and fought many battles—for in war there was none his equal—until his power extended to the borders of Eiré; the Tanist, too, he slew, who was Oileel Ainey, the son of Lorc. Then he was elected Ard-Rie of all Erin in Temair; and he depressed the ollavs and the druids, setting the kings and nobles above the law, whence, too, came his power. Thus Covac Cœl-Bray reigned, having slain his brother.

CHAPTER XVI.

A FLOWER OF THE FOREST.

" Then from the caverns of my dreamy youth
I sprang as one sandalled with plumes of fire."

SHELLEY.

But the boy Lara, son of Oileel Ainey, son of Lorc, was not slain; for, when a band of assassins surrounded his father's Dûn, hard by Gowra in the south, and slew his

brethren, one passing swiftly, with wild eyes, and a harp
in his hand, whispered a sudden word in his ear, which
he remembered and obeyed; for he counterfeited dumb-
ness and idiotcy, and they slew him not, partly from
contempt, and partly for that they were sacred whose
minds the divine people had disturbed. Thus was left
Lara amid his slain kindred and the loud lamenting
women, who were the slaves of Oileel.

But in the end an old man came, who had been the
swineherd of his father, and led him away by the hand,
and brought him to where was a sheeling on the edge
of the forest. For when Ugainey More had begun to
reign, he was rebelled against from the west; but the
rebels he had crushed in a red foray to the borders of
the Shannon, and he had brought back many slaves, and
amongst them him who now led out the boy from the
bloody Dûn. Then he put upon the young prince servile
weeds, a brown coarse bratta, with a wooden pin upon
the breast, and on his feet the shoes of a slave, un-
tanned skin of deer, with the haired side out, and fastened round the ankle with a thong passing through the
unshaped leather, and he set him to scutch flax and
break the ground for rue, for he had a small field which
himself had reclaimed from the forest. Then came
emissaries from the king, and they watched him, but
he deceived them too; and after that no man thought
concerning him, save only Ferceirtney the poet, and
Craivetheena the cunning harper, who were of the royal
retinue at Dinn Rie.

After this the king's Maor, for Covac had seized for
himself the estates of his brethren, levied the fine which
it was customary for men to pay when their lord had
died, in order that the funeral games might be worthy

of his rank, but the Maor levied a treble fine, and paid
no funeral honours to the body of the good king slain.
Moreover, with a strong hand, he compelled the old man
to perform double services, which it was not lawful should
be done, for Mœlken had served blamelessly under two
lords, Ugainey and Oileel, rendering regularly his tribute of curds and butter, water-cresses and rue, and the
stipulated labour about the king's Dûn, which was performed by his wife.   Moreover, he had done no act of
trespass or violence for which the new lord would have
been responsible before the law.   Now, although the
ollavs suffered none such to be driven out or ha-
rassed by cruel and unnatural lords, yet now their
power was set at naught by Cœl-Bray and the fierce
kings who supported them.   And now, again, the evil
days of yore were returning when the king was absolute
over the tuath, and the lord over his tenants, and the
rights of the tribute-paying classes were infringed, and
boaireys degenerated into bodács, and bodács into slaves.
The ollavs, too, fell away from their high place, and
became dependent upon the kings, forgetting those lofty
ranns in which were enshrined the wisdom and justice of
the Gæil, and the ramifications of far-spreading tribes
preserving the ancestral rights of men, and they
chanted now only songs praising lawlessness and
strength ; and the rights of women, too, and the laws
of marriage were relaxed.

   Therefore, through the whole of Lahan, and along the
shores of the three waters, and northwards to the Liffey
and mid-Erin, there was great affliction, and laws and
justice suffered throughout all Eiré, for in all the provinces strong lords, relying on his support, defied their
ollavs and the assemblies of their freemen, and mer-

cenaries multiplied about each Dûn and about each
chieftain's liss.

But every night two men set out from Dinn Rie
secretly, faring westward from the Barrow, and they
came to that lonely sheeling on the borders of the forest,
and, in the house of Mœlken, a deftly-touched harp
thrilled nightly, and the sound of a manly voice was
heard, and the sound of a boy's voice responsive.
For Ferceirtney the poet, and Craivetheena the harper
and shanachie went thither in the dead of night secretly, in order that in the mind of the boy they
might sow kingly thoughts. But as a child waters and
tends each day a flower which has been given to her,
hastening thither always with hope and fear, who has no
other, and is immured in the depths of the city, or as a
young mother watching over her first child, so anxiously
and fearfully tended those wise men the royal flower
that grew unnoticed in the wilderness ; or as that good
Hebrew priest and his wife watched over the boy whom
they had preserved when all the seed-royal of Israel
were slain.

Ferceirtney instructed him in the history of his people, in the laws of the Gæil, and the duties and prero-
gatives of kings, and taught him to adore the Tuatha
and the unseen might of the Fianna, and all the wide-
ruling children of Nemeth ; and Craivetheena chanted
bardic tales concerning the sons and kindred of Milesius, and the ancient wars which the Tuatha had waged
against the giants, and he played lofty strains upon the
harp, and a noble spirit grew within the boy's breast.

During the day, indeed, Lara ground corn for the
household, bruising it in a shallow mortar with a smooth
hand-stone, or worked in the field, or led the old man's

only cow into the forest to feed, for he had no rights in
the common land of the tuath, and he continually
revolved in his mind the things which he had been
taught.

Moreover, his foster-father used to send him twice a
year to the royal Dûn at Dinn Rie with the tributes of
his holding, in order that suspicion might be allayed;
but Lara studied closely the fortifications of the city of
Dinn Rie, and how it might be entered by an enemy.
Yet there he ever bore himself like an idiot, with open
mouth and slavering lips, obeying the stern injunctions
of those who watched over him.

Now one day, in late summer, Lara having brought
to the king's Maor the heavy dues of his foster-father,
and having with difficulty endured the words of the
grinding officer, returning passed by the plain of the
hurlers, in which were the sons and foster-sons of the
king driving the ball from goal to goal, and there pausing, he watched the princes at their play; but Craivetheena, afar off, observed him carefully, for this was his
custom whensoever the boy came to Dinn Rie. Then,
as it so happened, the ball was driven outside the
measured ground, and lay in the grass at the feet of
Lara, who, stooping, took it in his hand, and flung it
back into the ground. Then was one side pleased, for
he threw the ball awry, not knowing the rules of the
game ; but the son of Cœl-Bray shouted fiercely, and
running towards him, smote at him with his hurle, but
Lara, grappling with him, wrung it from his hands and
felled him with a single blow, smiting him above the
left ear with the brazen hurle. But when the companions of Maylvee rushed at him also, they were astonished and fell back, for he stood erect and wrathful,

with one foot upon the fallen prince, and uttered a fierce imperious speech. Therefore they retired, fear-stricken and amazed, saying, " Is this he that was dumb and an idiot ?" But Lara cast aside the hurle, and strode westward, indignant, across the plain.

Then, ere the princes returned to the king's Dûn, Craivetheena hastened to seek the ollav, for he walked in a quiet place beside the river, and there were with him two pupils having bardic staves in their hands, from which they read, and it was already evening. Straightway then, having concerted plans, they ordered chariots and swift horses to be yoked, and took trusty attendants, and left Dinn Rie, one to the north and one to the south, moving slowly till they were beyond the city; and then, making a rapid circuit, they met at the house of Mæl Ken.

There, then, delaying not for aught, they took up the old man and his wife and Lara, and drave westward through the night ; and there were those that pursued them, for a swift word traversed Dinn Rie, and there was a sudden meeting of the king's Saba ; and hardly had the flying prince and his aiders departed from the sheeling when the Airey Echta of Dinn Rie, with his armed men, rode up.

But Ferceirtney and the fugitives drave swiftly through the pass in the Slieve Margy Mountains, and along the northern spurs of the same, and they crossed the Dineen and the Nore, and entered the country of the Osree : but here the pursuit was stayed. Yet they feared to trust themselves with the Osree, and they went rapidly through that territory and crossed the Suir, ten miles north from Caiseal of the Kings, and they passed in among the tribes of the Corca Lewy. But after that they went westward again, past Slieve Felim, and they crossed the Maigue and the Deale, and so went on till they came to Slieve Mish, where was the capital and strength of the Fir-morca, the mighty children of Heber the son of Milith, and they saw afar off the mighty raths and fertas strewn over the plain, looking over Letter Lee, and beyond them the entrenched places and glittering palaces of the King Skoreea, who, with a strong hand, held Slieve Mish and the approaches to that sacred place.   But by the great King of the Shiel Heber they were joyfully received, for he was hostile to Cœl-Bray, and went not to the conventions at Temair, nor paid him the tribute and honour due to the possessor of Tara.   Now of Slieve Mish I desire to tell the history.

CHAPTER XVII.

COMING OF THE MILESIANS.

" And moreover we have seen the sons of the Anakims there."
                                          HEBREW CHRONICLER.

FROM Tor Brogan, of Espân, the sons and kindred of Milesius set sail for the invasion of Erin, and in each ship were fifty persons, not only warriors, but also their wives and little ones, their druids and poets, their craftsmen and slaves; for they had determined to occupy the island and make it their home.   For not only were they straitened for room in their own country, by reason of the multiplying of the Clanna Gædil, but vengeance, too, impelled them; for Ith, the son of Brogan, and uncle of Milesius, had been slain by the inhabitants of the isle.   For, having been borne northwards through the Ictian sea by violent winds, he had at last gained a quiet bay on the northern shore, whence with chosen comrades he had marched inland. But when after certain days he had not returned, the remainder of his people who were left with the ships, following in the same direction, if haply they might discover their comrades and their captain, had lighted upon him dead, in the midst of his dead warriors; but upon their bodies there were no marks of violence, and ever after men called this plain the plain of Ith.

But they, when they had mourned over their slain comrades, and had consumed the sad relics with fire upon the beach of Loch Febal, sailed back to Espân, bearing with them the charred bones inurned of Ith the son of Brogan, and they kindled a flame in the minds of his brethren and his kindred. Now the sons of Brogan, Brega, and Fuad, Coola, Cooalney, and Murthemney, were more impelled by vengeance; but the sons of Mihth, Heber, Heremon, Iar, Arannan, Colpa, Arech Febaroe, Donn, and Amargin, were moved by an uncos tral spirit prompting them to great deeds.

But an ancient fear invested the island, for a wondrous race was said to dwell therein, and men called it Banba, after the name of a great queen who dwelt there; and also Fohla and Eiré, and mariners told strange tales of noises heard upon its shores, and mighty forms of men and women seen afar upon the sides of the mountains; also of its beauty men spake, green and woody, and abounding in streams.

Nay-the-less, the Clanna Milith, set forth with undaunted heart, naught fearing, for of yore too the race of Gædil was accustomed to seek new lands, and from the east to Espân they had come in ships and heard the waves roar in the Torrian frith.

Moreover, in that galley in which sailed Amargin was borne the Lia Fail, which the Clanna Gædil in the ancient days had brought with them to Espân, and ancestral prophecies had foretold that the sovereignty of the Gæil should not cease around it, and men said that that stone was instinct with life, and that there came from it voices and lightnings and portents, and standing upon it, the kings of the Gæil were invested with sovereignty.

Therefore with undaunted hearts the sons of Milith came together to that hosting, and for them, as they left the harbour Amargin chanted the chant that shields those who travel upon the sea, and the Lia Fail gave forth sounds of good omen, and all the warriors shouted and chanted the crown-dord, striking with their spears the hollow shields, while the snoring galleys ran on, out into the open sea, bearing the Clan Milith to Inis Fail.

After this they rowed and sailed forward perpetually, for a good wind sprang up from the south, and the steady oarsmanship of the brave mariners ceased not day or night, but ever the white oars kept bounding forward constant-going, steady, unhesitating, as sang the ancient bard, over the wide plains of Lear.   But on the sixth day, at sunrise, they saw afar off the beautiful hills of Eiré, forest-crowned, whence, too, men named the island Na Veeva, on account of its woods.   Then were the Clanna Gæil glad when they saw the winding shores, and they all lifted up their voices together and shouted, both warriors and little children.   But there were on the decks also women looking forward with anxious hearts ; Scota, mother of the eight sons of Milith, for she had survived her great lord, and now sought Eiré with her heroic sons, and she sailed with Heber in his ship, for he was gentler than the others ; and there was Odba,

the wife of steed-loving Herēmon; but she sailed in
another ship. Also there was Faus the wife of Oon, a
wise druidess and held in great honour, and she sailed
with her husband and his three brothers, princes of the
Clan Gædil in Espân. But the fairest of the women
that came into Erin with the sons of Milith was Feale
the wife of Lewy, son of that Ith who had been slain by
the Tuatha of Erin, and she had lived alone with an
·aged relative in the western regions of Espân, in an
inland valley, until she was wooed by Lewy the son of
Ith, surnamed Laid-Ken for his love of poetry; and men
said concerning Feale that she was too beautiful to live.

Now the mariners that knew the coast guided the
ships forward to where there was a deep inver, for here
the Slaney poured his waters into the sea, and afterwards the place was named Cahirmān, and a great fair
was held there by the people of Lahan.

There then they landed on the east shore of the river,
and they wondered for that they saw no one there, only
cattle and deer feeding in the green glades of the forest.

Then Amargin, the son of Milith, chanted a druidic
song that the land might be blessed, and that the race
of Milith might be fortunate in their new country.

But after this they drew up their ships upon the
beach of the sea, putting props under them, and for
themselves they constructed booths out of the abundant
timber.

But after this, having prepared food to last for many
days, and having left behind them the women and children and the slaves, with warriors to guard them, and
also Arannan, for he was the youngest and not yet
inured to hardness, they themselves set forward to
march inland.

On the second day they found great foot-marks on the soft margin of the river, as of giants who went bare-footed, and after that, being alarmed, they went cautiously. But on the next day they came to a great plain cleared from the forest, and tame cattle and sheep feeding there, and men of great stature went in and out amongst them, unarmed and peaceful, bearing vessels of milk, or carrying young lambs after the manner of shepherds, for they were a pastoral tribe.

But when they saw this, Herēmon bade them advance, and they went on towards the giants, who received them with kindness, and answered them in their own language, and one went where, on the edge of the plain, were their houses, made of the stems of the highest trees, with wicker-work between, and returned with their king.

But the Fir-bolgs wondered at the beauty and martial bravery of the sons of Milith, and these admired the great stature of the Fir-bolgs. But the King of the Fir-bolgs, whose name was Crimthann, surnamed Skia-vale, led them into his house and entertained them there that night, and they inquired concerning one another's history.

But Crimthann told the sons of Milith that in the ancient days his ancestors alone held the island, and that they fought with and held tributary the Fomoroh, until they had been subdued by the children of Dana, a divine race, though of the same blood with themselves, and that they were immortal, and travelled upon the wind, and that they had power over the elements, and were very glorious to look upon Lear, whose dominion was over the sea, and his son Mananan, whose home was in the Muirnict and Loch Oribsen in the west,

beyond the great stream in which dwelt Shenàne, Yeoha
the Ollav with his sons, and Mac Cool with his Fianna,
Eadane the poetess, and many others, and that the
descendants of the Fir-bolgs were subservient to them
since, paying them tribute and reverence ; and he said
that they were now assembled together in the centre of
the island, for that it was the custom of the Tuatha
Eireen to gather together from time to time, like men,
to each other's fairy habitations, to consume the feast of
age, and to delight in one another's society ; but that
for the rest, they dwelt upon their hills over Eiré, de-
lighting themselves with infusing subtle influences into
the winds and waters, the earth and the sea, and into
the souls of men, having magic power over all things.
And he said that they were now assembled in a plain,
beyond a river which flowed into the sea westward, and
was called the Oun Liffey, and he described to Herēmon
and his brethren where that plain was.

CHAPTER XVIII

THE TUATHA OF ANCIENT ERIN.

Τὰς πάνθ' ὁρώσας Εὐμενίδας ὁ γ' ἐθάδ' ἄν
Εἴποι λεώς νιν ἄλλα δ' ἀλλαχοῦ καλά.

SOPHOCLES.

Now when they had eaten and drunk and conversed for
a long time, they slept upon couches prepared for them
by the women, and in the morning they marched onwards again, going still towards the north.   But having
crossed the Oun Liffey they turned to the east, and they
were amazed and terrified, so profound was the empti-

ness of the land, so that all things seemed to watch them as they passed, and no man spake to another, for their voices sounded strange and terrible, and they felt as if the place was enchanted.

But as they marched, following the advice of the good Fir-bolg, on a sudden, lo, a blaze of light, and they stood face to face with the Tuatha of Erin; for on a green knoll in the wood there sat a company of persons, male and female, in bright raiment, and themselves more glorious than the dawn, and they turned their eyes upon the children of Milith, and these were astonished, even as petulant citizens that burst into an assembly of grave and reverend elders. Now there sat upon the summit of the knoll one who seemed their king, of great majesty, and at his right hand were four youths, and one was of exceeding beauty, who held a tiompan in his hand, and above his head there wheeled slowly in the air birds of bright plumage, whose singing was sweeter than the harp, and on his left hand were three men of mighty stature, and one of them had hair like glistening silver, and at his feet were two hounds. Now at the feet of him who sat at the head of the knoll were three women, one majestic and gentle, and one slender and very graceful, with laughter-loving lips, and the third had thoughtful brows and earnest eyes that seemed to read the future, and in her hand were bardic staves, which was Fohla, the daughter of the Dâda, to whom the hill of Wisna in the west was sacred, and many more were there, both male and female.

Then there rolled above the heads of the warriors a terrible noise as of distant thunder, the voice of him who sat upon the crest of the knoll, and he said—

" O children of Brogan, not unexpected of us do you

come hither, for since the rising of the sun we have
been awaiting your appearance; and now ye are come.
Wherefore have ye thus rashly set your foot upon the
soil of Eiré, which, from the beginning, has known only
us and those who honour us, and are obedient to us, as
are the Fomoroh and the Fir-bolgs? but ye are haughty
and stubborn, honouring nought but yourselves and
your brazen weapons and your bravery; and though
now astonied, yet are your necks stiff and your hearts
hard.   Nevertheless your proud heads too we shall bend,
till ye render to us the honour which is our due, and we
shall teach you your own vileness, for we are strong and
everlasting, and great and fair, as ye see ; and upon those
who reverence us not we send affliction; and if they
continue stubborn we destroy them.   Ith, the son of
Brogan, we slew, for he concealed an unjust mind, and
ye, too, we would have destroyed, but that an ancient
prophecy forbade.   Return now straightway to Inver
Slaney, nor tarry by the way, and push down your ships
into the brine, and depart from our shores ; but when
ye have gone out nine tones of the broad sea, turn
backwards again the prows of your galleys, and return
again to Fohla if you can ; and then, when affliction
comes upon you and ye are in perplexity and woe, ye
shall call upon us, the children of Dana, for succour,
and particularly upon me, Yeoha the Ollav, the son of
Erc, for your hard hearts shall melt like snow in your
breasts, and your stiff necks I will bring low.   Therefore depart.''

But as he spake he frowned and beckoned with an imperious hand, and they, the sons and kindred of Milith,
alarmed, rushed together like sheep when they see an
enemy, so ran together those mighty warriors, disturbed

and abashed, with wild eyes, and hair that stood out from their heads, clutching one another as men who have seen some intolerable sight. But as nothing succeeded, they grew calmer, and whispered together, and some said that the people of the land were playing upon them, and that they should draw their swords and make a slaughter of the people upon the hill; but others said that it was a voice of great authority which they had heard, and of these was Amargin, who spake passionately to his brethren that they should depart; but Donn and Biela, Arech Febaroe and Iar, led on by Colpa, rushed forward suddenly, brandishing their spears, to slay the inhabitants of the land, and there followed them many of the Clan Brogan and others of the Clan Gædil, for nought that was created ever ere this caused the heart of these people to fear, for they were very mighty and with dauntless minds. But as they shouted and rushed forward, suddenly they stopped, and turning, looked upon one another, for the green knoll was all that was there, empty and silent, only a great voice came from the east saying, " Depart, and delay not."

Then a trembling seized the Clanna Gæil, and the spears fell from their moist hands, and in silence they set forward, marching day and night, and slept not nor ate, and took but little rest; and when they came to Inver Slaney they pushed down the ships, and put on board all their goods and their wives and children, and the horses which Herēmon had brought with him from Espân, and they wrought all that day and night, and in the dawn of the day they departed from the island, and they meditated flight again to Espân, such terror was in their minds, only Arannan spake petulantly, for he was youthful, and wagged an idle tongue. But they feared

also to fly to Espàn, lest the vengeance of the Tuatha
De Danan should overtake them, and Amargin and Heber
strongly counselled that they should obey the divine voice
and trust to the goodness of the Shee. Accordingly,
when they were gone out nine marine distances from the
shore, Herēmon bade the coruaira who was with him to
sound the signal upon his horn, and all at once they
turned shorewards again the prows of their many-oared
galleys ; but when they looked again towards the shore
they saw nothing, only the wet sea extending to the
horizon, and they were amazed, but they rowed forwards
all that day and saw nothing, and southwards again, but
in vain, for the Tuatha De had made the island no
bigger than a hog's back upon the waters; therefore they
wearied themselves with rowing. Then they brought
the ships together and held a council, and some were
still for flying to Espàn, but they had not provisions for
the voyage, and they thought that they should all perish.
But amongst them came forth Amargin in his sacred
robes, and the other druids that were with him, and
they invoked the aid of the Tuatha of Erin, and lay
prostrate on the decks of the ships, imploring humbly
that their lives might be saved, and that they might see
land; but as they rose, lo, the hills of Erin northward,
distant not many miles, and then all the people gave
thanks to the fairy princes of Erin, and to Yeoha their
king for the deliverance.

Now as they rowed forward joyfully, they beheld clouds
black as ink rising out of the land, and stretching out
into the sea, rolling along the green surface of the sea,
and soon they saw not the land, for, as it were, a great
bastion of darkness stood upon the level floor of the sea,
solid and firm like rock, only that the waves brake not

against its base, and it went eastward and westward across the wide sea, and above it was not cloudy or ragged, but as if planed and clean cut, and like a finished wall, higher than a tall forest tree, and the rays of the sun penetrated it not, but it stood steady like a wall above the quivering waves.

Then the children of Milith were distressed and terrified once more, and Iar said, " O that I had not drawn my sword at Cathair Cro-fin, for this people are powerful as they are merciful and glorious, and all the nations of the world they could repel from their shores. Yet we landed at Inver Slaney proudly, as though we alone were great." And that speech of Iar, the son of Milith, was heard by the Tuatha, and they beheld him where he wept.

But the ships rowed forward, and penetrated the darkness, and they stood with the prows in and the sterns out, for they feared to venture in ; but inside all was darkness, cold and intense, so that no man saw the face of his fellow ; but Colpa's ship, driven faster than the rest, went in altogether, and came not out again ; but as the oarsmen began to row backwards, like a wave that rises on the beach, that tide of darkness spread beyond them, and they were as if entombed. Then the children and women cried out, and many of the warriors, for they were terrified, and the ships struck against one another, and there were noises and hollow reverberations, and so they continued for about the space of half an hour, for all men were too terrified to think. Then Amargin lifted up his voice, that echoed through the darkness, and all heard it, and he uttered a prayer to Eiré, the great queen, whose throne was Ard Erin, in Slieve Blahma, and she was one of those

that sat at the feet of the Dàda, and that prayer has
been preserved by the poets of Erin, which Amargin
chanted when they were immersed in the deathlike
darkness. But straightway, a bright form, as it were of
a woman, very beautiful, glanced through the darkness,
and after that it dissolved away till the last inky blot
had vanished, and a second time they beheld the winding shores of Eiré, and the forest-crowned hills, and
their hearts returned in them, and those who wept dried
their tears, and many prayed that the Tuatha of Erin
would afflict them no more, but give a prosperous voyage
and happy landing. Nevertheless, not so easily was
Elga to be taken possession of by the sons of Milith;
for, as once more they rowed forward, and their mariners were guiding them to that great estuary, Cumar na
Tri Usca, where the three great rivers of Lahan roll into
the sea, the Tuatha De Danan came around them and
troubled them once more.

CHAPTER XIX.

TEMPEST-TOSSED.

" The sound of blustering winds that all night long
  Had roused the sea, now with hoarse cadence lulls
  Sea-faring men o'er-watched, whose bark by chance,
  Or pinnace, anchors in some rocky bay
  After the tempest."

MILTON.

THEN suddenly the wind descended upon the sea, and
clouds gathered in the sky, concealing the sun, and
there was a great storm. Soon the oars of the mariners
were broken, and the planks rifted, while the mighty

billows rose and fell, tossing to the sky the great galleys like balls in the hands of a juggler, or drawing them down into the deep gulfs of the ocean, till the ships struck against the sandy floor, and the secret chambers of the mighty Lear were revealed, and all the while the storm so roared that no man heard his fellow's voice, and the shrieks of the women and children, and of the unwarlike people in the ships, were not perceived, also the thunder bellowed around them, with lightning and heavy rain.

Then the fleet was divided, and half drifted eastward around the flag-ship of Herēmon, and half drifted westward around that of Heber; and while it was day, these last kept together, but when the night fell, they separated, drifting over the wide sea. But in the morning Heber looked out in the grey dawn across the tossing main, and saw none of his companions, but he stood on the deck encouraging his people, and his four sons stood around him.

But all that day and night the storm raged; and when the next day dawned, the sea ran high, though the storm was abated; and, looking round, Heber saw the land rising into mountains on the right hand and on the left, and he perceived that he had been borne into a deep inver in the island; and he saw around him many of the ships of the Gæil riding safely upon the waters, but he saw not the ships of Donn, Arech the Red-browed, or the long swift ship of Iar, nor could he see Arannan, though he sought anxiously, glancing from ship to ship, and he rowed through the ships seeking tidings, and of the fate of Arannan he learned then, but of the rest afterwards.

Now Arannan was the youngest of the sons of Milith,

and very petulant, and of his brethren Heber, alone regarded him; but he sailed in the ship of Gosten, a
chieftain of the Gæil, who came with the sons of Milith
as a volunteer, and he was an old man, and delighted in
the society of Arannan. But he was not terrified by
the storm, but rather exulted; and on the second day he
recalled a saying of Amargin's, that a storm excited by
druidic arts, prevailed only on the surface of the ground
and sea, and he said that this was a druidic storm, and
not produced by the divine powers, who have just authority over the sea and wind, saying, that at the top of the
mast it would be calm as a summer evening; then he
ascended quickly to the cross-tree of the mast, and cried
out that there was no wind there; but straightway a
sudden gust drove him from his hold, like a leaf from
its branch when the winds of autumn strip the trees,
and with a scream he plunged into the boiling sea, on
the larboard side of the ship, and some said that they
had seen a great hand in the dim air that smote him
from the mast, and all the people grieved greatly for
Arannan though themselves in sore perplexity and
trouble.

Westward in the Atlantic, beyond Inver Scena, rises
a lofty rock out of the mid-ocean. Thither, in later
times, came the disciples of the Talkend and builded
their oratory, and the ragged rocks re-echoed the noise
of the bell, and the singing of psalms. Against its in-
hospitable crags had been borne the ship in which sailed
Iar, the son of Milith, with thirty warriors, and women
and children, and the ship brake against the cruel
rocks, and there they all miserably perished. But not
thus was the race of the noble Iar doomed to pass
away. For to Iar was born a son named Heber, and he

sailed in the same ship with Herēmon, from which
Heber sprang, the Crave Roe, and all the Knights of
the Red Branch.   Thus perished Iar and his people in
the darkness and the tempest, and they heard not their
own cries for the thunders of the ocean against the cliffs.

But meantime, during the dark night, the ship in
which was borne Donn, the son of Milith, was carried
shorewards, and ere they knew the danger, the ship was
driven upon a quicksand and swallowed up with all its
unhappy freight.   Donn himself and all the people who
were with him perished in sight of the land, in the grey
tempestuous dawn.   Along with him perished Arech
Febaroe, and Diel, a daughter of Milith, and very dear to
Donn, with whom she sailed.   Now the place in which
Donn's ship was lost lies westwards from Inver Scena,
facing the great sea ; and that place has ever since been
named the House of Donn, and it was a sacred place
thenceforward for the children of Milith, and was called
the House of Donn, and it was one of the places to
which the unhappy children of Lear were wont to come,
for their sweet fairy singing was heard at many places
throughout Erin, and here last were they seen by the
Gæil.

Now Heber and all his people landed on the northern
shore of the inver, and they called it after the name of
Scena, the wife of Heber, for she died there while they
were encamped upon the shore.   But afterwards they
marched northwards through the wooded mountains,
which the descendants of Kiar, the son of Fergus Mac
Roy, afterwards possessed, and on the third day they
came to Slieve Mish ; but as they marched between the
hills of that range, they beheld an awful sight, for there
met them a lady of superhuman stature and dazzling

beauty, who, with fifty others, came down the sides of
Slieve Mish, and all the people trembled and fell down
when they saw them; but Heber alone stood erect,
holding in his hands the brazen cath-barr, while his
brown hair rolled back over his mighty shoulders; and
so he stood, waiting the approach of Tuatha and the
ever-living Shee that attended her.

But she addressed Heber, and smiling sweetly, said
that she was the queen of all that land, and that she
was Banba, the daughter of the great Dana, and
that it was from her men called the island Banba,
and she welcomed Heber to his new home, and prophesied for him and for his people a great future.
Moreover she said that now for the last time would she
be seen of the Gæil, but that she would dwell for ever
invisible in the hollow folds of Slieve Mish, and that
she would care for the children of Heber to the end of
time. But even while she spake, like a dream she
vanished from before the eyes of the Gædil, and before
them there was nought but the heathery hill side, with
white lichen-clad rocks, and sprinkled with small oak
and holly, and they heard nought but the noise of the
stream that flashed down the sunny mountain slope,
and their great captain stood bare-headed in front of
them, looking as if into vacancy while he conversed with
the Shee, receiving with a humble heart the monitions
and warnings of the Ban Tuatha of Slieve Mish.

Then Heber fixed upon this place as the capital of his
realm; and here he held his solemn convocations, and
here he interred his dead, and here he called upon the
Shee for succour and counsel, and especially upon the
great Queen who had presented herself to him as he
marched, and there, between the mountains and the sea,

are the graves of all the chief people that came over with Heber.

Here they buried Scota, the wife of Milith, for she had survived her great lord, and came into Erin with her sons, and she sailed in Heber's ship. The flower of Espàn, she was planted anew in the soil of Eiré, yet here not long did she bloom, yet her name is upon the Clanna Gæil to this day. But they made for her a lofty barrow, compact of earth and stones, and in a hollow cist within it they laid the sad leavings of the funeral pyre, and those who dwell around Slieve Mish point out to the traveller still the great ferta which conceals the bones of the wife of Milith, and the mother of the far-spreading Milesian tribes.

There, too, is the tomb of Faus in its glen, who was the wife of Oon, a chieftain of the race of Gædil, who came into Erin with the Clan Milith, and he was brother of that Gosten with whom Arannan sailed, and the glen in which she was laid is named Glen Faus to this day.

But that heroine of the children of Milith, for whom men most mourned of those who were there entombed, was Feale, the wife of Lewy, the son of that Ith whom the Tuatha had slain. She was young and very beautiful, and she had lived alone in the western regions of Espàn with an aged mother, until she was wooed by Lewy, the son of Ith, who delighted in the bardic art, and was named Laid-Ken. But as she sat upon this coast, looking out over the northern sea, meditating, with happy thoughts in her gentle mind, there emerged suddenly a bather out of the sea, and he came towards her. But she knew not her husband, and she stood up and screamed, and fell down in a deadly swoon from which she did not wake.

There, then, where she died, the children of Milith and the kindred of Lewy buried Feale, raising up on high a conspicuous rath looking over the waters. But ever after that, until he died, Lewy came thither at intervals and mourned over his bride, shedding tears and chanting mournful elegies ; and these lamentations and sorrowful threnes are preserved in the ancient literature of the Gæil.

Now the ships that remained with Herēmon were borne round by the Muirnict, and in the morning, when the storm was over, they saw a deep inlet in the land, into which they rowed, for there the waters of the Boyne were poured into the sea. At this place they landed; and here Colpa, surnamed of the sword, perished, for his impetuosity destroyed him. Down from the galley's deck he sprang into a frail curragh, that he might land ; but the tiny boat, unable to sustain the weight of the mighty warrior, was overturned, and Colpa, who had never learned the art of swimming, and was besides weighed down by his brazen armour and the weapons at his belt, was there miserably drowned before the eyes of his brother.

Then Herēmon landed with Heber, the son of Iar, Amargin, his brother, the druid, and the sons of Brogan, who were his cousins, and he took possession of all the country round about, and fixed his capital at Arget Ros, on the left bank of the Nore, and ruled over the Clan Milith and the Clan Brogan. But Amargin built a Dûn at the mouth of the Oboka, where it falls into the Muirnict, and where to-day there is a populous city, and the sons of Brogan occupied the east of Erin, north and south of the Boyne. Now the Fir-bolgs of Leinster gave tribute and homage to Herēmon, and he

made Crimthann his regent under him. But every-
where that the Clan Gædil encamped there was a noise
of woodmen, and the great trees kept falling perpetually,
scaring the doves from their ancient habitations.

CHAPTER XX.

SLIEVE MISH.

" Less than a god they thought could never dwell
  Within the hollow of that shell,
  That sang so sweetly and so well."

COLLINS.

THIS then, Slieve Mish of the Shiel Heber, was the
territory, and this the city to which the exiles of Dinn
Rie came flying from the unjust king; and first, as they
approached the city, they inquired for the house of the
Brugh-Fir.   There, in the wide court, they took their
horses from the chariots and washed them, and also the
chariots; and the slaves of the Brugh-Fir gave the horses
food and water, for they brought in green grass which
they had cut, for it was spring, and the meadows were
deep with abundant grass.   After that, they themselves
were led into the house of the Brugh-Fir; and his Maor
having inquired straitly concerning them, they were
provided with food and entertainment in proportion to
their rank, and there were other strangers and wayfarers
there also; and all were entertained equally in that hospitable house.

But when they had eaten and drunk, Ferceirtney and
Craivetheena and the Rie-damna went out, going to
where was the Dûn of the king, conspicuous from its
size and lime-white walls, and on account of the deep

foss that surrounded it, according to the law; but in the great lawn of the Dûn they beheld a crowd of the people in the open air, beneath a spreading oak, between the mountains and the sea, on the west side of the Dûn, and whence could be seen the groups of wicker houses scattered over the plain, which constituted the city of the Fer-Morca, and they, too, approached and stood among the people.

Now, it so happened that the Airechta of the king was held that day, and his ollav sitting, administered justice amongst the people, having in his hand the crave ceol of his office, shaking which, he compelled attention when there arose confusion, and beside him sat Scoreea, the King of the Fer-Morca, and on the other side the Tanist of the tuath, and also those of the flauts who were the public officials of that realm ; but the ollav in the middle decided for the people their rights.

Then was Fercoirtney glad, for the ancient and wise laws which were committed to the Gæil by Fohla, which she had taught to Fiontann, and Fiontann had taught to the ollavs of the Gæil, were wholly disregarded at Dinn Rie, and there, indeed, the kings and lords dealt out judgments as they pleased, and for firm law there was only the caprice of unjust men.

But when the exiles first mingled with the crowd, a debt had been proved against a citizen of the tuath, for a priest had shown how he had not received from him the dues that appertained to his office, for it was his duty to go to Wisna in mid-Erin, and return, bearing with him the sacred fire which was kindled by the Ard-Druid on the hill of Wisna, where men were accustomed to worship Fohla. This he kindled on the eve of Sam-hâne, and from it was lighted all the fires in all the

households of Eiré, and these dues were prescribed by
Fenechas of Fail.

Then, the airey against whom the claim was made,
stood forward, and an ollav, whose duty it was, explained
how the debtor was unable to meet all his engagements,
and after that, he who was the elected chief of the
debtor's kindred announced that he was willing to
undertake the debts and the property of the defaulting
citizen, and when all this was shown to the satisfaction
of the judge, then they entered into certain agreements
before witnesses, and pledges were given, and bonds
entered into before those who were the officers of the
court.

But after that there came forward a noble, and it was
shown to the court how a party of men had passed
through his land in pursuit of a wild boar, and that one
of them, Inal Garf the son of Asail, whose liss was upon
the left bank of the Fionglas, had smote with a stone
and slain one of the slaves of him who now sought re-
dress, because he, being faithful to his lord, desired to
prevent them from passing through a field in which was
growing flax.

And this, too, Ferceirtney admired, for that there
were trained ollavs having rights and privileges, who
set before the Ard-ollav of the king the complaints of
those who sued, and the justification of those who defended, being well skilled in the laws of Fohla, and
repeating the ancient ranns adroitly, and that there were
also men attending upon those who brought forward the
witnesses and pledges and suitors without confusion or
tumult, and assisted the ollavs in the conduct of each
case.

But when the ollav had finished speaking, then came

forward Inal Garf and denied that he had injured the
slave of him who complained, and he tendered twelve
men, aireys of the tuath, who offered themselves as
compurgators of the accused, and pledges to the flaut
that Inal Garf had not slain his slave, and they bound
themselves lawfully before the officers of the court, so
that if afterwards it should be discovered that Inal Garf
had done this thing they would be all liable in a heavy
bond to that flaut, whose slave had been slain.

But after that, there came forward a harper, whose
hand was bound up in a cloth, and he was a descendant
of Kis, the wondrous harp-player of Espàn, who had
come into Erin with the sons of Milith, and for him
before they left Tor Brogan, they had cast lots, for he
was a slave, and he hàd fallen to Heber and afterwards to
Orba son of Heber, and his posterity were greatly revered
in the south of Eiré. Now, a base fellow, a fudir of that
same Inal Garf son of Asail having drunk deep, bade him,
imperiously, to play for him that he might sleep, but the
harper, not deeming it right to flatter a drunken beast,
refused, and the other flung violently at him a house-
wife's spatula which chanced to be near, and smote him
on the back of the right hand, and his hand was dis-
abled for many days, and the nail had fallen from the
thumb.

Now, when there was no justification, the Ard-ollav
computed first the enechlan on account of the insult,
and this was determined according to his rank, and after
that the corp-diera for the wounding. Then stepped
forward Ferceirtney, who was tall and bearded, and of
a noble presence, and after greeting reverently the king
and his court, begged to be permitted to repeat an
ancient rann applicable to that case, he being himself

G

an ollav, though now an exile from his country. But
when this was gladly granted, he repeated a verse of the
laws of Fohla, compact and sure in the strong fetters of
alliteration and assonance, according to which there was
a special damage on account of the making of an artificial nail, to be fitted dextrously to the finger by a skilled
person in order that the harper might return to the practice of his art the sooner. Which, though a small thing,
he deemed the court would not unwillingly consider, seeing that so great a wrong had been done to the blameless
musician.

But this, too, the Ard-ollav gladly computed, thanking
Ferceirtney for the timely assistance, and the heavy fine
was delivered over to the airey ecta of the tuath to levy
upon the estate of Inal Garf, who was lord of that fudir.

Now the king wondered greatly when he saw the
bearing of the exiles, and after the assembly was broken
up he approached them, and Ferceirtney told all the
woeful history to the king, and the king and his nobles
listened to him relating that bloody slaughter of the line
of Lorc, for the fame of it had gone through Erin, and
wherever there were just men there was compassion and
wrath. But he told them also concerning the boy, and
kindled great joy amongst the Fir-Morca, when they
found that the blood of Lorc had not all been spent upon
the earth, and they easily believed him when they looked
upon the youth. Then the king charged his own sons
to attend to Lara, and they gave him royal raiment, and
took from him his servile weeds, and they all came in
to the king's feasting chamber in his Dùn, for they were
to abide henceforward with him, and Craivetheena and
Ferceirtney wondered when they saw Lara, for he conversed with the nobles of the Fir-Morca as though he had

ne'er been aught but a Rie-damna and honoured as a king's son, and he seemed to them nobler than the young princes who were in hostageship with the king, or were being brought up at his court.

Now, at the banquet that night there was present amongst the women the only daughter of the king, a young maiden on the verge of womanhood, and Lara observed her, and she observed him, for in the minds of both there sang the immortal birds, children of the breath of Angus of the Brugh, the beautiful son of Yeoha, and their minds trembled towards one another, and a strong compulsion led them on to love.

Then turned Lara to his friend Craivetheena, for he was wont to confide to him in all things, but towards the poet he felt an awe, and he said, " O Craivetheena, I greatly desire to converse with that young damsel who sits at the right hand of the queen ; she with the clear-flashing eyes and lightsome countenance, for surely now I think it is the singing of those birds of Angus that are said to bring little good that is arising around us two as we look at one another."

Then Craivetheena spake tenderly to the boy, and after that he conferred with Ferceirtney.

Now, when the feast was over and they began to turn their attention to music and singing and the chanting of tales, then Craivetheena took down his harp from where it hung upon the wall, which ran round the room separating the great chamber in the midst of the house from the sleeping chambers, which were next the outer wall. Then from its bag of otter-skin, adorned with partang, and lined with smooth fur, he drew forth his harp, bright with gold and findruiney, and from the strings unwound the white linen wrappers that preserved their lustre. After this he tuned the sweetly-sounding strings, and all at once brake forth and sang. Now, his song was of the making of the harp, and how, in the ancient days, when the Fir-bolgs were yet in the land, Cool, who was of that race of mighty hunters, the Fianna of ancient Erin, took to wife Canola, but ere long a dark spirit of discord arose between them, for as yet music was not, nor gentle thoughts in men's minds, and there was much strife and an evil mind between those twain. Then at length Canola fled from her husband, and he repenting, pursued her, but ever as he pursued she fled, and thus they traversed Erin perpetually, until they became a proverb and a jest amongst the Fianna of Erin and the Fir-bolgs. But in the end, as she fled along the shore of the northern sea, where the Bann rolls its waters into the Moyle, she paused in her running and listened, for long-drawn sweet sounds, sorrowful and thrilling, came upon her ear. Now, upon the beach there lay the bony remnant of a mighty fish, and from rib to rib were strained the dry tendons and quivering strings, and upon these the sea-winds played, making a mournful music. There Canola stood, suddenly pausing in her flight like one entranced listening to the sweet sounds. But Cool saw this from afar, and when he too heard the sound he departed and went into the forest, and having cut down a yew tree he shaped a hollow shell and strained deer-gut across the shell from lip to lip, and played thereon with his hands, as the sea-wind on the tendons of the whale. But as the night fell and the stars rose, Canola heard sounds sweeter than the nightingale proceed from the edge of the forest where Cool played upon his rude tiompan.

But Canola approached him, and after that they went

together back to where was their home at Slieve Awlin, in the south, leading happy days thenceforward.

So sang Craivetheena ; but as he played he struck that lethean note which, in the ancient days, those harpers whom the Tuatha loved were permitted to loose from the soul of the harp, and even as at the strain of that Colchian druidess, when one by one the stars of heaven faded from the sky, so one by one the kings and nobles of the Fir-Morca, their women and their warriors, drooped and slumbered, while the bright-eyed harper turned slowly this way and that, loosing upon each that magic note, till in the end only himself and Ferceirtney preserved their intelligence, and Lara and the maiden gazing at one another.

Then stepped Lara quickly to where was Moreea, and they conversed together for a long time, and the end of this was that they avowed to one another their love, and pledged a faithful troth.

Then Craivetheena recalled him to his side, and after that, changing gradually the tones of his harp, revived again the drooping banqueters.

Nevertheless that same night the secret of the lovers was discovered by the queen, and the king was enraged: But ere long he yielded to the entreaties and tears of the maiden, and in the end he equipped an army for Lara, and he went eastward with horses and chariots and many spearmen, and the greatest captains of the Fir-Morca with him. Nevertheless they were routed in a great battle by Covac Cæl-Bray at a place near Dinn Rie, and Lara and Craivetheena and a few warriors that remained with him fled southwards to Cahirmān, and escaped in a ship into Gaul.

Thence after a season he returned with a new army—

"a lance-armed host from over-seas;" and this time
with a small band of brave warriors he appeared under
the ramparts of Dinn Rie on the evening of the feast of
Samhâne, and Craivetheena went round the Dûn and
played; but as he played the warlike spirit fled from the
hearts of those within, and they drooped even as the
banqueters in the hall of the Fir-Morca, and in the end
Lara invaded the Dûn and slew Covac Cæl-Bray, and
with him thirty kings of the race of Herēmon who were
tributary to him, and burned his palace with fire and
in a great war after that he brake the power of the
nobles that supported Cæl-Bray, and he prospered both
in peace and in war, being blessed with a heroic wife,
for into her breast the great queen Moreega had breathed
a noble spirit, and to Lara she was equal to many
warriors, and from them proceeded a race of monarchs
and legislators whose fame was great amongst the Gæil.

CHAPTER XXI.

THE FAIRY BRIDE.

"I found in dreams a place of wind and flowers,
Full of sweet trees and colour of glad grass,
In midst of which there was
A lady clothed like summer with sweet hours.
                              SWINBURNE.

She shone before my eyes awhile,
        And then no more ;
The shallop of my peace is wrecked
        On beauty's shore ;
By Hope's fair isle it rode awhile,
        And then no more.
                    JAMES CLARENCE MANGAN.

Now Emain Macha and the warlike tribes, whose
centre and capital that city was, became greater and
more powerful as generation succeeded generation, for
the valour and genius of Kimbay Mac Fiontann wrought
in the nation which he and Macha had caused to be, long
after his own charred bones were inurned at Tailteen.
Thus far and wide the confederate tribes of Emain
Macha extended their authority, binding together the
scattered nations which were the posterity of Iar. But
when well nigh a hundred years had passed away, then
amongst them started forth a mighty warrior named
Rury, and under his guidance the clans of Iar brake
forth south-westwards and poured over territories in
mid-Erin, and in the south, driving back the clans of
Heber on those of Ith, and those of Ith upon the Fir-

bolgs and the sea, and men called him The Great, on account of these conquests. Moreover his posterity alone were eligible to the kingship of the Irian nations, and his name remained upon them, so that they were called the Clanna Rury thenceforward, for his fame and power spread far and wide, and, like seed from the hand of the sower, he scattered warlike colonies of the Clanna Iar in many lands, for he penetrated from sea to sea, so that the chroniclers record one great battle which he brake upon the southern nations at Glenamna, hard by Oileen Ard Nemeth and the estuary of the Lee.

But when he, Rury the Great, died, then gradually the warlike tribes whom he had planted in the south fell away from their allegiance to Emain Macha, entering into local confederacies and alliances in which the interests of the ancestral race and the elder branch were not regarded.

Then for a season the Clanna Rury, which was now also called the Red Branch, waxed faint, and the descendants of Ugainey More in the east began again to be very great, and they seized Tara and ordered the Temairian festival, and their kings were invested with the Ard-Rieship of all Erin. But of these Yeoha, surnamed Faydleeah, was the greatest and most noteworthy both for other things and because he was the father of Queen Meave, the famous warrioress, who in after days ruled over all the country west of the Shannon, and who feared not to enter the battle, and to fight with the heroes of Eiré, and this is the parentage of Queen Meave.

Yeoha, King of Tara, having been led thither by dreams and prophecies, went alone to Brugh Leeah in the north, for the women of Erin pleased him not, and there was no High Queen at Temair. Arriving there he left his chariot and horses in the plain, with the charioteer guarding them, and went forward alone to the sacred hills. This, then, he clomb, following the course of a bright stream that ran sparkling to the valley, winding between rocks and hillocks, and through hazel trees, and under grassy, hollow banks, for that Fairy Brugh was the most beautiful in Erin. Suddenly, as he came round a bend of the stream, he beheld a beautiful girl, of a loveliness such as he had never before seen. But when the king drew nigh she looked at him with wide, innocent eyes, remembering not her former state, for the Tuatha designed that she should become the High Queen of all Erin.

Then he spake to her in the Gælic tongue, and she answered him again, and in the end he profferred love, which she accepted, and she became the Queen of Tara, and celebrated in all that age for her beauty and goodness. Moreover, years touched her not, for she was always beautiful and young, though sons and daughters grew up around her, and all who saw her loved her, but especially her own husband and her children, and her name was Eadâne.

Now after her last child Meave had been born, as Eadâne and her maidens were one day bathing on the sea-shore at Inver Kikminna, they saw a blaze of bright light approaching across the plain far away, and presently they beheld a company of young men, from whose arms and bright garments that light proceeded. But in front rode out a youth of most noble appearance which was Meehir, the son of the Dâda. Beneath him pranced a steed of extraordinary beauty, and gorgeously caprisoned. On his back was slung a shield of silver with golden rim, a long bratta of bright green depended from his shoulders, and a great brooch shone upon his breast, a golden fillet surrounded his temples, and in his right hand he grasped a long spear, along whose tree ran gold rings that uttered a peal of faint melody; but, as the maidens gazed in astonishment, the gorgeous cavalcade suddenly melted into the air like a bubble.

That night was the feast of Samhâne, and the High King entertained his chief nobles in the Tec Meadcuarta at Temair—the chamber where the mead circles—and the noise of revelry arose upon the night, the tinkling of the harp and tiompan, and the voices of many trained singers singing before the kings. But as night advanced the guests retired each to his appointed place, and at last the hall was empty and the slaves were setting the place in order and putting away the instruments of festivity. But as the last of the great candles was being extinguished, the slaves were aware of a tall youth standing in the midst of the hall, of a most noble countenance and bearing. Then one went and told the king; but when the king came out the other started as if from a reverie, and made as though he would retire, saying that he had lingered pondering over the moves of his last game of chess.

"I am fond of chess, too," said the king. "If you are not in haste to leave I would be glad to test your skill."

But when the youth consented to this, "Alas," cried the king, "it escaped me that the chess-boards have been put by, and are now in the grianan of the women, and I do not desire to disturb my wife and her maidens, who have retired early to rest this night."

"That shall be no obstacle," said the stranger, "seeing that I have an excellent one with me."

Then he produced a beautiful chess-board, with squares of silver and pearl, and out of a bag of twisted threads of findruiney he took out golden men, and ranged them on the board, and they sat down to play; but the High King wondered more and more as he gazed at the stranger arranging the board, for rays of light seemed to pass out of him, and his skin was of dazzling whiteness.

" What shall be the wager ?" said the king.

"Let the victor demand what he pleases," replied the stranger.

After this they played, and the king was beaten.

" What do you demand now ?" said the king.

"This night next year I shall signify that," replied he, folding up the board and gathering the men into the bag. After this he bade adieu to the king, and left the hall.

But the king trembled and was afraid, for as the stranger left the hall sudden darkness fell upon the vast chamber, and he was aware that all but a few of the candles had been extinguished, and that the light by which they had played had emanated from the divine visitant.

Now all that year the king was troubled with gloomy forebodings, and when the eve of Samhâne came round again the king feasted his nobles, according to the ancient custom, and in the hall were many illustrious champions and noble ladies, and Eadâne, the Queen of all Erin, was amongst them. But all the avenues to the palace were strictly guarded that night, and no un- known person was suffered to pass into the hall. Then, as before, the sound of revelry arose, and the tinkling of the harp and tiompan, but the king's brow was troubled, and he moved anxiously around his own hall, and many times gave a charge to the armed men who guarded the doors. But as the night advanced, one saw and signified to the rest how a tall and noble youth sat among the harpers, having a small harp in his hands, and the eyes of all turned upon him, for he glittered like a star amongst the singing men and harpers. But ere the king could speak he arose, and crossing the hall to where the queen sat surrounded by her ladies, he stood before her, and, striking the strings of his lyre, he sang this lay, and his voice held rapt the whole house, but his eyes the while he sang were fixed upon Eadâne.

O Beafind, will you come with me
To a wonderful country that is mine,
Where the people's hair is of golden hue,
And whiter than snow the fair body.

Nor grief nor care approach us ;
Beauty that dazzles the eye is the gift of all;
Teeth are white there, eyebrows black,
And the hue of the fox-glove on every cheek.

The meadows grow crimson flowers,
Delicately speckled like the black-bird's egg ;
Though beautiful to see are the plains of Inisfail,
They are common to the plains of the great land.

Though exhilarating the drinks of Inisfail,
They are nought to the drinks of the great land ;
There is no land like my own land,
Where age wastes not, death slays not.

Soft, sweet streams traverse the plains,
Flowing with mead and with wine ;
There beauty is uncontaminated by sin,
And sweet love is never tainted by wickedness.

We see the world and all those who live in it,
But by them we are unbeholden ;
The cloud of man's sin and transgression
Is a veil before their eyes.

But, while all were amazed and their senses steeped in forgetfulness by the magic power of that sweet singing, suddenly he raised the High Queen in his arms and bore her through the midst. But ere the armed men could lay their hands upon him, both vanished into the air, and the nobles and the High King looked one upon another, speechless, in mute amazement and trembling.

This is the history of Eadâne, the island goddess, who had afterwards her fairy palace on the lofty heights of Insi Bēra, and who delighted always to succour and befriend mortals in their adversity. Owen More she sheltered from the wrath of Conn of the Hundred Battles, when at Cloc Barra the Shiel Heber were overthrown by the clans of the north.

But after this Yeoha was disconsolate, and roamed sadly around his palace, and all the joy went out of his life. Moreover, his sons, Bras and Nar and Lothar, rebelled against him, and out of the north and west they raised a great army to wrest from him the kingship. Nevertheless, his generals defeated them in a great battle at Ath Comar. But, as he was himself fording the river in this battle, one of his sons struck him on the breast with a battle-stone, which slew him not, for it first passed through the shield of Konal Karna, the Ultonian, who sprang forward to protect him. But afterwards on Droum Croca he was presented with the heads of his three beloved sons—a ghastly trophy; and after this he was never seen to smile, and his surname became Faydleeah, on account of his heavy sighs.

CHAPTER XXII.

AILEEL MORE'S PALACE.

"The ascending pile
Stood fixed her stately height."

MILTON.

ABOUT this time arose a powerful prince in the regions
west of the Shannon, and, supported by the authority of
the King of Tara, began to extend widely his dominions.
To him, Yeoha Faydleeah, the High King, gave his
daughter Meave in marriage, heroine of the great war
of the Tân-bo-Cooalney, which is approaching.   In
order to receive the daughter of the High King with due
state and honour, Aileel More designed the erection of
a great palace in the city of Cruhane, which he had
founded as the centre and capital of his dominions, and
he collected the best architects and builders of Olnemacia to assist in the work.   So all these came together,
and encamped that night in booths.   But the next day,
when the white dawn was diffused over the land, all arose,
and orders went forth to commence the erection of the
great Dùn.   So the men swarmed forth under the guidance of their chiefs, and first the girth of the Dùn was
measured round and of the encircling fosses, and after
this they raised in the middle a strong mound, compact
of earth and stones, and broad and flat upon the top.
But meantime others had hewn down and prepared in
the forest the straight stems of tall and slender trees,
and these they drew and lowered into their recepticles,

and set them up erect upon the mound in the form of
an oblong circle, and fixed them firmly into the earth to
form the walls of the palace all around. But within
this again was erected a lesser circle, but of greater
height, which should form shafts for the support of the
roof, and which should enclose the great feasting chamber of the Dûn, and within these again, in the centre,
strong and massive, was set up the roof tree. But from
tree to tree of the outer circle ran tough rods, securely
fastened to each tree like a lattice, and upon this frame-
work was woven by deft fingers a close covering of
pliant osiers. But from the top of the great roof-tree
to the tops of the shafts that ran round the Tec Meadcuarta, and thence to the outermost circle, extended
many cross-trees and tough long upholding beams, and
over these they laid in order long shingles of oakwood,
overlapping one another, to be the roof. Meanwhile
others were plastering the sides with clay, to exclude the
cold wind. But in the sides of the house were set many
windows of glass, fitted with strong bolts of findruiney;
but those on high near the roof were large, and not protected with bolts and bars ; but all around the Dûn they
fixed weather-boards, board above board. Then they
coloured the walls snow-white, to be seen afar, and with
divers colours the roof.

After this they erected a second Dûn, not as large as
the first, but finished with greater elegance and art,
and raised up on high from the ground on strong piles,
so that the winds blew freely between that palace and
the ground, but it was attached to the great Dûn, and
there were communicating passages and stairs. This
was the Grianan of Queen Meave and her maidens, the
sunny palace of the women, without which it was no

Dûn for a king. The door of the Grianan was approached by steps; it was painted green, and beautifully carved. It was provided with fittings of silver, and the lintel above the door was of bright silver. The door opened into a portico, and that into the Grianan, and the portico was most lightly and beautifully constructed, and the roof decorated all over with the wing-feathers of bright-plumaged birds, feather overlapping bright feather.

Below the Dûn, all round the raised mound, they excavated a deep trench, throwing up the earth on the inner bank of the dyke, and with this built, encircling the Dûn, a rampart firm and strong, with palisades and bristling spikes of sharp timber. Without this again they built another rampart, and sunk a second foss; also they built a strong wall of massive stones, with all the muniments of an ancient strength. From bank to bank of each dyke extended a strong level bridge of timber—even, smooth, massive beams fastened firmly together with clamps and bolts of bronze. At the inner end of each bridge was a gateway in the rampart, defended with towers, and fitted with chambers for the keepers of the gates. The bridge was fitted with strong hinges at the inner end, and at night and in times of danger was drawn up, and, standing upright, filled the gateway, and being secured with bars, completed the defensive circuit of the ramparts. Now, when the ramparts, ditches, and bridges had been fully prepared, they diverted a portion of the neighbouring stream, which flowed from that sacred well where the Talkend afterwards met the daughters of the Ard-Rie, guiding it along a slender covered way, and the rivulet fell gurgling into the deep trenches till they were filled with the brown water; but elsewhere there was provided a drain, which carried off the overflow.

Within and between the dykes and ramparts, and on the level places at the foot of the rath, and in many places on every side, were built booleys for the cattle, and sheep-folds for the sheep, and dairies, and magazines, and stables for the king's stud, with the workshops of the smiths and kerds, and all the appurtenances and environments that belong to a noble Dûn.

But within the Dûn many expert workmen had been preparing the great hall and the chambers. The roof-tree, and the encircling shafts that supported the roof and ran round the Tec Meadcuarta, they planed and polished, and decorated with carvings, and the capital of each pillar was lustrous with ornamentations of glittering findruiney.

But from pillar to pillar ran a wooden partition, reaching half way to the roof, so as to enclose the Meadcuarta, and to divide the great central chamber from the others. Between the polished roof-shafts the large windows set on high in the walls of the Dûn poured in their light, and illuminated the hall. The walls of the Tec Meadcuarta, even the wooden partition that ran from pillar to pillar, were sculptured by cunning hands, kerds and carvers in timber, with edged tools, tracing spiral lines, subtile and elegant convolutions of intertwisted and inextricable serpents, and the forms of animals and of men and faces. All the timber-work of the Tec Meadcuarta, the shafts, and the walls, were of red yew. Fixed also in the pillars and in the walls were brazen sconces for holding candles, some large to support the great candles, taller than the spear of a warrior, that burned behind the couches of kings, and others of lesser size; also

H

armour racks to receive the shield and spears of those who feasted.

The Tec Meadcuarta, like the Dûn itself, was shaped like a lozenge. The entrance was from the south, and the royal couch was at the north end of the hall. Thence, on both sides of the hall, rounding like a horse-shoe, the tables and couches of the kings and nobles extended through the hall on both sides towards the door ; but between the couches and the walls was a clear space, along which men passed and repassed. This portion of the hall was higher than the middle, for on the middle-floor, and harmonizing with the arrangements of the raised part of the hall, were the couches and tables of mere warriors and persons of lesser note.

Between the pillars of the Tec Meadcuarta and the walls of the Dûn were constructed the chambers, those for cooking and sleeping, and the lavatories. When Cuculain came afterwards, as an ambassador from the men of Ulla, Queen Meave ordered a bath to be prepared for him in one of these.

A third of the chamber, towards the north end, was set apart for the king, and there was the champion's seat of honour in front of the king, and the seats of those whom the king desired to have about him ; and between this part of the hall and the remainder was the fire-place, where glowed a fire of red charcoal.

But all laboured at the Dûn with alacrity, and after not many days the palace was completed. Then Aileel More carried away his bride westward from Tara, with a great cavalcade, and they crossed the plains of Meath and the great ford of the Shannon, which is to-day the ford of the Loin, and they entered Olnemacia and came to Cruhâne, to the noble Cathair which had been built to receive the daughter of the High King ; but, while still far away, Queen Meave beheld the lofty Dûn, snow-white and glittering.

CHAPTER XXIII.

DEATH OF CONAIREY MORE.

Ard-Rie Erenn Uili, B.C. 53;
Slain near Ath-a-Cliah, B.C. 23.

" An eagle so caught in some bursting cloud
On Caucasus ; his thunder-baffled wings
Entangled in the whirlwind, and his eyes
That gazed on the undazzling sun now blinded
By the white lightning, while the ponderous hail
Beats on his struggling form, that sinks at length
Prone, and the aërial ice clings over it."

SHELLEY.

WHILE Meave and Aileel More ruled over Olnemacia, and Concobar Mac Nessa over the Ultonians, Tara and the Ard-Rieship was seized by one of the noblest figures of the heroic period, Conairey More the Beautiful, the son of Eterskel, of the race of Heremon. In the Irish bardic firmament there shone three stars of pre-eminent and unsurpassed beauty, Angus an Vrôga, Eros of the Gæil, whose habitation was the Fairy Brugh upon the Boyne, Conairey More, the son of Eterskel, and Cormac, the son of Art, who is yet to come.

All Erin, say the bards, had peace in the days of Conairey. Nature herself, the rivers, soil, and winds of Erin, responded to the call of the son of Eterskel, and unlearned every evil propensity. In his reign the hazels and apple-trees all but broke with the abundance of the fruit with which they were bent to the ground. The winters were not thunderous, or storm-producing, or cold. From March in one year, to April in the next, the hair of the kine was not roughened by any wind. The rivers teemed with salmon, and the sea annually cast up the secret treasures of her depths upon the strand of Inver Colpa.*

But in the end, evil portents began to disturb his reign. One day Conglass, his master of the hounds, went forth from Tara to hunt, and many of Conairey's chieftains went with him, and young princes in fosterage at his court. They never returned, and not for many days did he learn their fate. At last, messengers came out of Borda Coolan who said, that on the day on which Conglass had left Tara labourers at work in the fields beheld a stag of strange and ill-omened hue pursued madly by the royal hounds, which ran into a cave in the mountain hard by, and that the hounds and all the hunters pursuing him entered into the mountain also and disappeared. In alarm they rushed to the cave. It was empty; but far away, as it were in the heart of the mountain, they heard the noise of hunters, which gradually died away, and that place bears his name to this day.

After this, Conairey was obliged to pronounce sentence of banishment against Ferrogane and his brothers, his own foster-children, sons of Donn Dess, a prince of the province of Lahan, who were educated at Tara along with his own sons. These young chiefs were passionately attached to Conairey and their foster-brothers, and the sentence of banishment, pronounced by one they loved, poisoned and perverted their whole nature. Like later

---

* *C. f.* the statement of Tacitus, that in his time the ports of Erin were more frequented by merchants than those of Britain.

exiles, they crossed the frith and sought assistance from one of the Princes of Cambria. From him they procured ships and men, and put to sea as pirates, resolved to harass the territory of their foster-father, and thirsting for vengeance on him who had cast them like offal out of their country.

Landing at Inver Colpa, they pillaged the whole country as far as Tara. The king, who was away just then, returned, but fearing to meet the pirates with a retinue so small, he turned southwards into Lahan to raise an army there. Meantime, the pirates, having put to sea, beheld in the distance the royal banners and the king with his household troops hastening southwards, and crossing the Oun Liffey at the Bridge of Hurdles, Atha Cliah.

Now, on the banks of the Dodder was one of the houses of hospitality which Conairey had established and endowed in many parts of Erin. Here the pirates knew that Conairey would sleep that night.

Then said Ferrogane to his comrades, "Who will go this night to the palace of Daderga, which is upon the Dodder, and bring me tidings of the disposition and numbers of the warriors that are with my enemy the High King of all Erin?" And Inkel, son of the Cambrian prince, volunteered to go. Then, taking guides, Inkel set forth, but while he was away Ferrogane's spirit was disturbed, for revenge and affection held alternate sway over his soul, and he shed many tears, as he leaned alone by himself against the bulwarks of his galley, looking over the dark sea.

But at last Inkel returned, and Ferrogane hastened to meet him, and the other chieftains, and the assembly was convened. Then Inkel related all things concerning the

number and disposition of the warriors that were with
Conairey, for undetected, he had entered the great
chamber of the palace, that wherein the mead circles,
and seen the High King feasting amongst his knights,
and all the glory of his retinue.   But Ferrogane leaned
to hear him with greedy ears, for the thought of all that
dear life from which he had been cruelly cast away came
over him and unmanned him, and he wept and shed
tears as he listened, and thus, as wrote the ancient bard,
Ferrogane questioned, and thus Inkel answered him
again.

"Whom saw'st thou, O Inkel, in the champion's
throne of honour, right in front of the High King?"

"I saw a huge warrior of resolute mien, his countenance broad above, and narrow below; his eyes full of
light and fire; his teeth well set and regular.   Ruddy-
faced was he, and with hair like unto flax.   Behind him
on the armour-rack shone his burnished shield, gold-
edged; a sword by his side, and in his hand a flesh-
seeking spear."

"Pass him by for the present," said Ferrogane.
" And after him whom didst thou see?"

"I saw around the champion and close to him nine
men.   All nine seemed of one size and shape, age and
colour.   Their long hair clustered over their shoulders.
Green brattas they wore, fastened with gold brooches on
the breast.   Also they had curved shields of red bronze,
ribbed spears and swords hilted with white bone."

"It is Cormac Conlingas," cried Ferrogane, "the
mighty champion of the Ultonians.   Well I know him,
son of Concobar Mac Nessa, High King of all Ulla,
with his nine comrades; he stands for the fidelity of his
tribe."

"I saw there," said Inkel, "nine persons on one couch, with pipes piping before the king. Most beautiful were they to look upon, with golden hair. Square caps had they upon their heads; brilliantly decorated brattas, too, they wore, of rich hues."

"These are no mortal pipers," said Ferrogane. "From the fairy hills of Meath have they come down to do honour to the High King."

"I saw there a couch, and one man alone occupied it. His hair so strong that if a sack of wild apples had been emptied on his head not one of them would fall to the ground. When he speaks you might hear a pin fall to the ground."

"That is the controller of the king's household," said Ferrogane. "His decisions are not to be impugned."

"I saw there on one couch three youths, with brattas of crimson silk, and wheel-brooches of gold. Lustrous and yellow was the thick fleece of hair that rolled from the head of each. Wondrous truly was that hair. Like their vivid countenances, it was full of light and life. Now it would descend lower than their shoulder-blades, and anon gather itself together more curled than the forehead of a bleating ram. Over each of them hung a golden shield, and burned the candle of a royal house. Men cannot remove from them their gaze, so beautiful are their countenances and their behaviour."

"Continue thy identifications, O Inkel," cried Ferrogane, bowing low his head and weeping. Ferrogane now shed tears and moaned till the third part of the night was past, and the front of his cloak was wet with tears, and no word was heard out of his mouth. "Alas and alas," cried Ferrogane, "a good cause truly have I

for these tears, for they are my own foster-brethren—
Oball and Oblini, and Coirpry Finn More, the three sons
of the High King."

"I saw there on an ornamented couch the fairest and
bravest of the champions of Erin. Of glistening crimson was his bratta, bright with gems the gold brooch
upon his breast. White as snow was one of his cheeks,
whiter and ruddier than the fox-glove was the other.
Violet blue was one of his eyes, blacker than the chaffer
was the other. Like a reaping basket was the bright
golden hair that flowed from his head. It fell lower
than the tips of his shoulder-blades, more curled than
the forehead of a bleating ram."

"It is Konal Karna, fairest and bravest of the Red
Branch. He, too, is a hostage for the fidelity of the
Ultonians." *

"I saw there a couch, its ornamentation more splendid than that of all the rest, and curtained around with
cloth of silver. On each side sat two splendid champions, but he who sat in the midst was of dazzling
beauty. In his countenance was the fire and majesty
of a sovereign, the grace and tenderness of a bard. Like
the colour of the clouds at sunrise were the changing
hues of the bratta that wrapped his mighty shoulders,
On his breast glistened a huge wheel-brooch of gold,
and like the sheen of burnished gold was his hair.
Beside him lay his sword. A hand's-breadth of the pure
steel was exposed from the scabbard ; but from that
hand's-breadth a light blazed that illuminated the house,
and before which the candles burned dim, and from it
came forth music sweeter than the sounds of harpers
harping in kings' houses."

* *C. f.* Hugo's description of the Duchess Josiana.

So far proceeded the Briton, till borne away by the
memory of that vision, he brake into sudden song and
chanted this lay—

> " I saw a tall, illustrious prince
>   Start forth against that bright ground,
>   Full-flowing in the springtide of dazzling beauty,
>   Gentle and brave.

> " I saw a renowned, placid king
>   His kingly place fulfilling,
>   In his couch that crossed the hall
>   From wall to wall.

> " I saw his cheeks white and crimson,
>   Dazzling white and like unto the dawn
>   Upon the stainless colour of snow ;
>   And pupils sparkling black
>   In dark blue eyes that glanced,
>   Drooped o'er by lashes chaffer-black.

> " The glittering princely diadem I saw,
>   With regal splendour
>   Flash forth its high refulgence,
>   And flood with light his noble countenance.

> " I saw the splendid Ard-rōth
>   Circle his head, enwreathing
>   With his hair its brightness ;
>   The sheen of gold most brilliant
>   Above his curling yellow locks.

> " I saw his crimson bratta, silken,
>   Of many hues,
>   Embroidery of gold o'er-ran it,
>   Traversing its gorgeous folds.

> " The mighty brooch with golden spear I saw,
>   Bright like the full moon,
>   Thick-sown with gems along the edge ;
>   It filled the noble spaces of his breast
>   From shoulder to manly shoulder.

" His splendid tunic of pure linen,
    With striped and silken borders,
    Bright as a face-reflecting mirror,
    Closed round his princely neck,
    Thence flowing on his bosom
    Down to his manly knees.

" At his right hand a kingly wand I saw,
    Of white silver ;
    Therewith, like eagles from their aeries,
    Those long-haired warriors
    He summons forth."

Anon the High King drooped and slept ; at his head sat one of his knights, at his feet the other.

Suddenly he started out of slumber and looked around, and cried aloud :

"I have dreamed of phantoms bearing death,
    Of a host of creeping, treacherous enemies,
    Of a combat of men upon the banks of the Dothra,
    And, early and alone,
    The King of Temair was slain."

" Identify for me, O Ferrogane, who it was that spake these words."

" I do not know his like," cried Ferrogane. " It was the vision of a king, and indeed it is the king, most noble, most dignified, most comely and powerful that has come of the whole world ; the most beautiful and perfect that has ever appeared. It is Conairey More, the son of Eterskel. It is he that was there, the High King of all Erin. Ard-Rie Erenn Uili."

That night, as darkness was waning, dim figures stole through the trees along the banks of the Dodder, silently wading the foss, and creeping over the ramparts of the Dûn. Suddenly a mighty shout awoke all who slept. There was a combat of men on the banks of the

Dothra, and, early and alone, the King of Temair was slain.

Next day the Ultonians, who held the frontier fortress, and guarded the southern border of the province, saw a party of fugitives hastening northwards along the great road leading out of Mid-Erin into Ulla. It was Cormac Conlingas and Konal Karna, with their comrades, flee-ing homewards from that massacre in which the High King of all Erin was slain.

CHAPTER XXIV.

BOYHOOD OF CUCULAIN.

" And wears upon his baby brow the round
And top of sovereignty."
SHAKESPEARE.

" Cuculain filius Sualtam, fortissimus heros Scotorum."
TIERNA.

FERROGANE calls Konal Karna the bravest of the Red Branch. Perhaps he was at the time; but his pre-eminence was soon to be taken away. A sun was rising before which his star was to grow pale.

Dectera, one of the sisters of Concobar Mac Nessa, married a prince whose patrimony lay along the shores of the Muirnict, and whose capital was Dûn Dalgan. They had one child, a boy, whom they named Setanta.

As soon as Setanta was able to understand the stories and conversation of those around him, he evinced a passion for arms and the martial life, which was so pre-mature and violent as to surprise all who knew him. His thought for ever ran on the wars and achievements of the Red Branch. He knew all the knights by name, the appearance and bearing of each, and what deeds of valour they had severally performed. Emain Macha, the capital of the Clanna Rury, was never out of his mind. He saw for ever before his mind its moats and ramparts, its gates and bridges, its streets filled with martial men, its high-raised Dûns and Raths, its branching roads, over which came the tributes of wide Ulla to the High King. He had seen his father's tribute driven thither, and had even longed to be one of the four-footed beasts that he beheld wending their way to the wondrous city. But above all, he delighted to be told of the great school where the young nobles of Ulster were taught martial exercises and the military art, under the superintendence of chosen knights, and of the High King himself. Of the several knights he had his own opinion, and had already resolved to accept no one as his instructor save Fergus Mac Roy, tanist of Ulster.

Of his father he saw little. His mind had become impaired, and he was confined in a secluded part of the Dûn. But whenever he spoke to Dectera of what was nearest his heart, and his desire to enter the military school at Emain Macha, she laughed, and said that he was not yet old enough to endure that rough life. But secretly she was alarmed, and formed plans to detain him at home altogether. Then Setanta concealed his desire, but inquired narrowly concerning the partings of the roads on the way to Emania.

At last, when he was ten years old, selecting a favourable night, Setanta stole away from his father's Dûn, and before morning had crossed the frontier of the tuath. He then lay down to rest and sleep in a wood. After this he set out again, travelling quickly lest he should be met

by any of his father's people. On his back was strapped
his little wooden shield, and by his side hung a sword
of lath. He had brought his ball and hurle of red-
bronze with him, and ran swiftly along the road, driving
the ball before him, or throwing up his javelin into the
air, and running to meet it ere it fell.

In the afternoon of that day Fergus Mac Roy and the
king sat together in the park that surrounded the king's
palace. A chess-board was between them, and their
attention was fixed on the game. At a distance the
young nobles were at their sports, and the shouts of the
boys and the clash of the metal hurles resounded in
evening air.

Suddenly the noise ceased, and Fergus and the king
looked up. They saw a strange boy rushing backwards
and forwards through the crowds of the young nobles,
urging the ball in any direction that he pleased, as if in
mockery, till none but the very best players attempted
to stop him, while the rest stood about the ground in
groups. Fergus and the king looked at each other for
a moment in silence.

After this, the boys came together into a group, and
held a council. Then commenced what seemed to be
an attempt to force him out of the ground, followed by a
furious fight. The strange boy seemed to be a very demon
of war; with his little hurle grasped, like a war-mace,
in both hands, he laid about him on every side, and the
boys were tumbling fast. He sprang at tall youths like
a hound at a stag's throat. He rushed through crowds
of his enemies like a hawk through a flock of birds.
The boys, seized with a panic, cried out that it was one
of the Tuatha from the Fairy Hills of the Boyne, and
fled right and left to gain the shelter of the trees.

Some of them, pursued by the stranger, ran round Concobar Mac Nessa and his knight. The boy, however, running straight, sprang over the chess-table; but Concobar deftly seized him by the wrist, and brought him to a stand, but with dilated eyes, and panting.

" Why are you so enraged, my boy?" said the king, " and why do you so maltreat my nobles?"

" Because they have not treated me with the respect due to a stranger," replied the boy.

" Who are you yourself?" said Concobar.

" I am Setanta, the son of Sualtam, and Dectera, your own sister, is my mother; and it is not before my uncle's palace that I should be insulted and dishonoured."

This was the debût and first martial exploit of the great Cuculain, type of Irish chivalry and courage, in the bardic firmament a bright particular star of strength, daring, and glory, that will not set or suffer aught but transient obscuration till the extinction of the Irish race; Cuculain, bravest of the brave, whose glory affected even the temperate-minded Tierna, so that his sober pen has inscribed, in the annals of ancient Erin, this testimony: " Cuculain filius Sualtam fortissimus heros Scotorum."

After this, Setanta was regularly received into the military school, where, ere long, he became a favourite both with old and young. He placed himself under the tuition of Fergus Mac Roy, who, each day, grew more and more proud of his pupil, for, while still a boy, his fame was extending over Ulla.

It was not long after this that Setanta received the name by which he is more generally known. Culain was chief of the black country of Ulla, and of a people altogether given up to the making of weapons and armour, where the sound of the hammer and the husky noise of the bellows were for ever heard. One day, Concobar and some of his knights, passing through the park to partake of an entertainment at the house of the armourer, paused awhile, looking at the boys at play. Then, as all were praising his little nephew, Concobar called to him, and the boy came up, flushed and shy, for there were with the king the chief warriors of the Red Branch: Leairey Bewda, with his heavy brow and deep-set, observing eyes, Fergus Mac Leda, King of Rathlin, Conn Mac Morna, and his friend Felim, son of Kelkar, Cormac Conlingas, the High King's son, and Fergus Mac Roy, besides others. But Concobar bade him come with them to the feast, and the knights around him laughed, and enumerated the good things which Culain had prepared for them. But, when Setanta's brow fell, Concobar bade him finish his game, and after that proceed to Culain's house, which was to the west of Emain Macha, and more than a mile distant from the city. Then the king and his knights went on to the feast, and Setanta returned joyfully to his game.

Now, when they were seen afar upon the plain, the smith left his workshop and put by his implements, and having washed from him the sweat and smoke, made himself ready to receive his guests; but the evening fell as they were coming into the liss, and all his people came in also and sat at the lower table, and the bridge was drawn up, and the door was shut for the night, and the candles were lit in the high chamber.

Then said Culain, "Have all thy retinue come in, O Concobar?" And when the King said that they were all there, Culain bade one of his apprentices go out and let loose the great mastiff that guarded the house. Now this dog was as large as a calf, and exceedingly

fierce, and he guarded all the smith's property outside
the house, and if anyone approached the house without beating on the gong which was outside the foss,
and in front of the draw-bridge, he was accustomed to
rend him. Then the mastiff, having been let loose,
careered three times round the liss, baying dreadfully,
and after that remained quiet outside his kennel, guarding his master's property. But inside they devoted
themselves to feasting and merriment, and there were
many jests made concerning Culain, for he was wont to
cause laughter to Concobar Mac Nessa and his knights,
yet was he good to his own people and faithful to the
Crave Rue, and very ardent and skilful in the practice
of his art. But as they were amusing themselves in
this manner, eating and drinking, a deep growl came
from without, as it were a note of warning, and after
that one yet more savage; but where he sat in the champion's seat, Fergus Mac Roy struck the table with his
hand, and rose straightway, crying out, "It is Setanta ;"
but ere the door could be opened they heard the boy's
voice raised in anger, and the fierce yelling of the dog,
and a scuffling in the bawn of the liss. Then they
rushed to the door in great fear, for they said that the boy
was torn in pieces; but when the bolts were drawn back,
and they sprang forth eager to save the boy's life, they
found the dog dead and Setanta standing over him with
his hurle, for he had sprung over the foss, not fearing
the dog. Forthwith, then, his tutor, Fergus Mac Roy
snatched him up on his shoulder, and returned with
great joy into the banquet hall, where all were well
pleased at the preservation of the boy, except Culain himself, who began to lament over the death of his dog, and
to enumerate all the services which he rendered to him.

" Do not grieve for thy dog, O Culain," cried Setanta, from the shoulder of Fergus, " for I will perform those services for you myself until a dog equally good is procured to take the place of him I slew."

Then one, jesting, said, " Cu-Culain," and thenceforward he went by this name.

It was about this time that he was presented with a companion and attendant, Læg, son of the King of Gowra, for Rury More had brought his father a captive to the north, and his son Læg, born to him in old age, in the north, was given to Cuculain when he returned to Dûn Dalgan for the first time from Emain Macha, and he was four years older than Cuculain.

CHAPTER XXV.

DEIRDRE.

" Yea, for her sake, on them the fire gat hold."
SWINBURNE.

WHEN Concobar Mac Nessa was called to the Ard-Rieship of Ulla he celebrated his inauguration by a great banquet at Emain Macha, and all the knights of the Crave Rue were there, and the chiefs and kings of the Clanna Rury, and the kings and ambassadors of the tribes and nations of Erin that were favourable to his succession. There were also there noble ladies, and amongst them the bride of Felim, chief bard of the Ultonians. It was a year of prophecies and portents, and Cathvah, the druid—he who had eaten of the nuts of knowledge—the interpreter of dreams and omens—had

I

announced that an age was then in its inception, which would be renowned to the ends of the earth, and the last age of the world.

That night the Ultonians feasted with more magnificence than had ever before that been used in Erin, and the sounds of revelry arose out of the vast and high Dûn into the night, and the lights glared far and wide, and there was the sound of the harp and of singing voices, for Emain Macha was wholly given over to festivity.

Then about the time that the shrill cry of the cock is first heard, a rapid fear swept like a wind through the whole city, and smote an universal silence, and men held their breaths awaiting some prodigy. Anon there arose upon the night a shrill and agonizing scream, as of an animal pierced, that utters a cry in its agony. And three times the cry shrilled through the city. But simultaneously were heard low thunder-like mutterings, whereat the earth trembled; but this came from the Tayta Brac, wherein was the warlike equipment of all the Red Branch; and aged warriors who had fought under Rury recognised that solemn warning, and they knew what shield it was that announced impending disaster. And, after this, there arose sounds of battle, crash of meeting hosts and shattering spears, the shoutings of warriors, and the war-cries of the Clans of Ulla, and between these noises was heard, far away, the roaring of the sea. Then the prodigy died away, and men saw the reflection of their own fear in the white faces of their comrades.

But in the king's palace the feast was broken up, and the king summoned a council of his great men, and there it was determined that Cathvah the seer should be interrogated concerning the import of the prodigy. Then Cathvah arose with his druidical instruments in his hands, and chanted the chant of divination; and under the power of that chant the veil that hides futurity was rent before his mind, and in a sacred phrenzy he walked towards the Grianan of the women, and the king and his knights followed him reverently. Then he approached the bride of the chief bard of Ulla, singling her out from amongst all the women in the Dûn, and he stood above her and prophesied :

"No common child bearest thou in thy womb, O lady. Beneath thy zone, veiled yet in infancy, I see a woman of wondrous beauty, bright gold her hair, eyes piercing and splendid, tongue full of sweet sounds, her countenance like the colour of snow blended with crimson; but out of her beauty shall arise a sword. It is the destruction of the wide territories of Ulla that thou bearest in thy womb, O lady—wasting wars and conflagrations and blood. I see the Red Branch divided against itself, and the sons of Usna slain, and the son of Duthrect, and I see the son of the High King, and Fergus, and many kings of the tribes of Ulla flying across the boundary into exile, and wars yet greater arising out of that expatriation which shall consume away the children of Iar."

After this, Concobar convened his council, and he himself desired that the child, when born, should be slain ; but it was finally determined that a tower should be built in a remote and inaccessible spot, and that she should be immured there until she died, for they reverenced the interpretations of Cathvah.

The child was born a beautiful blue-eyed babe, and she was called Deirdré, and Concobar selected a prudent and wise woman named Lowrcam, to whom he committed the child, and she was immured according to the resolution of the saba of the kings, at Emain Macha.

The child Deirdré grew up so beautiful, gentle, and
tender, that she drew to herself the whole heart's-love
of the lady who guarded her, so that her loyalty to the
council of the kings, and to Concobar Mac Nessa, was
dissolved, and the memory of the portents that attended
Deirdré's birth, and the vaticinations of Cathvah, faded
away. Therefore she relaxed the severity of that im-
prisonment, and suffered her to wander in the forest
that surrounded the tower, to gather flowers, and listen
to the songs of the birds.

There were at this time amongst the knights of the
Red Branch three young warriors, the glory of all Ulla
for their beauty and their accomplishments, Naysi, and
Anly, and Ardan, the three sons of Usna, and they were
loved by all who knew them, and chiefly by Fergus Mac
Roy, who was the great sheltering tree of all the noblest
and best of the young knights. And now that I have
likened Fergus to a great sheltering tree, I mind me
how afterwards, in the wars of the Tân-bo-Cooalney, one
seeing him moving in the fore-front of Queen Meave's host
said, "He seems to me, observing him, to resemble a
great tree that stands alone upon the lawn of some noble
Dûn." But to him the children of Usna were dearer
than all the rest of the Red Branch. Naysi was the
most beautiful of the brothers, black as the raven were
his eyebrows and curling hair, and white and ruddy his
countenance.

It so happened that, in a great chase, Naysi, the son
of Usna, got separated from his companions, and as he
wandered through the forest, seeking to recover his way,
he came to where was the lonely tower in which Deirdré
was immured. But he presented himself to her as she
walked among the trees, and the end of that meeting

was, that they gave each other their love, and plighted
a faithful troth.

Then Naysi took counsel with his brothers, and with
the chiefs of his clan, and they were troubled and afraid,
and besought him to cease from that upon which he had
resolved. But, when they could not persuade him, they
resolved to perish along with him before the wrath of
the High King, if it were necessary, rather than suffer
him to be unbefriended.

So there was a sudden hosting of the clan, and they
bore away Deirdré from her tower, and marched rapidly
northwards to the Moyle. But at Dûn Kermnah, upon
the sea, a fleet was prepared. Thus the Clanna Usna
deserted Concobar Mac Nessa, and they passed into
Alba, and went into the service of the king of that land.

Then there was great lamentation over all Ulla, for
the loss of the children of Usna, and in every Dûn,
from Assaroe to Dundalgan, the poets chanted mournful
strains about the exile of the sons of Usna, and the
wondrous beauty of Deirdré, and the noblest of the youth
of Ulla, and of the rest of Eiré, passed into Alba, to
see Deirdré, and many of them took service under them,
and the Clan Usna grew mightier every day. But Concobar Mac Nessa passed sentence of perpetual banishment and exile against the clan, for he feared the words
of the prophet prophesying the Red Branch divided
against itself.

But, from the time of their departure, Fergus Mac
Roy had no rest, for he was disconsolate for the perpetual
exile of Naysi, Anly, and Ardan, and he was wroth with
Concobar Mac Nessa, and uttered bitter gibes and scoffs
against the High King and his star-gazers. But, in the
end, he procured a reversal of the sentence of perpetual

exile, and forthwith, taking his household troops, and his sons, Illan the Fair, and Bewney the Ruthless Red, he passed over into Alba; and when the sons of Usna heard of the reversal of the sentence, they gave three shouts of joy, and shed tears of pleasure; but Deirdré uttered three cries of lamentation, and shed tears of sorrow, for she said that evil was impending over the children of Usna. Then Fergus Mac Roy said that they were under his protection, and that no harm could happen them, for that there was no king in Erin who could break through his protection. But Deirdré would not be comforted, and all the day and night she shed tears, and related dreams and omens, and predicted the treachery of Bewney the Ruthless Red; yet they did not give heed to her, but hastened forward the sailing. But innumerable were the lamentations of Deirdré concerning the children of Usna, and they are preserved in the books of the poets. And, both in Alba, before they set out, and while they sailed across the intervening sea, were they warned by many portents. But beside many other, it was permitted them to hear the mournful chanting of the unhappy children of Lear. For, as they rowed across the cold expanse of the Moyle, they heard the children singing, and it was night. There the hands of all the mariners were relaxed, and every oar suspended. Then the whole host wept together, and the warriors and strong men sobbed aloud, when they heard the children singing, for the cry of them, as they sang, pierced the starry night, and dissolved every heart.

After this, they rowed on in silence, and came to Dûn Kermnah, and the children of Usna hastened onward to Emain Macha, trusting in the High King, that he would not violate the protection of Mac Roy.

Nay-the-less, Concobar Mac Nessa gave no heed to the protection of Fergus, for he saw that his authority and sovereignty were set aside, and that now the wars predicted by Cathvah were about to burst, and that Fergus and the children of Usna were confederate against him. Therefore, he made a swift and sudden excursion into the north, with his bravest and most agile warriors; but Fergus Mac Roy had delayed at Dûn Kermnah, having been detained there by a stratagem, and Bewney the Ruthless Red, went over to his side, and betrayed the children of Usna. But Concobar Mac Nessa seized Deirdré and Naysi, Anly and Ardan, and he slew the children of Usna, and Illan the Fair, and many of the Clan Usna, and despised the protection of Fergus Mac Roy.

But, when Fergus Mac Roy heard how his protection had been set at naught, and his son slain, and the sons of Usna, he passed into rebellion, and drew away with him two-thirds of the Red Branch; for wide territories passed into rebellion along with him, and amongst them Cormac Conlingas, the High King's son, and the children of Iar were divided against themselves, and the whole realm was shaken with war, and Emain Macha burned to the ground; but, in the end, Fergus Mac Roy was defeated, and driven over the border into the country of the Olncmacta, west of the Shannon, and all these exiles went into the service of Aileel More and Queen Meave, and Fergus Mac Roy was the greatest of her generals at the breaking out of the wars of the Tanbo-Cooalney.

CHAPTER XXVI.

THE NUTS OF KNOWLEDGE.

" And a river went out of Eden to water the garden ; and from thence it was parted, and became into four heads. The name of the first river is Pison, and the name of the second river is Gihon, and the name of the third river is Hiddekel, and the fourth river is Euphates."

MOSES.

IN the heart of green Banba a fairy garden, and in the garden an ever-springing fountain of pure translucent water. But, unseen of the Gæil, that well leaped and bubbled, and the Tuatha De Danan alone beheld it, themselves unseen, a divine race. There for ages it leaped and sprang, feeding the great streams of Fohla.

Around the well grew hazel-trees, seven in number, with leaves of tender green, and berries of bright crimson, and the nuts that grew on these trees filled with knowledge the mind of any who ate them, so that to him the past and present and future were revealed, and the Tuatha Eireen alone had access to that garden, and ate not of the fruit of those trees, for holy fear and ancient prophecy forbade.

But Sinān, who was of the race of Lear, the marine god, having an evil mind, resolved to eat of the fruit, and she approached the fountain by stealth. But the divine fountain arose in wrath with a roaring, with billows and water-spouts and foam, and it caught and surrounded her, and overwhelmed her as she fled, and whirling her along and around, brake forth westward and southward. And, like a dead leaf, it bore her

past the Great Ford, and past the city of the host-
ings and the fairy hills, where Bove Derg had his habitation, and past Limenich, and cast her into the great
sea westward. But thenceforward the waters of western
Erin flowed along the channel which had been made by
the flood which the sacred well-head had cast forth
against the grand-daughter of Lear, and after her it has
received its name.

Unseen by the Gæil the fountain still springs, feeding the great stream of Fohla, and the hazels shed their
crimson fruit on the mossy ground, and into the clear
water, and beneath the ground it sends forth rills feeding the great streams. But at the time of the shedding
of fruit, a salmon, the Yeo Feasa appears in that garden
in the clear well, and as each divine nut falls upon the
surface, he darts upwards and devours it. He is larger
and more beautiful than the fishes of his tribe, glittering
with crimson stars and bright hues; but for the rest of
the year he roams the wide ocean and the great streams
of Inis Fail. Now when any of the Gæil excelled in
wisdom, men said he has eaten of the nuts of knowledge, and of Cathvah, too, the Ard-Druid, men said
this.

CHAPTER XXVII.

CUCULAIN IS KNIGHTED.

" Then felt I like some watcher of the skies
When a new planet swims into his ken."

KEATS.

ONE night in the month of the fires of Bel, Cathvah, the
druid and star-gazer, was observing the heavens through
his astrological instruments. Beside him was Cuculain,
just then completing his sixteenth year. Since the exile
of Fergus Mac Roy, Cuculain had attached himself most
to the Ard-Druid, and delighted to be along with him
in his studies and observations. Suddenly the old man
put aside his instruments, and meditated a long time
in silence.

" Setanta," said he at length, " art thou yet sixteen
years of age ?"

" No father," replied the boy.

" It will then be difficult to persuade the king to
knight thee and enroll thee among his knights," said
Cathvah. " Yet this must be done to-morrow, for it
has been revealed to me that he whom Concobar Mac
Nessa shall present with arms to-morrow, will be renowned to the most distant ages, and to the ends of the
earth. Thou shalt be presented with arms to-morrow,
and after that thou mayest retire again for a season
amongst thy comrades, nor go out amongst the warriors
until thy strength is mature."

The next day Cathvah procured the king's consent
to the knighting of Cuculain. Now, on the same

morning, one of his grooms came to Concobar Mac Nessa, and said, "O Chief of the Red Branch, thou knowest how no horse has eaten barley, or ever occupied the stall where stood the divine steed which, with another of mortal breed, in the days of Kimbay Mac Fiontann, was accustomed to bear forth to the battle the great war-queen, Macha Monga-Rue; but ever since that stall has been empty, and no mortal steed hath profaned the stall in which the deathless Lia Macha was wont to stand. Yet, O Concobar, as I passed into the great stable on the east side of the court-yard, wherein are the steeds of thy own ambus, and in which is that spot since held sacred, I saw in the empty stall a mare, grey almost to whiteness, and of a size and beauty such as I have never before seen, who turned to look upon me as I entered the stable, having very gentle eyes, but such as terrified me, so that I let fall the vessel in which I was bearing curds for the steed of Konaul Clareena, and she approached me, and laid her head upon my shoulder, making a strange noise."

Now, as the groom was thus speaking, Cowshra Mend Macha, a younger son of Concobar, came before the king and said—"Thou knowest, O my father, that house in which is preserved the chariot of Kimbay Mac Fiontann, wherein he and she, whose name I bear, the great queen that protects our nation, rode forth to the wars in the ancient days, and how it has been preserved ever since, and that it is under my care to keep bright and clean. Now, this day at sunrise, I approached the house, as is my custom, and approaching, I heard dire voices, clamorous and terrible, that came from within, and noises like the noise of battle, and

shouts as of warriors in the agony of the conflict, that
raise their voice with short intense cries as they ply
their weapons, avoiding or inflicting death. Then I
went back terrified, but there met me Minrowar, son of
Gerkin, for he came but last night from Moharne, in
the east, and he went to look at his own steeds; but
together we opened the gate of the chariot-house, and
the bronze of the chariot burned like glowing fire, and
the voices cried out in acclaim, when we stood in the
doorway, and the light streamed into the dark chamber.
Doubtless, a great warrior will appear amongst the Red
Branch, for men say that not for a hundred years have
these voices been heard, and I know not for whom
Macha sends these portents, if it be not for the son of
Sualtam, though he is not yet of an age to bear arms."

Thus was Concobar prepared for the knighting of
Cuculain.

Then in the presence of his court, and his warriors,
and the youths who were the comrades and companions
of Cuculain, Concobar presented the young hero with
his weapons of war, after he had taken the vows of the
Red Branch, and having also bound himself by certain
gæsa. But Cuculain looked narrowly upon the weapons,
and he struck the spears together, and clashed the sword
upon the shield, and he brake the spears in pieces, and
the sword, and made chasms in the shield.

" These are not good weapons, O my King," said the
boy.

Then the king presented him with others that were
larger and stronger, and these, too, the boy brake into
little pieces.

" These are still worse, O son of Nessa," said the boy,
" and it is not seemly, O Chief of the Red Branch, that

on the day that I am to receive my arms I should be
made a laughing-stock before the Clanna Rury, being
yet but a boy."

But Concobar Mac Nessa exulted exceedingly when
he beheld the amazing strength and the waywardness
of the boy, and beneath delicate brows his eyes glittered
like glittering swords as he glanced rapidly round on the
crowd of martial men that surrounded him ; but amongst
them all he seemed himself a bright torch of valour and
war, more pure and clear than polished steel. But he
beckoned to one of his knights, who hastened away and
returned, bringing Concobar's own shield and spears
and sword out of the Tayta Brac, where they were kept,
an equipment in reserve. And Cuculain shook them
and bent them, and clashed them together, but they
held firm.

" These are good arms, O son of Nessa," said Cuculain.

Then there were laid forward a pair of noble steeds
and a war-car, and the king conferred them on Cuculain.
Then Cuculain sprang into the chariot, and standing
with legs apart, he stamped from side to side and shook
and shook, and jolted the car until the axle brake, and
the car itself was broken to pieces.

" This is not a good chariot, O my King," said the
boy.

Then there were led forward three chariots, and all
these he brake in succession.

" These are not good chariots," O Chief of the Red
Branch," said Cuculain. " No brave warrior would enter the battle or fight from such rotten foot-hold."

Then the king called to his son Cowshra Mend Macha
and bade him take Læg, and harness to the war-chariot,
of which he had the care, the wondrous grey steed, and

that one which had been given him by Kelkar, the son of Uther, and to give Læg a charioteering equipment to be charioteer of Cuculain. For now it was apparent to all the nobles and to the king that a lion of war had appeared amongst them, and that it was for him that Macha had sent these omens.

Then Cuculain's heart leaped in his breast when he heard the thunder of the great war-car and the mad whinnying of the horses that smelt the battle afar. Soon he beheld them with his eyes, and the charioteer with the golden fillet of his office, erect in the car, struggling to subdue their fury. A grey long-maned steed, whale-bellied, broad-chested, behind one yoke, a black, tufty-maned steed behind the other.

Like a hawk swooping along the face of a cliff when the wind is high, or like the rush of the March wind over the smooth plain, or like the fleetness of the stag roused from his lair by the hounds, and covering his first field, was the rush of those steeds when they had broken through the restraint of the charioteer, as though they galloped over fiery flags, so that the earth shook and trembled with the velocity of their motion, and all the time the great car brayed and shrieked as the wheels of solid and glittering bronze went round, for there were demons that had their abode in that car.

The charioteer restrained the steeds before the assembly, but nay-the-less a deep purr, like the purr of a tiger, proceeded from the axle. Then the whole assembly lifted up their voices and shouted for Cuculain, and he himself, Cuculain, the son of Sualtam, sprang into his chariot, all armed, with a cry as of a warrior springing into his chariot in the battle, and he stood erect and brandished his spears, and the war-sprites of

the Gæil shouted along with him, for the Bocanahs
and Bananahs and the Geniti Glindi, the wild people
of the glens, and the demons of the air, roared around
him, when first the great warrior of the Gæil, his battle-
arms in his hands, stood equipped for war in his chariot
before all the warriors of his tribe, the kings of the
Clanna Rury and the people of Emain Macha. Then
Cuculain bid Læg let the steeds go, and they flew away
rapidly, and three times they encircled Emain Macha.
Then said Cuculain—

" Where leads the great road yonder ? "

" To Ath-na-forarey and the border of the Crave
Rue," said Læg.

" And wherefore is it called ' the Ford of the Watch-
ings ? ' " sad Cuculain.

" Because," said Læg, " there is always one of the
king's knights there keeping ward and watch over the
gate of the province."

" Guide thither my horses," said Cuculain, " for I
have sworn not to lay aside my arms to-day until I have
wetted them in the blood of one of the enemies of my
tribe ; and who is it who is over the garrison this day ? "

" It is Konal Karna who commands there this day,"
said Læg.

Now, as they were drawing near to the ford, the watchman heard the rolling of the chariot and the trampling
of the horses, and they sent word to Konal that a war-
chariot was approaching from Emain Macha, but Konal
came out of the Dûn with his people, and when he saw
Cuculain in the war-car of the king, and his glittering
weapons around him, he began to laugh, and said,

" Is it arms the boy has taken ? "

And Cuculain said, " Indeed it is, and I have sworn

not let them back into the Tayta Brac until I have
wetted them in the blood of one of the enemies of Ulla."

Then Konal ceased laughing and said, "You shall
not do this Setanta, for you shall not be permitted, and
he held back the horses, but Cuculain forced the horses
onwards, and Konal fell back.

Then cried Konal to his charioteer, "Harness my
horses, for if this mad boy ventures into the territory of
the enemy and meets with hurt I shall never be forgiven
by the Ultonians." Now the territories of Mid-Erin
were hostile to Concobar through the expatriation and
defeat of Fergus.

But the horses were quickly yoked, and Konal Karna
dashed through the ford, and straightway he came up
to Cuculain and drave for a while abreast of the boy, urging him to return. Then Cuculain stood up on both feet
with his legs far apart in the car, and raising high above
his head in his hands a large stone which Læg had
picked from the highway, he dashed it with all his force
on the pole of Konal Karna's chariot, and the pole was
broken in twain, and the chariot fell down, and the chief
of the Red Branch, Konal Karna, the beauty of the
Ultonians, was rolled out of the chariot upon the road,
and was defiled with dust.

"Do you think that I can throw straight?" cried
Cuculain; "and now that you remind me, it is one of
the vows of our order never to go out with insecure
trappings, rotten chariot-poles, or the like."

Then Konal got up out of the dust, and swore that if
a step would save Cuculain's head from the men of
Meath he would not take it.

But Cuculain laughed again, and Læg urged on the
steeds. Now as they drew near the Boyne and the point

where it receives the waters of the Mattok, there was a
great Dûn. In this Dûn lived three brothers, the three
sons of Nectan, renowned amongst the tribes of Meath for
valour and strength. Then as they drew nigh the Dûn,
Cuculain shouted insults and challenges with a loud
voice, for the brothers had seen the war-car of Concobar
Mac Nessa far away, and their own chariots were prepared, and they had despatched messengers on every
side to cut off the retreat of the men of Ulla. Then
Læg checked the horses, and Cuculain descended upon
the ground, and fitted an iron bullet to his sling, and
he slung and killed the first of the warriors, and slung
again and killed the second, and he slung the third time
with all his might against the warrior, who was almost
upon them, his strong shield held before him, while he
crouched down in the chariot, and the iron bullet passed
through the bronze shield and through his forehead, and
went out behind. Then Cuculain drew his sword, and
ran and cut off the heads of the slain, and sprang into
the chariot, and Læg flogged the steeds, who flew northwards again, swifter than the wind, for already they saw
signals and fires, and horsemen galloping across the
country to intercept their passage to the north. But
they escaped out of the jaws of the enemy, and reached
Ath-na-Forary, and when Konal saw the heads of the
men of Meath, and recognized who were those warriors,
he was filled with wonder, and he sent men-of-war to
conduct him back to Emain Macha, and the whole city
came out to welcome the young knight. Then his arms
were hung up in the Tayta Brac, but Cuculain himself
went back to his comrades, and he slept with them, and
did not go out with the Red Branch.

K

CHAPTER XXVIII.

THE DONN COOALNEY.

" I met a lady in the meads,
Full beautiful, a fairy's child."

KEATS.

LIKE a bright star, when the wind is high, revealing and concealing itself, a moment seen, and then again deep-buried in the driving clouds, Cuculain is revealed and hidden, crossing the spaces of the bardic sky, ere attaining the region where he blazes out with surpassing splendour, dimming all the lesser lights in that heroic age. We see him still a boy helping to subdue Mananan's isle in the Muirnict, or sacking the Dûn of Curoi Mac Dary, or learning subtle feats of arms under Skaáh, the Amazon of the northern seas, or, in spite of obstacles, bearing away with his swift steeds the beautiful daughter of the Brugh-Fir of Lusk, or, like another Samson, thinking it a little thing to raise the wall-pillars of Bricrind's Dûn, that his wife Emer might come in when the warriors of Concobar shut to the doors of the great Dûn, fearing a strife amongst the Red Branch, year after year, his fame waxing greater, if not throughout Eiré, at least amongst his own people, though as yet but a stripling.

Now, all this time, the sovereignty of Aileel and Meave was growing stronger over the regions west of the Shannon, and after the expatriation of Fergus, when he

entered into the service of Queen Meave, the borders of
their realm extended further into the heart of Erin, so
that many foreign chieftains in the uttermost parts of
the island entered under her protection, and her name
and power were felt from the borders of the Crave Rue
to the southern sea.   For the queen, she ever went out
to war beside her lord, hurling the javelin like a man of
war, and evermore were martial works a delight to her,
the hosting and the battle, the subjugation of foreign
kings, the driving away of booty and lines of weeping
captives, and her authority extended over the four provinces of Erin.   For age came slowly upon her lord, and
his strength was relaxed, but the flush of a divine origin
made full her veins, and her eyes waxed not dim for
years, nor was her authority diminished, and ever she
marshalled her warriors, and went out to battle in their
midst, and Fergus, the exile, was the captain of her battalions under her.   But the Clans of Ulla alone refused
to give her honour, for the Red Branch held the province firm under the authority of their mighty king; and
as when the founder casts many pieces of rusty metal
into the furnace, and they come forth one strong and
shining bar, so was the province of Ulla beneath its
king.

Now, Meave had many herds of cattle and flocks of
sheep, nor neglected she the arts of peace, and amongst
her herds was a snow-white bull of a pure and noble
breed, brought from over-seas in her ships, and many an
ounce of red gold, and many finely-woven garments, and
hard swords, had she given in barter for the Fion-
bannah.   But the Ultonians also imported from over-
seas a bull of the purest and noblest breed that ever
came into Erin, and he was the marvel of all who beheld

him, for his exceeding size, strength, and beauty. And not without a divine discernment was the Donn Cooalney, for it was his pleasure each day to see armed youths play at arms before him, and to hear harpers harping, and the recitation of noble tales; but at night in his keep he loved music sweeter than the harp, and it filled the whole cantred, and some say that he had the gift of speech. Like a god was he honoured by all the Gæil, and Dary, King of Southern Cooalney, was he who had the custody of the bull. Blacker than the cock-chaffer was the Donn Cooalney, there was no white spot upon his body.

When Meave saw the honour in which he was held, and how her vassals and tributary kings went often to Ulla, and how her authority was imperilled, she resolved to possess herself of the bull; therefore, she sent Fergus Mac Roy as an ambassador, beseeching the King of Cooalney that he would permit the bull to be brought to her to Rath Cruhane, that his blood might be mingled with the herds of the Olnemacta, and that he would be received with all honour, and restored back straightway with an armed escort. Nevertheless, she concealed another mind, and revealed it not to Fergus, for she feared him. Then Fergus took horses and horsemen, and fared eastward, and on the third day he reached the Dûn of the King of Cooalney. It was night, and the bridge of the foss had been drawn up, filling the gateway at the other side, so they beat upon the brazen gong, and at the noise, the three sons of Dary—Ros and Fiechna and Iomna came down, and received Fergus and his people hospitably.

Then was the old king glad when he knew who it was that was come unto him, even the mighty Fergus

Mac Roy, and how the great queen in the west had
sent him an ambassador to himself, and he arose from
the place where he was crouched before the fire with
alacrity, and shrilly ordered a feast to be prepared, and
the great candles to be lit, the bards and jugglers to be
summoned, and the chess-tables set in order, and ever
he bustled to and fro with many words, and oftentimes approached Fergus with assiduous hospitality; and
though his sons would gladly have conversed with the
renowned warrior, and he with them, he would not
suffer them, but ever despatched them to and fro; and
many times he declared that though Concobar Mac
Nessa might make him an exiled king, yet would he
send the Donn Cooalney westward to the great queen,
and the brows of the young princes darkened when they
heard it.

After that, supper was set before Fergus and his
knights, and the old king sat beside Fergus, and related
to him how he, above all the Ultonians, had been
elected to the custody of the Donn Cooalney, and how
the chieftains of Erin came humbly to him beseeching
him that they might be permitted to see the bull; and
he brought to Fergus a bard who chanted the pedigree
of the bull, and he related minutely all the habits of the
Donn Cooalney, even to such as by themselves were not
agreeable to hear. Then at last Fergus, for the ruddy
ale was circling in his veins, and his mind was hot and
choleric, laughed aloud, and uttered words in which the
scoff was thinly veiled. This, when the king perceived,
he was enraged; but dissembled, and presently he rose
up and left the hall, striding wrathfully amongst the
hounds and servants. Also there came one to him and
said, "The horsemen who have come with Fergus Mac

Roy are openly boasting that it was through fear that you consented to send away the bull." But this was a device of the king's sons, for they feared the wrath of the High King, and they themselves were knights of the Crave Rue. Then the king would have hastened back to let loose upon Fergus the flood of anger which had gathered in his breast, but the young men suffered him not.

There, then, Fergus and his people slept in the Dûn, unconscious of the change; but in the morning, when the strangers were outside the foss and rampart, the people of the Dûn suddenly drew up the bridge, and bade them return back empty to the queen, for that he should not bring away the bull. Then was Fergus mightily enraged, but nay-the-less, he departed, and fared rapidly westward, and on the third day arrived at Rath Cruhane; and when he related all to the queen, she wept tears of bitterness and anger, and reviled Fergus Mac Roy.

Then Meave sent messengers, through the four provinces, to all who were confederate with her, or feared her, and from Eyrus to Cahirmán, and from the borders of the Crave Rue to Oilean Arda Nemed, and the utmost limits of Borda Lu, there was a stirring and commotion, as when the summer wind shakes the forest with its leaves. For out of every rath, green-sided and fossed, and out of every strong cathair came forth the warlike children of Milith, with their weapons and their bravery, their horsemen, and scythèd chariots. Fiacha Mac Fireaba and Eiderkool, headstrong and silly, Nath-crandal, with his salves and incantations, and lying druids, and strong Bras Mac Firb, Lord of the Osree. From the pleasant harbour in the south-west, where

the Isle of Bera raises its lofty head out of the sea,
came the two sons of Neara. Young were they and
brave, and eager for the war, but they escaped not the
red hands of Cuculain when he met them in the forest
advancing in front of the host. Out of the east came
Brōn and Breena, ruthless warriors, joint kings of Ben
Edar, and they took tribute from the timid merchants
of Bal-a-Clia. With a fierce crew came they, thirsting
for the destruction of the Clanna Rury. Not so warlike
came Lon, and Uala, and Dill, the three sons of Gara,
with their bards; from the wooded Lake of Derryvara,
they came, and they were dear to the Shee, for that
their people had cherished the unhappy children of
Lear, when they abode swan-like in the lake, lurking in
the coverts along the shore, and Lehûne, of the children
of Ith, whose white Dûn glittered amid its trees above
the waters of the Bandon. Lewy Mac Neesh, the true
friend of Cuculain, and Fir-Mac-Be, the false friend,
and Fireaba Larna, with arrows by·his side, and songs
in his mouth, light as a gossamer, from the sources of
the Lua; Lōk Mac Favash, King of the Shiel Heber,
o'er whom fluttered unseen the daughter of Ernemine,
a spectre terrible and foul; but she did not escape
the spear of Cuculain, though she vexed him. Dûn
Coffey was his palace and capital, and strongly he
governed his territories; the sons of Kior from the
Berba, and of Cumeyrga from that sweet vale among
the Galtees, down which rolls the Aherlow.

But out of Olnemacia, out of the ancestral territories
of Aileel and his kindred clans, came the six strong
sons of Magach, the son of the Horse, Ket, and Mohcorb,
and Awlin, Endee and Skanal, and Atga; and there
came Cormac Conlingas, he that escaped out of the

massacre in which Conairey More was slain, the ally he, and dear friend of Fergus. Also there came bands of the Fianna, fair, pure warriors, for out of every mountain, dell, and river, and sacred forest, and out of their haunts upon the sea shore, congregated the lesser Fianna, putting on vulnerable flesh to assist the great queen. But the greater Fianna cared not for the children of Milith, but disregarded them altogether.

Then all these came together with their battalions to Magh Ai, and the four plains of Ai, Moa and Markeen, Sleshin and Keeltān, were filled with the uproar of the warriors, the whinnying of horses, and the creaking of the innumerable chariots.

But Meave was troubled in her mind as she thought of the great prowess of the Red Branch, and how the province was bound together, firm and strong, beneath its king. Therefore, while the kings of Olnemacia and the foreign confederates were gathering themselves together to the four plains of Magh Ai, Queen Meave set forth to go to Moy Tura, to consult with the prophet that dwelt there, and she left Aileel sitting in the door of the Dûn, looking forth with dim eyes, and his heart was warmed when he heard the martial din around him, and she left Fergus moving about among the battalions upon the plain, distinguishable from afar, and Cormac Conlingas directing the evolutions of a squadron of swift chariots.

But this time the vision of the prophet was darkened, and he said no intelligible word, save that the brains of Mesgœra alone would slay Concobar, but of the result of the war he spake not, but unmeaning noises came out of his mouth. Then the High Queen was troubled and disturbed, for a great fear came upon her, and she bade

the charioteer urge the steeds back again to Magh Ai,
but in spite of shame she bowed her lofty head, gold-
crowned, into the chariot and wept. But anon, weeping,
she was aware that a maiden of divine aspect sat at her
feet in the chariot, weaving a strange-hued web, and, as
she wove, she sang. Fair and sweet was the maiden,
with smooth, gold hair, the ruddy blood glowing in her
tender nails.

" Who art thou ?" said the queen.

" I am Faythleen the prophetess, I am the guardian
of thy race ; from sacred Tara have I now come, and I
am weaving good for thee, O my queen."

" How look my hosts southwards in Magh Ai ?"

" Bloodied all, and crimson."

" And how look the Clanna Rury, in the north ?"

" Bloodied all, and crimson. I see the young hero
of Murthemney—Culain's swift hound—his war-mace in
his hand, beating down the four provinces. Beware of
him, O my queen. Beware of the youth with the deadly sling. Make no bargain with him, for that bargain
thou shalt rue. Hence must I speed away quickly, to
spread amazement in the hosts of Ulla. They shall not
return to their right mind for a season. And do thou
hasten forward the expedition, for thou shalt conquer
the province ere they be aware "

So saying, she passed away quickly, like a shadow
that flees across the plain when the March wind blows,
and Meave returned to Magh Ai. And when they saw
the royal squadron, and the queen's chariot in the midst,
the whole host shouted. Then they drew back the
covering of the chariot, and the great queen stood erect
in her chariot, her spear in her right hand, and the golden
cath-barr upon her head, and before her great bosom a

round shield, and, on high above the glittering shield, her countenance, serene and pure.

Now Fergus Mac Roy was moving through the whole host, marshalling and directing, conspicuous among the warriors as an antlered stag that stalks amid the herd, and his voice resounded above the din and clamour of Magh Ai. But when the royal cavalcade appeared from the north, and the whole host was confused, and shouted, he bore it with difficulty, and turning half round, and leaning on his spear, looked askance and slightly to where the great queen stood erect armed in her chariot; but when she saw Fergus, her pale, pure countenance was disturbed, and she sat down quickly, and bid them draw to the covering of the chariot, and urge the steeds onward to the royal Dûn. Now Aileel sat in the doorway, and Orloff, their youngest son, sat by his side, preparing a scourge for his steeds. With a shrill voice Aileel chid his wife; but she answered softly, and led him into the Dûn, for it was evening.

CHAPTER XXIX.

AFFLICTION OF THE RED BRANCH.

" If such astonishment as this can seize
   Celestial spirits."

MILTON.

BUT the beautiful Ban Tuatha passed away northwards, to where the Red Cataract pours the waters of the Erne into the sea, and on the black cliffs, standing like a bird, she chanted druidic lays and incantations. Then from

the west, out of the deep, arose a cloud, and travelled
shoreward till it touched the shore, when it broke and
diffused itself into a thin mist that overspread all the
territory of the Red Branch from sea to sea, and travelled
along its boundaries upon the south. And all the
knights of the Red Branch, even the strong and acute
warriors of the Clanna Rury, when they inhaled the evil
mist were stupefied and amazed, as though they had
drunk the juice of some noxious herb.

In his hall at Emain Macha, Concobar Mac Nessa remained in one place for hours, holding a chessman in his
hand, or roamed through the Tayta Brac, gazing upon
the weapons and armour of his knights, understanding
no word that was spoken unto him, and his knightly
countenance was ofttimes marred with a foolish smile,
and the captains of his household troops went with him,
and the faces of all were sad, and their eyes without intelligence.

But away in their own Dûns all the great chiefs of
the Red Branch were stricken likewise by the insane
mist. At Dûn Sovarchey, on his crags, lay Kelkar the son
of Uther, like a stranded whale, his dense hair shed out
upon the rocks, his eye fishy and glazed; nor thought
he any more now of the raising of massive ramparts,
and his brood of giant sons, and the huge warriors in
whom he delighted, clustered around and behind him
on the upland, silent, motionless, in an evil slumber
and stupefaction, like cormorants or rooks.

On their ramparts sat the three sons of Dary, the
keeper of the Donn Cooalney, chucking stones into the
foss, for they said that the bull had been taken away,
and that the High King was approaching to slay them,
and they wept day and night, and moaned, for it seemed

to them better to die by the hands of Concobar Mac
Nessa a just death than to flee into exile or to resist.
But the old man went about chattering incessantly like
a foolish bird which nobody regards.

On the isle of Rachlin, Fergus the son of Leda took
the gold apples out of his hair, and unplaited his shining locks, and cut down the nut groves, and destroyed
the orchards, and defiled the pleasant streams that he
had as an ornament to his Dûn, and he consumed with
fire his palace and his galley variegated and gilt, and
he and his men of war wailed together upon the shore,
for they said that Fergus Mac Roy had slain the king,
and that the Red Branch was dissolved, and he brake all
the instruments of music, and drave away with shouts
and blows the bards and augurers in whom he used to
delight.

Follomān, the king's son, the clear-minded and subtle,
sat on the beach of the northern sea, and he traced in
the sand military combinations, and much he meditated
as he roamed to and fro, and forgot the mimic warfare
with his battalion, which was his wont, and when any
spake to him he looked vacantly, comprehending not
their words.

Leairey Bewda fought all day long before his Dûn an
unreal fight, and disappeared southwards, he and his
warriors, chasing the enemy, but at even-fall, when the
stars began to rise, they returned. Now upon the plain
there lay the straight trunk of a great fir-tree, which
slaves had that morning hewn down in the forest, and
with brazen axes shorn away the brown, small branches
below, but the top with its green feathery plumes they
had spared to be mingled with rushes for the floor of the
Dûn, and they had harnessed to it a yoke of oxen, and

drew it towards the Dûn. But when they saw Leairey and his warriors bearing down upon them with wild cries, they slipped the ropes from the trunk, and fled with their oxen and jingling harness to the shelter of a nut-grove hard by. But when Leairey and his warriors beheld it returning from the pursuit of the visionary foe, they raised three shouts of lamentation over the High King slain, and they chanted threnes, and far away men heard the loud lamentation. Then they gathered logs together, and consumed with fire the druidic cheat, and gathered the embers into a vase of clay, engraving the sides with oghamic characters and cryptic signs, and lines curving and intervolved. But in the plain they dug a chamber, flagged at the bottom and at the sides, and at both ends, and placed the urn there while all the people wept, and covered it above with heavy, smooth flag-stones, and over that with earth and green turves. Then they set upright upon the plain, around the chamber, great stones, and surrounded them with earth so that there was a sloping mound of earth all around. After this they rolled with levers and ropes an enormous pebble up the sloping mound, arranging it skilfully on the heads of the stones, which had been set upright. Then they removed again the earth, and the Cromlech of the High King stood upon the plain, for they adhered to the ancient Fomorian custom in that western region.

Then all day long, and for many days, Leairey and his warriors celebrated funeral games, and the woods and hills re-echoed with the din as the red-shielded, fierce warriors of Leairey contended around their king.

Some leagues thence, hard by the Erne, Iliach, the father of Leairey dragged out his remaining years. Thin and feeble was Iliach, for old age had come upon

him.   Not now such as when in his youth he had spread
the fear of the Great Rury in the regions of the south,
and with his ships devastated the shores of the great
bay in the south-west of Erin, planting there groves of
Irian spears.   There in later days Banat, the son of
Concobar, established himself amid hostile peoples, re-
newing the ancient conquest, and his clan took root there,
and flourished.   But he, Iliach, in his pleasant Dûn dwelt
alone with an aged woman who waited upon him.   For
the Rie-ship of the territory he had transferred to Leairey,
and he busied himself with pruning his fruit trees, and
prouder was he of his nuts and apples than of the purple
scars that covered his body.   But his chariot, neglected,
was falling to pieces in its house, and his harness upon
the rack and his war-steeds, weak with age and heavy
with fat, wandered about the Dûn.

   At Calânn, around his splendid Dûn and well ordered territory, Conn, the son of Morna, roamed disconsolate, for he said that Concobar Mac Nessa, with
his retinue, was coming to him, and that there was confusion in all his dominion, that his brehons were loud
and ignorant, and his bards hoarse-voiced and dull, that
his Dûn was not fit to lodge a fudir, and his warriors
drunken, unkempt, and quarrelsome, and he sought desolate places and stagnant waters, and wept there.   But
Felim the Beautiful, son of Kalcar, sat silent beside him,
his blue eye glazed, a bursting wave of war, stiller than
the field-pond at which cattle quench their thirst.

   In the hollow mountain-folds of Slieve Few, with its
horrid crags, crouched Factna Mac Mahoon ; Factna the
Bear's son, like a sick lion crouched on the hill-side, his
shaggy arms resting upon shaggy knees, and between
his hands he glared out before him towards Emain

Macha. Below the far plain was dotted with his cattle, and slaves on horseback went through them, and the smith's work ceased not, nor the carpenter's and weaver's, but he crouched still all day and night with his warriors on the hill-side, dark, motionless, terrible, like a bottomless tarn in the hollow of the mountains.

At Derry Galga, on the northern sea, the twin sons of Concobar, Fiecha Donn and Fiecha Gall, the brown-haired and the fair-haired, inseparable as the night from the dawn, active as wild cats of the mountain, forgot all knightly exercises and raced like squirrels around the forest, springing from tree to tree and bough to bough, pursuing one another with screams and ape-like chatterings, and their battalions brake loose in like manner, and the swine-herds in the forest hid themselves in heaps of the dry leaves.

At Isca Bo Nemeth, the water of the sacred cow set about with the roan-tree and the holly, where the druids walked and pondered in the religious groves; Glas and Mainey and Conairey, ruling the western regions of their father's realm with a triple sway, sat silent at the council table. Straight as pillars they sat, with grave countenances full of authority. Silent they sat, ringed round by an armed cohort, silent too. A solemn stillness weighed upon all the place. Through the wide doors of the Dûn one could see the sacred water glitter between the roan-trees, green and scarlet. The tribute-paying tribes came and went, silent with restrained breath.

Round his Dûn, on the northern sea, Cethern, the fiercest spirit of the Red Branch, head-long as a rushing cataract, pursued his own cattle with frightful yells, and ever he shouted the High King's name and the battle-cry of his clan, erect in his chariot, with shield and spears, and the charioteer, mad as he, urged the steeds hither and thither across the plain, against the flying herds, and his warriors did likewise, while all the people wept, and ever as he felled some gentle beast, he raised the cry of victory, drawing to him with its twisted thong the spear, red with ignoble blood. Then one let loose his many hounds that bayed and raged in their kennels, and they joined in the havoc till all the plain was dotted with dead and dying beasts. But his warriors straightway skinned them, and bore the dripping pelts to the armour chamber with exulting cries, and hanged them upon the armour racks in triumph. Then the devilish mood blazed out, and Cethern fell with his clashing weapons upon the plain out of the chariot, and lay like a dead man. But Iondan, the daughter of Yeoha, whose lofty Dûn gleamed through trees above the waters of the Bann, his faithful wife, approached him with her women, for she watched him with steady eyes from afar, and she bore him to the Dûn, and stripped off his battle-dress, and washed him, and laid him enveloped in soft, clean linen upon his bed, and she collected all the weapons and defensive armour into the armour chamber, and barred the entrance with strong bolts and locks, and returned to where he lay, and wept.

In the King's Dûn, at Emain Macha, stalked the two Roscathals behind Concobar Mac Messa. For they moved when he moved, and stood still when he stood still, awaiting his word. Round their mighty breasts, stronger than ten bulls, was fastened their ploughing harness. Ploughers were they that ploughed through hostile battalions, and they looked from the king to the bronze battle-plough with its scythes, and thence again to the king. Thus they walked behind their king like hounds behind their master.

At Ath-na-Forarey, Konal Karna, when he inhaled the druidic mist, took down his hurle from its rack, oiling anew the shining curve of its tree, and polished the brazen head till it glittered from the oil and the friction, and made rougher the rough haft, and replaced it upon its rack. But the sentinel on the white carn came down, and busied himself in the Dûn, and the scouts out in the hostile territory came back, and the armed warriors that stood beside the harnessed steeds and ready chariots, laid aside their armour and their weapons, and Konal regarded them not. Then he took a fishing-rod from its place, and a servant, and went up the river. But the craftsmen and the cattle masters were astonished, and they said, "Is it Konal who has left us in this jeopardy?" But they came towards him and said, "The watchman has come down from Carn Fion, and the scouts have come in out of the enemy's country, and the armed band of warriors prepared for battle have laid aside their armour, and we have no defence against a sudden hosting of the men of Meath." But Konal waved them away, saying, "I know this river well, my friends. Pray, stand back from the brink, for you disturb the fish." Only his martial intelligence was taken away, for his mind was temperate and gentle.

CHAPTER XXX.

ONLY A NAME.

"Have ye seen his face?
Have ye beheld his chariot?"

KEATS.

ON the next day the whole host of Queen Meave was put
in motion, and the sons of Neara, riding in one chariot,
went on in front, and they came that evening to Delvin
and camped there, and after that they went on continuously, and they crossed the Shannon and the Inny, and
went past the great lakes of Meath, and thence past the
rath of Odba, wife of Heremon, and they were within
two days' march of the frontier, and yet saw no sign of
the Red Branch. But on the morrow after that, the sons
of Neara met the tracks of two chariots, faring southwards in the direction of Tara, and they followed the
tracks and came to a glade in the forest, and they saw
that those whose were the chariots had slept there that
night, and the glade was partly rough and stony, and
partly good pasture, and they saw that two horses had
been tethered in one part, and two in the other. Moreover, they saw that one of the chariots had departed
thence towards Emain Macha, and the other in the direction of Tara. Then they returned to their route, going
on always to Cooalney. But the host was very great,
and the place woody, and they spent that day hewing
down trees and tearing away brushwood, and the passage
that they made through that wood was called ever after,

the Track of the Chariots. Now the next day the sons of Neara advancing again, came upon the wheel-tracks of a chariot going on before them to Cooalney, and they said: "It is the same chariot that went southwards yesterday to Tara." Then they pursued the track till they came to an ancient pillar-stone, the grave of some warrior slain long since in the glades of that forest, and upon the pillar was a hoop of fresh-cut osier, and upon it Ogham characters, newly inscribed, and in the evening they came to the council of the kings, having the hoop in their hand. Now Aileel sat at the end of the pavilion nodding, and the silver wand trembled in his hand, and the queen sat upon his right hand, and Fergus stood upon his left hand, wrangling with the assembled kings; but the queen was incensed at the authority with which he spake. Then when she saw the sons of Neara, she smiled and beckoned them to herself, for they had been brought up with her own sons, and she took the hoop from their hands and gave it to the Ard-druid to read, but he could not. Then it was handed to Fergus, and with difficulty did they persuade him to look into the Ogham, for the kings desired one thing, and Meave supported them, and he was enraged with her and them. But when he read the Ogham, he started as one starts when stung by an ant, and inquired of the sons of Neara how they came by the hoop, and they told him.

"It is an Ogham taught by Cathvah to the youths of the Ultonians," said Fergus. "Cuculain is the name inscribed on the hoop. He is the youngest of the Knights of the Red Branch."

"Then, have we not much to fear?" said Meave.

To return to Cuculain. In his paternal territory, when not at Emain Macha, or in the service of Concobar,

he ruled his father's clan, having been elected to the
kingship of Cooalney by the chiefs, and inaugurated by
Concobar.   Very gradually he withdrew from the control of Dectera, the battalion of the territory, and the
governance of the' port and shipping, and the imposition
of the tributes.   He released his father from his confine-
ment, and always Sualtam moved around the territory
along with his son, but avoided Dectara his wife.

Now, at the time that the host of Meave had commenced their march eastward, Cuculain rose early one
day, for he had made an appointment with Faythleen,
the deceitful prophetess of Tara, and in the grey of the
morning he set forth from Dûn Dalgan alone; but in the
chariot Emer had put many things, as for a long journey.   Presently Cuculain, hearing wheels, looked round,
and he saw his father in his chariot following behind.
Then was Cuculain displeased, nevertheless he did not
send his father back.   Thus they rode on together, and
crossed the frontier of the province, which was the Oun
Dia, and Cuculain looked back and saw the druidic mist
covering the province like a great fleece, and he marvelled what it meant, and so they rode on, and when it was
evening they came to a glade in the forest, and Cuculain
let down his father's chariot and arranged the rugs for
him to sleep, and he tethered his father's horses in the
northern grassy part of the glade, and his own among
the moss and stones and coarse grass.   Now, very early
the next day, in the still morning, he awoke, and heard,
as it were, the clamour of a mighty host, and he climbed
up into the branches of a lofty elm-tree, and, far away,
he saw the standard of Queen Meave, and the banners
of the sons of Heber and Ith, and the standard of Tara,
and of the children of Leairy Lorc, and the whole host

preparing to set out north-eastward to Cooalney, to the
borders of the Crave Rue. Then Cuculain made haste
and came down, swinging rapidly from branch to branch
like a wood cat, and he awoke his father, and he bid
him urge his steeds swiftly northward to Ath-na-Forarey, and to Emain Macha, and to arouse the Red
Branch far and wide, for that the Four Provinces of Erin
were gathered together for the devastation of Ulla. Then
Sualtam made haste and scourged his steeds, and they
flew northward swiftly, but Cuculain held on upon his
course southward. Nevertheless he found not the deceitful prophetess where she had appointed, and he was enraged, for it was to gratify Emer he had gone thither,
and the same night he travelled northwards again, and
skirted the sea, and went round the forest, and proceded
the Four Provinces, moving on before them to Cooalney.
Then he cut down a twig with his sword, and notched
his name upon the twig, and made a hoop of it, which
hoop was found by the sons of Neara and brought unto
Fergus. For he said, " I shall give them warning, and
not fall upon them unawares."

Now Cuculain was not quite alone upon that expedition, for there were with him two companions, yielding,
indeed, no great succour in war, but whose clear voices
and comradeship he did not despise when loneliness and
sorrow encompased him after each fierce combat at the
Oun Dia, when alone he held the gates of the province
against the men of Meave. For at Dûn Dalgan, while
he was yet a boy, there was an old man, a worker in
leather, who wrought sandals and shoes for the household of Dectara. He had no children, and his wife was
long since dead, and he had lived alone in his house by
the wayside, on the road leading out of Dûn Dalgan,

eastward to Drum Rury, to the patrimony of Bricrind
the satirist.   But both himself and his father before him
had been accustomed to rear singing birds, nor did they
confine them in prisons of wicker-work or twisted findruiney, and the birds sung in and around the house en-
livening the mind of the old man.   Now, Cuculain was
accustomed to sit with him, and the old man taught
him the mysteries of his art, so that, while yet a child,
he became skilful in that craft, and he wrought at the
old man's side.   Moreover, Æd Enver boasted to him
that he was of the race of Luprachān, a descendant of
Dana, who, in ancient days, occupied Tara, and he told
how the Clanna Luprachān ruled widely over Erin,
teaching noble arts to the Gæil, and how they dwelt now
immortal in fairy-land.   So spake the old man, and he
taught the boy also much concerning birds, and the
birds came to Cuculain equally with the old man.   Now
when Cuculain was raised to the Rie-ship of the tuath,
and all men brought him presents, Æd Enver, who was
now very aged, and received from his clan the maintenance which was the old man's right according to the
law, came to the palace and presented Cuculain with two
young black-birds of the purest breed, and these attached
themselves closely to Cuculain.   Vale Darig and Ceolān
were their names, and they accompanied him on this
journey.   But after the fight with Lōk Mac Favash they
were no more seen, whether that they were washed away
in the spray of that fierce conflict, or, fluttering round
were smit by the weapons, or, being terrified, had flown
afar, but Cuculain was sorrowful that night, being alone
in the hollow forest.

Then the next day the host of Meave moved onward
once more, and the sons of Neara advancing not far

from the camp, and following the track of the chariot
that preceded them, came to where was a spear fixed
deep in the ground; and it seemed as if two-thirds of
the spear was sunk into the hard ground, and one third
only remained above. Now, that morning Fergus had
gone round to the out-posts, and had given strict injunctions not to slay the man whose chariot track they had
seen, but that he should be taken alive; and as the
sons of Neara were wondering at the cause why the
spear had been fixed there in the ground, Fergus and
his people came up to them. But Fergus uttered a cry
of joy when he beheld the spear where it stood erect
between the two wheel-tracks, and he saw that it was
cast from the hand of the warrior turning round in his
chariot, as he rode, to be a challenge and attestation of
his prowess to the host of Meave; but the sons of Neara,
light-chattering, were curious to know why Cuculain
should have delayed to drive that spear into the ground,
for they said it was driven in with blows. Yet it was
plain that the chariot had not stopped, and there was
no foot-mark, nor was the extremity of the spear marred
at all as with blows. Then the sons of Neara urged on
their horses; nevertheless, their haviour was not so
gallant as before, for their minds misgave them, and
they were astonished at the great size of the spear-
tree.

Then Fergus Mac Roy found Orloff among the van in
his gilded chariot, while he danced along the chariot-
pole, brandishing his light spears, and Fergus bade him
return, and he would not; wherefore he drave him back
to the host with blows, and he returned weeping to the
queen, where she rode with chariots before her, and
behind, and on each side of her, and she was incensed.

Then a vast rumour diffused itself through the host concerning Cuculain, and that night in the council there was dissension, and the voice of Fergus might be heard through the camp contending with the kings of the four provinces. For Fergus desired that the great warriors of the host should form the van, and the kings derided him. But when the council was dismissed, Fergus returned, and he found the queen alone in the pavilion, and he addressed her and said :—

"Fitter were it for thee, O queen, to have remained in thy own Dûn and seen to the government of thy household, than to march upon this foray with thy lord, silly from age, and thy son, Orloff, silly from youth. At home in thy own palace thou shouldst have remained with these, for here thou art a disturbing influence, and partest from me the authority over the loose array of this great host. For thou art not thyself fit to govern men, and make provision to secure victory, or to give the necessary commands in battle, and against me, who am, thou dost countenance the headstrong and mutinous kings. And this thou too thyself well knowest, but it is a delight to thee to appear before all the people with thy weapons and martial bravery, and to hear them shout when they see thee shield-bearing in thy great war-chariot, and thy head gold-crowned above the host. For it is because of this, and not for thy knowledge of war and government, that the clans of Aileel have not long since put him aside, and raised the Tanist to the Ard-Rieship of the province ; for with thy fair face and thy stature beyond women, and thy shining shield, thou hast bewitched them, and also the far coming kings of the south. For if thou hast sometimes in the edge of battle cast thy spear into the hostile ranks, well knowedst

thou that thy chariot was thick-ringed with warriors,
the mightiest in the land, and not one of those that
would not die a thousand deaths rather than that one
tress of thy yellow hair should receive any hurt. And
no such great accomplishment is this of thine, for many
a time in warlike forays have I seen women contend
with spear and shield against opposing warriors with
more cunning and ferocity than have been granted to
thee. And this I tell thee, for thy greater behoof. Like
an eagle that hovers above the moor-fowl on the mountain side, there hovers one above this host who delays
his stroke, but will quickly deal out death. Far-shoot-
ing Cuculain, the son of Sualtam, goes before us, his
sling is in his hand, and no stronger than the leaf of
the sycamore will thy shield be against his bullets,
and well I know he will not err if against thee he bends
the Crave Tawl. For verily in Emain Macha have I
seen him smite far aloft the wheeling swallow. Therefore, now be persuaded by me, O queen, and return with
thy lord and with the boy. For greatly I fear for thee
when I see thee amid the host with the gold cath-barr
upon thy head, thy shield far seen, and thy god-like
stature, and with difficulty do I draw away my mind to
the care of this great host."

Now, ere Fergus had uttered many words, the queen
arose from where she sat, her fair, pure countenance
marred with great anger, and with trembling hands she
seized a javelin, and cast it at Fergus, but he watched,
and stepped aside, and the javelin hissed through the
wattled walls, and passed out into the camp ; but ere
she could seize another, he ran to her, and seized her
with his strong hands and forced her back into her
throne, and held her still, and she spat at him. But

he took up his speech where he had stopped, and went on to the end, and when he had made an end he gathered together the weapons that were at her side, and went out of the pavilion, stalking moodily to his own booth.

Now, outside the Royal Pavilion there was a throng of men, and amongst them a warrior slain, for a javelin had pierced him behind the ear; Yeoha Glûnduff was his name, and he was a Rie-damna of the Province of Lahan.

CHAPTER XXXI.

DEATH OF ORLOFF.

" And in the morning twilight wandered forth,
  Beside the osiers of a rivulet,
  Full ankle deep in lilies."

KEATS.

BUT Yeoha Glûnduff lay upon the ground slain, and when they drew out the javelin they knew that it was the High Queen's, and there was great wrath. But Fergus set a guard about the queen's pavilion that no one should tell her of the death of Yeoha Glûnduff until the morning.

Now, all that night the great queen raged in her house, nourishing the angry fire in her breast, weeping and gnashing with her teeth; but as the darkness began to abate she slept, and, not long sleeping, she was awaked by a cry, and, fearing an assault, she fitted her cath-barr to her head, for it was upon a ledge beside the couch, and, looking forth through the window, she

beheld the warriors gathering together, and men rushing from all sides out of their branchy booths, looking eastwards, and the sun had not yet risen. But
she looked too, and behold a chariot approaching from
the east, with horses galloping wildly, all awry, as
though they had seen a spectre, their heads bare of
trappings, and she recognized the horses of the sons of
Neara, and behind them in the chariot were two figures,
headless, lolling against one another, as the chariot
bounded onward, for Cuculain had met them in the
forest, and fought with them, and cut off their heads,
and he took the bits from the mouths of the horses, and
the head-stalls from their heads ; and he took the rein
and fastened it to the right side of the chariot, and
round one of the brothers, and then round the other,
and made it fast to the left side of the chariot, and
turned the faces of the steeds towards the camp, and
scourged them, and they flew madly back to the host.

But when the queen saw them from behind the osiered
walls of her pavilion, she screamed such a cry as a widow
renders when they bring back her husband slain, for
she looks up from happy household labours, and lo, the
faces of them that bear her husband in the doorway, so
screamed the great queen, and thinly clad, and regard-
less of her dignity, she rushed from the tent, and Fergus
saw her, and bade one bring out her robe, but as she ran
men heard the war-cry of the Clans of Ulla, and lo, far
away a warrior stood upon an ancient cairn, shaking in
his hands two heads, held by the long yellow hair, and
forthwith, he dropped them, and took his sling, and
slang towards the camp, and the gold cath-barr fell from
Meave's head shattered upon the ground, and a thousand
warriors ran forward to the cairn, but Cuculain disap-

peared into the forest; but while the warriors went
eastward men heard a shrill cry towards the north, and
lo, Orloff, the Queen's son, in his chariot flying towards
the camp; but suddenly, as though smitten by a javelin,
the reins fell from his hand, and he rolled out of the
chariot.   Then trackers went through all that country,
but they found no warriors, and the host encamped there
that day, and the queen remained in her pavilion, and
saw no one, but in the evening she sent out a messenger
to bring in Fergus Mac Roy.

Now, Cuculain had crossed the Oun Dia, going on
before the host, and he had disposed his chariot and
horses in a labyrinth of the forest, which he had found
beforetime, for he and Læg were accustomed to chase
the wild boar in this forest.   But, after he had slain
the sons of Neara, and uttered his challenge to the men
of Meave, running westwards through a forest that
skirted the Oun Dia at this point, as he brake through
into a certain glade he came upon Orloff, but his horses
stood beside him harnessed to the light, splendid racing-
chariot, and Orloff kneeling down with his carpenter's
tools beside him, was smoothing an ash bough to be a
wheel-spoke for his chariot.

Then, hearing the noise, he looked round, and he saw
Cuculain standing over him, stained with the blood of
the sons of Neara, and Orloff stood up trembling, and
said:

" Surely thou art that Cuculain of whom the warriors
converse, and now, having met thee, I must die."

Then Cuculain laughed, and said, " Not so, O youth,
but thou shalt be my captive.   Follow now quickly and
I shall not harm thee, nor will I bind thee, for I think
that thou art a king's son.

But Orloff, pretending to follow, presently turned and fled to where was the chariot, and he bounded over the rim of the chariot, snatching the goad from its place, and turned the horses' heads to the camp, deceiving the generous Cuculain, but Cuculain pursued him, and overtook him as he was emerging upon the grassy plain, and in the sight of the camp, and he drove his spear through the back of Orloff, piercing the crimson fuan, and it came out above the brooch upon his breast, and he rolled forward out of the chariot upon his head. But Cuculain recovered his spear, and was not any more seen by the men of Meave.

CHAPTER XXVII.

THE CROWN TAWL.

"Ἕζετ' ἔπειτ' ἀπάνευθε νεῶν μετὰ δ' ἰὸν ἔηκε
Δεινὴ δὲ κλαγγὴ γένετ' ἀργυρίοιο βίοιο."

HOMER.

THEN the next day they began to draw nigh to the frontiers of the territory of Concobar Mac Nessa, and that day the best warriors in the host went together, in bodies of ten, in advance of the main army, and they sustained no hurt. In the evening they encamped, and the sun set, and not long after the moon rose and the stars began to shine, and the blue hills all round, and the wide horizon were bathed in the moony glare. Then, when the host was preparing the booths of the chieftains and their sedgy beds, cooking suppers, and cleaning chariots and horses, and a vast din arose out of the camp, suddenly there

was a cry as of a warrior smitten to his death, and the
whole host became silent, like the sea beneath frosty
stars when its waves fall down and are still, and in that
stillness was heard a faint, clear, far-off twang, mingled
with hissing, followed by another cry, as of a man smitten.   Then one uttered the word, " Cuculain," and the
whole host was in an uproar, and numerous battalions
sallied forth, scouring the forest and the hill-sides the
whole night.   But now in front and now behind, from
the south and from the north, sounded the clear twang
of the Crave Tawl, and ever some warrior cried out,
smitten by the deadly bolt.   Then there was held a
council of the kings, and Meave was not there, but Fergus Mac Roy occupied her place on the right hand of
Aileel, and the authority of Fergus was great over the
kings, for Meave had sent messengers to each of them
that they should obey Fergus.   But when men inquired
of Fergus concerning Cuculain, Fergus related the first
coming of Cuculain to Emain Macha, and the dispersion
of the young nobles before the king's palace, and Cormac Conlingas took up the tale, and told how he had
slaughtered the huge mastiff of Culain the smith, and
acquired his surname, and how he had attached himself
to Fergus above all the other knights, and other Ultonian exiles told many surprising things concerning Cuculain.   Then the kings proposed that Fergus should
go to him and offer a great bribe, so that he might pass
over to the host of Meave, and forsake the Red Branch.

And Fergus said, " Ye will not persuade him, for
when I rebelled against Concobar Mac Nessa, one, not
sent by me, urged him to leave the school at Emain
Macha, and come out and join our hosting, but he wept
bitterly, and would not come out.   Neither will you

persuade him now, when he is the sworn knight of the King of Ulla."

Nevertheless, the project was pleasing to the assembled kings, and Fergus consented to bear the conditions to Cuculain. Then the next morning, ere the sun rose, Fergus mounted his chariot and drove far out in front, and he bid the charioteer guard the horses till he returned, and advanced by himself, and clomb an eminence, and lifted up his voice on high, and shouted, calling Cuculain by his old name, Setanta; and Cuculain heard him in his secret place, and he cast aside his arms, and ran through the forest, and he threw himself upon Fergus and kissed him, and wept.

Then Fergus told him the conditions which he had come bearing, and Cuculain answered resolutely that he would not forsake the Red Branch, nor the king. Then Cuculain led Fergus along with him, and brought him to his secret place, and there were his horses feeding, and his chariot, and no wheel-tracks leading thither. Then he arranged skins for Fergus, and went down to the stream below and speared two salmon, and with his sling he slew two wild goose in the marshes of the river, and he returned to Fergus and cooked them, and he took mead and ale out of his chariot, and they caroused and conversed until the evening star arose. Then Fergus went away to where was his chariot, and returned to the camp.

But amongst the assembled kings that night he told them how Cuculain had scorned their bribe, and even as he spoke, the Crave Tawl sounded from the distant hills, and the people died. But the kings said that the bribe was not sufficient, and they urged Meave to offer her daughter Fionavar in marriage, and Meave answered hotly and proudly ; but after a space, she smiled an evil smile, and consented to the arrangement, and that Cuculain should be governor of Olnemacta under her, to the exclusion of her own sons, and that, if he preferred it, she would make him Monarch of Ulla, in the room of Concobar Mac Nessa.

Then Fergus arose in great wrath, and dashed his spear upon the ground, but his eyes burned like coals of fire, and his voice rattled in his throat.

" Full well I know thy meaning, and in vain wouldst thou conceal from me the thing that is in thy mind, O crafty and perverse woman.   Yet Cuculain thou shalt not this time ensnare to his destruction with lies.   Nevertheless I am willing to go to Cuculain with these conditions if the assembled kings will guarantee their performance, and take the young hero Cuculain under their protection."

But the High Queen trembled before the wrath of Fergus, and the assembled kings, Ket the son of Magâh, Lewy Mac Neesh, and Nathcrandal, and Lōk Mac Favash guaranteed the performance of the conditions, and extended their protection to Cuculain.

Then in the morning Fergus Mac Roy went forth to Cuculain's secret place, and he found Cuculain lying on the ground upon his back, with a red-billed blackbird on his finger, and he and the blackbird whistled to one another alternately, and when he saw Fergus he started to his feet, and received him hospitably as the day before. But when Fergus told him the conditions which he had come bearing, Cuculain looked down upon the ground, and traced with the point of his spear upon the ground. Then Fergus said no more, and after that they feasted and caroused till the evening star arose.

Then said Fergus, " Is there any condition on which thou wilt cease slaying the people ?" and Cuculain said, " There is, but it would not be seemly for me to put it forward."

After that Fergus departed, and returned to the camp, and Cuculain took his sling, and clomb to the brow of the hill, and looked northwards, and saw no sign of life throughout broad Ulla, and he was astonished at the coming not of Concobar and his knights.

But before the assembled kings, that night in Meave's camp, Fergus Mac Roy related how Cuculain had despised their conditions, and Meave said, " There are a hundred of our people slain every night, and my trackers and scouts cannot surround him ; but when seen, he ever evades them with his light feet, and if my people so perish night by night, I think not many of us will cross the Shannon returning to Olnemacia, nor of our allies to their own homes. Are there any conditions which this bloody youth will accept, and so cease from his slinging and slaying ?"

And Fergus said, " There is such a condition, but he refused to make it known to me, but said that we ourselves should propose it."

Then they all debated what this should be, and when they came to no result, they appealed again to Fergus, and Fergus said :

" Brave, and not bloody-minded, is Cuculain, and he loves not this nocturnal slaughter which he inflicts upon us, nightly guarding the borders of the Crave Rue. Let us make a treaty with Cuculain after this manner : That the host of Meave shall not cross the Oun Dia invading the lands of Ulla until Cuculain be subdued in single combat, and that he engage to meet a warrior each day."

Now the kings were surprised if Cuculain would accept such conditions, but nay-the-less, they and Meave ratified the proposal.

Now when it was morning, and Fergus was ascending into his chariot, he saw a youth of the camp entering his chariot also, making as though he would follow him. Then said Fergus:

"Who art thou, O youth?"

And he said, "Eiderkool, am I, a flaut of the Clan Farna, and I desire to give my horses exercise."

"Beware that thou followest not me," said Fergus, " for I shall slay thee."

Then Fergus and his charioteer rode away northwards, and after a space Eiderkool and his charioteer went after; but in his silly heart he threatened great things, and deemed that huge renown would be his before the setting of the sun. From the shores of Inver Scena had he come, where his Dûn looked across the great mere, and chieftains not many were around him in that barren region, and he was great in his own eyes, loquacious and empty, and he buzzed around the camp like a bee. But his mother sent him forth boasting that no braver warrior followed in the Tàn, and she lamented that she had permitted him to follow arms, for that in science and poetry his excellence was as great, and that he might be Ard-Druid or Ard-Ollav of all Erin, had he chosen to excel in those arts; and much she boasted amongst her women, and the wives of her vassals. And she trusted to a prophecy of Fiontànn, for he was Ard-Druid of the nation of Kasàr, and when all that people perished, he was preserved, and he dwelt in the dells of Carn Tuhall, leading a divine life, like the Tuatha, teaching those who resorted to him, for he conversed equally with the Shee, and with the sons of Milith, and he had eaten of the nuts of the sacred tree. Now when she wearied him, he uttered a doubtful prophecy—"that no one would go into danger so lightly as her son;" but the father of Eiderkool was a noted ollav, and his wife was a weariness to him.

Now Fergus went forward to where Cuculain was, and Cuculain hastened to meet him. Then Fergus unfolded the terms to Cuculain, and Cuculain rejoiced when he heard. After that, Fergus returned to the camp, but ere long he observed the double track, and he feared treachery, and bade the charioteer return at full speed.

Eiderkool, on his side, had followed till the chariot of Fergus stopped, and after that he drew aside into the forest, and descending, followed Fergus Mac Roy, treading the intricacies of the labyrinth; but he went cautiously, for great was his fear of Fergus Mac Roy. Now when Fergus had departed from Cuculain, he returned to his charioteer exulting, and they gallopped up to the dell, and Cuculain looked out and saw a warrior advancing towards him, and Cuculain came out to meet him hospitably, and he inquired the cause of his coming.

"I am come to see thee," said Eiderkool, "to know whether thy fame is equal to thy deserts."

And Cuculain laughed and said, "And now having seen me, how do I appear unto you?"

And Eiderkool answered, "Thou art comely, indeed, and not unwarlike to look upon, but amongst great warriors thou wouldst not be noticed at all, nor even amongst forward striplings wouldst thou attract any considerable attention, and I believe that I myself could easily subdue thee."

And Cuculain said, " Return now, O youth, unharmed to the camp, for under the protection of Fergus, my friend and tutor, hast thou come here. Therefore, I would not harm thee. Return again to the camp."

Then Eiderkool began to be very brave, and he reviled Cuculain, and stepped forward to slay him. Therefore Cuculain made haste back to where were his weapons, and facing Eiderkool, he executed a dexterous sword-stroke at the feet of Eiderkool, by which he jerked a clod of the green turf into his breast, cone-shaped, cut neatly with a rapid turn of the wrist. " Return back to the camp, now, for I would not slay thee," cried Cuculain ; but he would not ; and after that Cuculain made a rapid stroke behind the shield of the other, and shore clean away the apple of gold into which his hair between his shoulders was fastened—for Eiderkool delighted in adorning himself. But when he still pressed on, Cuculain's anger rose, and he smote him so that he died, and his charioteer took away the body and bore it back to the camp, and Fergus met him, and turned back likewise to the camp.

Now, that night among the assembled kings, Fergus related how Cuculain had accepted the terms proposed by the four provinces.

Then said Meave, " I greatly desire to behold this youth, and I prythee, O Fergus, bring him down with thee into the camp, that we may see him ;" and Fergus looked narrowly upon the queen, but she said :

" I meditate no guile against the youth, though my dear son, Orloff, was slain by his hands ; for well I know that if he accepts those conditions, not many hours longer will he behold the sun, but these kings and myself extend to him our protection, and guarantee to him a safe departure out of the camp."

Then the next morning, ere the sun rose, Fergus set forth for the last time with chariots and warriors, and he returned with Cuculain, and Cuculain's friends who were in the camp ran forward to meet him—warriors who had been fostered at the court of Concobar Mac Nessa, ere enmity had arisen between the Red Branch and the remainder of the children of Milith, through the expatriation of Fergus, and the supremacy of the great queen—Lewy Mac Neesh, and Fir Mac Bé, and many others, for Cuculain had many friends; but there came not Fardia, the son of Daman, the son of Dary, chief of the western Fir-bolgs. He had learned feats of arms along with Cuculain, at the hands of Scaáh, the warrior queen of the ragged Isle, far away in the northern seas, and they had together sacked the City of Cahirman, sailing thither in their ships, for Cuculain's territory bordered on the sea, and he had a naval station, and much shipping.

But the kings of Erin were astonished when they beheld Cuculain, for smooth and pleasant was his countenance, and his stature not great, and that day he played at goal with the men of Erin, and they gave him changes of raiment and keeves of water in his wattled house, and he dressed himself and came in to the feast. And the great queen had pity upon him when she saw him, and knew that ere long he would be slain, guarding the frontiers of his nation, and she relented from her wrath for the slaying Orloff and the sons of Neara, and she placed him between herself and Aileel at the banquet, and Cuculain hearkened to Aileel when he spake, and the old king forgot his churlishness, and conversed pleasantly with Cuculain. And on the morrow, when the time came that he should depart, the great queen kissed him before the whole host, for very gentle was the aspect of Cuculain, and all the women grieved when they saw Fergus lead away the youth to the other side of the ford.

CHAPTER XXXIII.

AT THE FORD.

Cuculain filius Sualtam fortissimus Heros Scotorum.

TIERNA.

THEN came Far-Cu, of the Fairy Bank of the Nore, fierce, dog-headed, and demanded permission to slay Cuculain upon the morrow, and Meave trembled upon her throne when he thrust himself into the assembly, and with hateful clamour and vociferation, declared that he alone was the hound of battle among the Gæil, and that he would mangle and devour the northern mongrel before the eyes of the four provinces. Then, on the morrow, Cuculain came down from his dell, and Far-Cu rushed upon him, and Cuculain slew him there before the whole host, and left his carcase lying half in and half out of the river-ford, and the eels came around him feeding, for he was loved by none ; but in the evening Cormac Conlíngas sent certain of his people, and they took him away and buried him.

After that, on successive days, came the two Cruags, rough warriors from the sources of the Bandon. From their strong Dûn in the hills they ruled a wide territory, and the people feared them. But though fierce and brave they fell before Cuculain and his brilliant sword-play.

Then said Cas Fohla, the cunning swordsman of Tara, strength and courage are not sufficient to subdue this hound, and he went down to Cuculain to the ford, and like the glittering of the sea at noon-tide was the bright, quick, flashing of their swords and nimble shields; but after not many passes, Cuculain drave his sword through the lungs of his enemy, and he fell splashing into the ford. But it was the evening of the fourth day, and Cuculain, looking forth, saw no signs of life through broad Ulla, and returned in amazement to his retreat.

Then arose Nathcrandal before the assembly and said, "By magic alone will the hound of Ulla be subdued, and it is not unknown to you that from my youth up I have studied this art, and my companions have been subtle druids, wiser far than those impostors of Tara, honoured so highly and so ignorantly by the Gæil, and I think that in Erin there is none my equal in druidic learning and magic, and I shall subdue and slay Cuculain through their aid."

Then said Lōk Mac Favash: "Lying druids and ignorant are those who are with and honoured by none but by themselves, and thee, not like the wise men of Moy Tura and Tara and Knock Ainey in my own land; and long ago would the people of Erin have expelled them out of Banba, but for the honour in which they hold thee for thy knowledge of war and wise government of thy territory. For in these arts dost thou excel, and not in magic and the subtle science of the druids. Verily if thou goest against Cuculain, trusting only in

these, much magic wilt thou need when the spear of
Cuculain is driven through thy lungs."

Then Nathcrandal answered him again with insult
and clamour, and the assembly was confused, for some
took one side and some another. Then started Aileel
from his slumber, and smote the canopy with his silver
staff, for there was much wrath, and the great queen
herself was mingling unqueenly in the wordy war. But
when there was silence Fergus Mac Roy lifted his strong
voice and said :

" Fools are ye both, and fools are all they that trust in
this lying magic. Verily, if your own strong hearts will
not give you the victory, not much gain will ye secure
from incantations. For when I see the soothsayer, his
belly swollen with the soup of a grey bull, slain after
foolish rites, retire to slumber and dream, more ready
am I to smite him with my spear across his druidic
paunch, than to gape around him till he start forth bel-
lowing with a nightmare got from over-much feeding; yea,
when he has put his thumb into his mouth, mumbling
chants, or slunk behind the door to chew raw flesh, oftentimes ere this have I chopped his chin upwards, to
the hurt of his druidic thumb, or bruised him against
the wall behind the door till he roared again. Dearer
to me is the strong cry of warriors entering the battle
than any jabbering of birds, or prosperous signs in the
heavens or on the earth."

Nevertheless, it seemed good to the assembly that
Nathcrandal should be permitted a trial of his arts
against Cuculain. Then, ere morning dawned, Nathcrandal and his druids went out into the forest with
chants and ceremonies, and they hewed down holly-
trees with consecrated axes, and fashioned javelins out

of the sacred wood, plain timber were these, untipped with brass or iron, and they smeared them with salves and sacred ointments, and returned to the camp. Then went down Nathcrandal to meet Cuculain, unarmed save with his druidic javelins, and he advanced to the ford and cast them at Cuculain, but Cuculain caught them all dexterously with his right hand, and his left was filled with the harmless javelins, and he was astonished. These then he chucked into the stream, and when he saw that the other was unarmed he returned to his retreat; but the stream carried down in its eddying current the druidic spearlets, and some were caught in the overhanging willows, and some, arrested by stones and weeds, stood up erect out of the rushing water, and the whole host shouted with laughter, and Nathcrandal returned foolishly to the camp.

Then came Brōn and Breena, the strong kings of Ben Edar, who ruled over Moy n'Alta and the borders of the Liffey, and took tribute from the timid merchants of Bal-a-Clia. Now they had learned many warlike feats in foreign lands, and they were enraged with Cuculain on account of his ships at Dûn Dalgan, and fierce was their bearing, and huge their stature, and like the mast of a galley were the trees of their great spears. Yet, notwithstanding the many ox-hides sewn fast together that surrounded their mighty breasts, they were subdued and slain by Cuculain, and their fallen carcases made red the stream.

Now it was the evening of the seventh day when Breena fell by the hands of Cuculain, and again he clomb to the brow of the mountain and looked northwards. But he saw afar off a chariot approaching slowly, and one in the chariot scourging the steeds, and with his right arm hanging limp by his side, and Cuculain ran to meet him, and lo, his father Sualtam returning alone.

Then Sualtam gave thanks to the gods that Cuculain was yet alive, and said, "Ill is the news that I am come bearing, O Setanta. Enchanted are all the warlike clans of Ulla, so that they are sunk in a mortal stupefaction, or wildly raving like men whose intelligence has been taken away." Then was Cuculain very sorrowful; but, nevertheless, he led his father to his secret recess, and unharnessed the horses and gave them drink, and he led his father to the stream, and drew up the sleeve of his flaxen lena, and washed the blood away from his elbow, and dried it carefully, and bound up the arm. Then he lighted a fire, and cooked supper; but as a servant who has come out of great jeopardy, having faithfully discharged the commands of his master, and has returned to him in safety, so was the feeble mind of Sualtam that night when he had come back to Cuculain, and they drank ale and metheglin beneath the trees, and Sualtam told his son all things that had happened to him.

CHAPTER XXXIV.

THE CLANNA RURY.

"Thus, in alternate uproar and sad peace,
Amazed were those Titans utterly."

KEATS.

"Parting from thee, O Setanta, I urged my steeds to Dûn Fachtua, in the first place, for it was nigh me, and passed through many flocks and herds feeding in the rich pasture, and ascended the high road to where

was the king's Dûn, and many craftsmen were labouring
there, and there was a noise of much industry. But
when I inquired for the king, they pointed upwards, and
like a flock of crows, I saw many warriors in dark brattas on the hill-side sitting. Then, leaving the chariot,
I ascended to where they were, and inquired for Factua,
the son of Mahoon; but ere I was aware, for I distinguished him not, being so great, he roared like thunder
above my head, and waved with his left hand towards
Emain Macha, and I was seized with terror, and escaped
out of that place joyfully.

"I came to Ath-na-Forarey, and on the white carn
there was no sentinel, nor any that kept watch and ward.
in all the place, nor chariots yoked, nor men of war prepared to meet the enemy. On the lawn of the Dûn lay
Konal himself, carving an ogham upon the blade of his
sword, and he did not look up when I spake unto him,
but answered mildly, 'If what thou sayest be true, then
thy wares must be good. Pass into the province, and
see that thou impose upon no one.' And though many
times I told him of thy peril, yet ever he took the drift
of my speech away.

"I came to Emain Macha, and cried out in the city
as I went through, and the timorous citizens flocked
after me. Now, as I approached the royal Dûn, I heard
the war-steeds neighing in their stables, and pulling
madly at the halters, and I beheld Læg leaning against
the gate of the chariot-house, in which was thy chariot,
and from the house within came voices dire, clamorous,
and mutterings."

Then Cuculain groaned, and clasped his hands; but
Sualtam continued:

"'What doest thou here, O Læg,' said I, 'when thy

master is contending alone against the four provinces?'
But he raised sorrowful eyes, and gazed on me without
reply.

"Then, even as I spake, I heard a great clamour in
the king's Dûn, the shouts of many warriors, and the
clash of smitten shields, and lo, in the Tec Meadcuarta
all the great knights of Concobar Mac Nessa, the chiefs
of the permanent battalion of Emain Macha, and at the
end of the chamber, Concobar Mac Nessa, and he
harangued them. Of ancient prophecy, then much he
spake, and of the ancestors of the Crave Rue, of Rury
Mōr and Ollav Fohla, of Kimbay Mac Fiontann and
Macha, and of Iar, the great son of Milith ; and he
spake of the Gæil, how they were one race, and of one
tongue, and of the Clanna Rury leading the children of
Milith, and the subjugation of foreign lands, and of an
empire reaching to the Torrian sea, and I know not
what other childish talk ; but the face of every warrior
was like a flame, and there was a huge uproar. Then
said the king, ' Yet are these foreign lands too distant,
though our ships are many and swift, therefore shall
the Roscathals be harnessed to them, and hale them
thither, so that we may be one people, not many, and
we will commence to-morrow with Manaan's Isle, which
we have added to our realm, subdued by my brave
knight Cuculain.' And all the warriors shouted again,
and there was no laughter ; but when I heard thy name
I sprang into the midst of the assembly, crying out,
' Cuculain is alone contending against the four provinces in Southern Cooalney,' and Concobar answered
with a triumphant cry, ' Thou bringest good news, old
man ; bid him be regent of the four provinces until the
rest of the Red Branch come back.' Then I hastened

from the Dûn, and mounted my chariot weeping, but the timorous citizens flocked after me, and every face was pale.

"I came to Isca Bo Nemeth, going swiftly through the sacred groves and along the shining water, and I came to the door of the Dûn, and cried, 'Arise, O sons of Concobar, and haste with your battalions to Southern Cooalney, for the four provinces are invading Ulla, and Cuculain alone defends the frontier.' But the sons of Concobar sat erect at the council-table, and they moved not at all, ringed round by a silent cohort; but two strong warriors advanced without word spoken, and seized me and bore me without the Dûn, and beyond the rampart, and cast me forth as when from their house of industry bees hale forth some worthless drone, and cast him beyond the precincts of the hive, and it is death to him if he should return. So cast they me forth among the Fir-bolgs and tribute-paying kings that gathered, pale-faced and amazed, around the Dûn.

"I came to the Dûn of Leairey Bewda, the victorious son of Iliach, far-seen resplendent amid its trees, and all around the deep foss were chariots and horsemen and many warriors, for there was a great hosting of the kings and the warlike tribes of his territory ; but upon the lawn was a mighty cromlech, such as I have never before seen now raised, and the green plain all around embrowned with earth. But within, at the end of the great hall, stood Leairey, erect as a tall poplar that grows alone upon the wet inches of the river. In robes of peace he stood and as though prepared for travel, and he brandished in his right hand two spears. But so standing he harangued his captains and said, 'For now that the great son of Nessa hath fallen, I, the chief of

the Red Branch by tanistry, must hence without delay
to Emain Macha to assume the Ard-Rieship of the province, the royal brooch and silvern wand of rule.   Yet
surely, though slain, his projects shall not fail through
us.   Concobar has fallen, but Macha, the red-maned
daughter of Ay Roe, is still amongst us. Her high place
at Emania hath she not deserted.   I see the gathering
of the clans of Iar, the borders of the Crave Rue burst
as by a great flood when the Red Branch rush forth to
overwhelm Inis Fohla to the House of Donn and the
strand of Cliona.   Not in vain hast thou cast thy
thoughts, O Concobar, like lightning into the children
of Rury, great son of Nessa, second founder of our race,
binder together of scattered clans, expulsor of Fergus
and his impure crew.'

"Now, as he noised along in this fashion, while his
warriors shouted approval, I, fearing he would never
make an end, for his eyes blazed like fire beneath his
white brows, and much he gesticulated, shaking about
neck and broad shoulders his fleece of black hair, I
rushed into the midst of the assembly, crying out
that the four provinces were invading Ulla, and thou
alone defending the frontiers against them.   Then he
paused a moment and bade them remove me ; but when
two strong warriors laid hands on me, a poet who was
present said, 'Deal tenderly with him ; it is the father
of Cuculain.'   Then at the word was the whole assembly silent, and the king dropped his spears and
came forward humbly, and took me by the hand and
said, 'Forgive me, O Sualtam, father of the great
Cuculain, for I knew not who it was.   Verily ere this
have I grieved, hearing of thy affliction. Our own minds
too the Shee may one day trouble and impair.'   Then

led he me to the best chamber, and gave me keeves of
water, and his people attended to the steeds and washed
the chariot, and I feasted with them that night, held in
great honour amongst them all, listening to the silly
speech of Leairey, for he spake as though he were
already King of all Erin, and Irian knights ruled from
every Dûn within her borders, and to me amazed at his
folly he would incline at times tenderly as though I were
a child. But in the morning an armed escort conducted
me to the borders of the territory, and he himself,
Leairey, the son of Iliach, accompanied me many miles
beyond the Dûn."

"After that I came on to the small Dûn of Iliach, remote from the great road, and a small lane led thither.
But the land around his Dûn was green and fertile,
though in the midst of a wild moor, and as I approached,
the air was filled with sweet smells, for thére were many
blossoming fruit-trees there, and there were trim hedges
and well-cared-for cattle there feeding. But in the door
of the Dûn sat an aged woman grinding with one of the
new mills brought from over-seas, for in the upper mill-
stone was set an upright handle, with which she turned
round the stone easily, and always the yellow flower
spurted forth from a hole in the side upon a clean,
white flaxen cloth spread beneath it upon the ground.
But when I inquired for Iliach, she led me forth through
a fragrant nut-grove to where was an open space, and
there saw I him, the mightiest of the great Rury's warriors, a stained and rent bratta around him, fastened
with a rusty brooch, and he himself kneeling down before a hive, was fixing an addition to the lower part
of the hive, and the slant beams of the descending sun
smote between the well-pruned trees. But he received

me joyfully, for we two had been comrades in the wars
of Rury, though he was much my elder, and he led me
straightway to the house. But when I told him of the
affliction of the Red Branch, and how thou here on the
borders of the province contendedst alone against the
four provinces, then, though the day was far gone, was he
filled with wrath and zeal for thy sake, and he ran to the
fields and brought in his two horses, their necks now
for a long time disused to the yoke, and drew forth the
creaking chariot, and the aged woman brought forth his
battle-dress, and arrayed him in it, but it was far too
big for his shrunken frame. But with ropes and stones
I helped him to cobble the chariot and the harness, for
both were rotten with age, and his shield was eaten
through in places with rust, and the spear-heads rattled
upon the extremities of the spear trees. Nevertheless,
as the work went on, his form seemed to grow, and his
figure to become erect and martial, and his voice and
countenance became more noble. But I left him there
raging around his chariot, and urged my steeds to
the north and east. But I think that Iliach will soon
be here. Nevertheless, the way is long and his steeds
lazy with old age and fat, and he alone of the Red
Branch cometh to help thee." Then Cuculain groaned
and shed tears, gazing into the red embers of the fire,
and in the silence they heard the hum ascending out of
the camp of Meave's mighty host, and the drowsy twit-
ter of Cuculain's blackbirds where they slept upon their
branch.

" After that," said Sualtam, "I came through young
plantations to the noble Dûn of Kethern. Now it was
night, and the bridge was up. Therefore I beat upon
the gong and shouted, but in their kennels the wolf-

hounds answered me with fierce yellings and clamour, and there came down many women and slaves from the Dûn and lowered the draw-bridge on the creaking hinges. But Iondan, the daughter of Yeoha, whose Dûn shines above the waters of the Banna, laid her finger upon her lips signifying silence, and she led me into the Dûn. There upon their couches lay all the fierce warriors of Kethern in an evil slumber and stupefaction, and between white linen sheets Kethern himself, his face hollow and wan, and his grey eyes, full of trouble, rolled round like an animal's, and upon his lips and jaws was sprouting the red unwarlike stubble. Then amid silence and tears the discreet queen prepared food for me, and a couch, and I told her wherefore I had come. But I rested there that night, and departed in the morning ere the sun rose.

"I came to Dûn Kermnah where was Follomān, son of Concobar, with his battalion, and the sun had not yet risen. Nevertheless below me on the sand I beheld the king's son, tall and straight, tracing, with his spear, lines upon the sea-sand, and his war-galleys were afloat, crowded with armed men and rowers, suspended in the washing brine, and other warriors stood armed upon the shore, awaiting some signal, which never came. Thus were they also like those I had beheld enchanted at Isca-Bo-Nemeth. There no man regarded me, but eyed me sternly when I spake unto them.

"After that I procured a fisherman's boat, and one who undertook to row me across the frith to the isle of Rathlin. But far away I heard the wailing of the son of Leda, and a smoke went up from where stood his pleasant Dûn, and the white streams that we have seen glittering down the slopes of the mountain around it

N

were all gone, and the groves cut down, and his galleys
shattered and consumed, and a vast and mournful clamour sounded across the sea as when pirates have suddenly descended upon some prosperous isle and slain
many warriors, and pillaged and wasted the whole place,
and borne away many women and children into slavery,
but in the evening they depart, and when their galleys
are far away, disappearing below the horizon, all those
who hid themselves in woods and caves, or fled to the
mountains, come forth upon the wasted plains and into
the smoking town, and they all howl together upon the
shore.   So wailed and lifted up their voices the warriors
and people of Fergus, and I feared lest they should slay
me, and returned."

"As I passed through the fertile land of Calann, reclaimed from the wild moor, and bright with many a
well-built wattled cot, and many a strong clean cathair
and painted liss, with hedges and bridges and firm roads,
in a wild mountain glen beneath oak-trees, I beheld Conn
the Beautiful, the son of Morna, and Felim Mac Kelkar
by his side.   But they moaned plaintively like wood-
doves in the forest, and their splendid raiment was
soiled, and their countenances marred with grief and
dishonoured by unwarlike growths of unshaven hair,
and I said:

"'What doest thou here, O son of Morna, and leadest
not thy battalion southwards to Southern Cooalney,
where my son Cuculain defends the frontiers of Ulla
against the four provinces of Erin?'

"But he moaned pitieusly, and said:

"'No more is the Rie-ship of Calann with me.   For
the High King hath driven us from the kingdom, most
worthily, in that we neglected our people and territory,

and busied ourselves only in hunting and chess-playing, and hither have we fled from the wrath of our dread sovereign, the son of Nessa.'

" After that I came to Dûn Sovarchey upon the sea, and from afar beheld the mighty rampart, every stone great enough to be the top stone of a king's cromlech, with its Dûn, great and strong, looking over the sea. But on the crags, like the dead carcass of a whale cast aloft there by some mighty storm, lay Kelkar, the son of Uther, a black bratta around his shoulders, and a great pin of iron in his chest, and his breath went out and in like the hollow-sounding waters in a great cavern, and round him, on the rocks and the upland, gathered his mighty men, thick as seals or cormorants upon the ledges of Carrig-na-Rōn, and I spake to them, but no man regarded me, for I feared to approach the great son of Uther. But as a thick cloud that crosses the noon-day sun, so brooded a great horror and darkness over all the place.

" I came also to Derry Galga, and passed through the forest to the Dûn ; but as I rode, and the noise of the chariot echoed in the hollow-sounding forest, there gathered above me in the trees, as it were apes or wild cats with unintelligible chatterings, and I saw there Fiecha Donn and Fiecha Gall, the High King's sons, whom also I have seen at Dûn Dalgan with thee, brave youths, comely and laughter-loving. But when they beheld me, they wrung off the green fir cones and cast them at me, rushing from bough to bough with great agility, and, hardly with my life, and with a broken elbow, did I escape out of that forest.

" I approached Dûn Dalgan, passing through our own territory, meaning to arouse thy warriors, O Setanta, but men told me that they too were sunk in a mortal stupefaction, and I beheld thy mother standing in the door of the Dûn, and went not thither.

" But after that I came to the Dûn of Dary, and far away I heard the roaring of the Donn Cooalney, roaring with a voice of anger and expostulation, articulate accents like a man.　Then the old king received me hospitably, and much he spake concerning the bull, and of ancient warlike feats done by himself.　Lies were they for the most part, for he was my coeval, and he recited for me long rhythmic pedigrees which he had composed, and would have detained me, nevertheless I departed.　But the sons of Dary, tall and noble youths, spake not at all, but gathered at the fire, silent, with pale faces, for they said that the Donn Cooalney was stolen away by Fergus Mac Roy.

" But after that I came on here to thee, having done what thou desiredest, and I will stay with thee now, and fight by thy side, for I desire not to leave thee any more."

Then Sualtam slept amid his rugs and skins, wearied out and travel-worn, but Cuculain slept not, and he was astonished, for the words of Sualtam were more wandering than they have been here set down.　But in the morning Cuculain caused Sualtam to go again to Emain Macha.

CHAPTER XXXV.

PERFIDY.

> " But sea it met
> And shuddered, for the o'erwhelming voice
> Of huge Enceladus swallowed it in wrath,
> The ponderous syllables—"
>
> KEATS.

Now, the same night the whole host of Queen Meave was troubled, and, in the Royal Pavilion, the kings of the four provinces sat silent, and an evil thought festered in their hearts, and each man desired that another should be first to speak it out openly. Then to them so sitting grim-silent arose Bras Mac Firb, the strong lord of Osree, and with stubborn brows he harangued them, and said :

" O Queen of the Olnemacta, and ye kings of the children of Milith ; how long shall we sit here idle, and delay to waste the rich plains of Ulla before the hosting of the Red Branch, and make for ourselves the dribbling stream of the Oun Dia, a barrier stronger than a rampart of brass ? Surely the fairy princes, the powerful children of Dana, have conspired to grant us the destruction of the Clanna Rury, who have relaxed the minds of Concobar and his knights, seeing that now for many days they haste not to the assistance of the hound. Yet ever the sun sets on our mighty host sitting here as though enchanted, bound in the toils of a foolish compact. Not for this have we come together, the far-sum-

moned tribes of Eiré, to be bound here with fetters of
air, that Cuculain may bar the progress of the four
provinces, setting before us that silly compact, as in a
narrow way the herdsman stops his cattle, putting a tree
across the path from fence to fence.   Not thus, I think,
will the warriors of Eiré be restrained here on the borders of Ulla, when we have come to trample and extin-
guish the fatal flame that threatens to devour us all.
For surely if in this hosting we break not the power of
the Red Branch, quickly will the yoke of Concobar Mac
Nessa be upon the necks of the kings of Eiré.   Not
here, indeed, are the borders of Crave Rue, they cease
not but with the sea that encircles Banba.   From
Emain Macha, the strong bole of the Red Branch, run
roots diverse, innumerable, ceasing not, but with every
shore whence, at a moment, will start forth groves of
Irian spears, even mutinous warriors who love the Red
Branch.   Well ye know that the bards of Eiré are not
our friends but his, for the son of Nessa hath bewitched
them.   With gifts and flattery and attentive ears doth he
even receive them coming.   The historians and makers
of tales, and every slanderous and sharp-tongued satirist
finds a welcome at Emain Macha, and the more we
curtail their privileges, and crop their sprouting pride
and domination, the more are they honoured and advanced in dignity among the Crave Rue.   Therefore,
like a ground through which rabbits have widely bur-
rowed, where the wheel sinking, the chariot is overset,
and those within it are rolled forth upon the grassy
plain, so is the soil of Eiré beneath the feet of her kings
undermined by the strolling vermin, for in every territory they came, chanting the greatness of the Red
Branch,   Therefore, at the first descent of the children

of Rury, will there be vast anarchy and rebellion, and many a smooth-faced chieftain will show a mutinous front when the Red Hand of the Ultonians is apparent. Shall we then sit here idle and miss an opportunity of gold, sending daily our bravest to be slaughtered by that youth whom Macha hath made invincible? Shall airy words bind us here as if with fetters of brass? Better far that we break this convention which ourselves have made, than that the Red Branch break us, and the tributes and hostages of all Erin go to Emain Macha."

So spake the strong king of the Osree, and the assembly murmured doubtful approbation; but Queen Meave looked sidelong at Fergus where he sat on the left hand of Aileel.

Then, ere the murmur had ceased, up rose Fergus Mac Roy, and fear and strength rose with him, bending fierce brows upon the assembly; but his dense hair shook around his neck and broad shoulders, and like near thunder his voice came forth out of his hollow chest—

"King, do they call thee High King of the Osree, O Bras Mac Firb?—King rather of some base Fir-bolgic clan, a tribute-paying people, scorn of the warrior tribes of Erin. Even so do the fudirs of Fohla make a promise and straightway break it, for fear has made them vile. Hateful to me is the treaty breaker, more loathsome than the night-stalking ghoul. Fear, I plainly see, hath eaten away thy manly heart that thou dreadest the bard-loving captain of the Red Branch, and the crooning of the bearded poet, which the brave man no more regards than the idle rail that crakes at sunset in the meadows. Verily, if the warriors of Meave were no more magnanimous than thee, very quickly would I cross the sea to

Gaul, like Lara of Dinn Rie, fleeing the presence of the vile, or into España, whence came forth the heroic sons of the great Milith, fleeing from Fohla as from a land accurst. But well I know that the noble kings of Eiré thou wilt not persuade to break faith with the generous Cuculain, and this I say, and by the great Dâda I swear it, which man soever of the host of Meave, I care not who, shall cross the Oun Dia invading the land of Ulla until Cuculain be subdued, according to the compact, quickly shall this spear drink his blood, and the wolves and grey-necked crows shall eat his body, unburned and unburied."

So spake Fergus, and sat down in his place raging; but the kings feared and were ashamed, and Bras Mac Firb retreated into the crowd of the kings scared and dazed, as when a young girl, expecting indeed rain, nevertheless steps briskly out of the house, but hardly has she passed the threshold when the white lightning strikes her blind, and the thunder crashes around her ears, and not slowly does she shrink back into her wattled house. So shrunk in among the kings the haughty Lord of the Osree before the great wrath of Fergus.

CHAPTER XXXVI.

QUEEN MEAVE AND LEWY.

" Then Jonathan and David made a covenant, for he loved him as
his own soul."

HEBREW CHRONICLER.

THEN arose Fionmowl, King of the Dairtheena, and
said, " O Meave, Ard-Rian of the Olnemacta, and ye
Kings of Erin, no home-nurtured warrior can compete
with Cuculain, so quick and dexterous is he in the management of his weapons, no swordsman or spear-thrower
of Fohla hath taught him the art of the duellio. My
counsel is, that we choose out one of the two warriors
who along with him have learned feats of arms at the
hands of Skaäh the warrior-queen who, with her martial
daughters, rules strongly the ragged isle in the northern
seas, teaching only select champions of the men of Erin
and Alba. But these are Lewy Mac Neesh, the glittering chief of Clan Falva, and Fardia, the son of Daman,
the son of Dary, chief of the western Fir bolgs, not
honoured indeed by the Milesian kings, but to my mind
the foremost warrior in all Erin. One of these, therefore, shall we select, who shall slay for us the hound of
Ulla, and remove for us this intolerable obstruction."

So spake the old wise king ; but amongst them arose,.
Lewy Mac Neesh, and said :

" Another champion than me shall ye select to go out
against Cuculain, but that dear friend my spear shall
never pierce, nor shall his pierce me."

Then was Meave enraged, and from her throne, not moving, she harangued :

" Must then this great host sit here idle day after day, bound in the toils of a most pernicious compact, into which we were driven by certain persons, more friends to Cuculain than to the four provinces, and now our warriors must shun the brunt of his brazen spear, putting forward forsooth some pretext of ancient friendship, but in their hearts restrained by fear. Small love has Cuculain for thee, I verily believe ; for, hearing of the ancient amity, I scanned his commerce with thee narrowly when he came to the camp, and more did he avoid thee than seek after thee. Not much would he think of driving his spear through thy very faithful breast."

But Lewy Mac Neesh, bearing himself humbly, but with a stubborn heart, made answer :

" I fear not the charge of cowardice, though made by thee, dread queen, before the chiefs of my nation and the far-coming kings of Eiré, nor is thy judgment right concerning Cuculain ; I will not go out and fight."

Then said Meave, paling with sudden anger, " Thy kingship, O Lewy, is in the hands of Aileel and myself. If thou goest not out against Cuculain I will strip thee of thy sovereignty, and expel thee out of my realm."

But, harder than the black rock over which the mad wave pours, but it always reappears, and the briny streams run white down its stubborn ribs, the son of Neesh made answer :

" The sovereignty which thou gavest me thou mayest again take away, and across the Shannon, or beyond the sea-swept borders of Eiré thou mayest expel me. All this thou mayest do, nor is my life safe against thee, though by birth of the noblest tribes of Herēmon, the

great son of Milesius, but against Cuculain, the son of
Sualtam, I will not lift up my spear."

Then Meave, subtle-minded, unweariable, laughed
lightly, and as the sun emerging from a black cloud pours
forth its light, causing the rain-drops lately fallen upon
the grass and the trees to glisten like pearls, so she
smiled upon Lewy Mac Neesh, and said :

" Thy sovereignty, O son of Neesh, I will by no means
take away, nor would I do myself and the nation of the
Olnemacta an injury so great, for well I know thy wise
government of thy territory, both in all that relates to
the provident rule of the tribute-paying people, which
greatly I value, for these are the soil whence the noble
tribes with their spreading branches draw sap and sus-
tenance, and also in the splendour and efficiency of the
rising-out of thy territory, not to speak of the moderation
and loyalty of thy bards, the rectitude of thy brehons,
and the skill of thy musicians. But this I said, trying
thee, to the end that thou mightest throw off this old
boyish tie, and slay for us the prime enemy, working
deliverance for the four provinces. For truly, as said
the lord of the Osree, I fear the subjugation of all Erin
at the hands of the Red Branch, if we break not their
power in this hosting. But upon me, especially, will
fall great shame and dishonour if I lead back my army
ineffectual, though attended by the rising-out of the four
great provinces of Erin, Meath and Lahan, Mooan and
the Olnemacta. For never before has such a great host
been gathered together in this island; and if misfortune
awaits us, never again will I show my face in a gathering of the kings, never go out with my warriors, or enjoy
my sovereignty any more ; and at night my bed is wet
with my tears, for I see no escape from the cloud of

dishonour preparing to burst upon my head. But upon
thee I counted as a sure refuge whenever disaster should
threaten to swallow me up, as now, for both thy father and
thy father's father were my dear friends, and I honoured
them above all the far-coming kings when the eve of
Samhâne brought to Tara the chiefs of all Eiré. And
thee thyself I have watched, as a king who in his youth
plants a tree beside his father's Dûn, and hopes one day to
see it an ornament to his palace, and a protection against
wintry blasts, and yearly marks how it stretches out
strong arms, and knows that its roots are firm and deep
in the nourishing earth. Thus have I watched thee
grow into the mighty champion that thou art, an ornament and a bulwark of my realm, for all thy poems and
music, the bravest and most agile warrior of the clans of
Aileel, and a pillar of our sovereignty from the Shannon
to the great sea westward. Come now, O Lewy, slay
me this northern hound, whose claws have already torn
so many of thy comrades in arms, and release me, your
queen, from this pit of ignominy into which I fall, and
Fionavar I will betroth to thee with a great dowry; yea,
and make thee regent of Ulla, when we have driven out
or slain the spreading tyrant that rules from Emain
Macha. Great then shall be thy renown over Erin, and
Alba, across the Muirnict also, in Gaul and Espân, and
wheresoever dwell, or shall hereafter be found, the great
race of the Gæil. Verily not far from thee shall be the Ard-
Rieship of Erin, as King of all Ulla, and my son-in-law,
and thy own birth, too, not ignoble."

But as she spake the great queen beckoned him to
herself, and she took his right hand in her's, and placed
her left upon his strong wrist; but instead of the cath-
barr a royal Ard-roth of slender gold encircled her pure

white forehead and lustrous hair. On her noble breast, beneath the white neck, was a fibula of gold, confining the robe of crimson silk, along whose collar and the partings in front ran a spiral embroidery of silver thread, and in her eyes gathered the glistening tear as she looked into the face of Lewy Mac Neesh. But at the other side of Meave sat Fergus Mac Roy, grim and silent.

Then, in spite of shame, the moist tear arose too in the eyes of Lewy Mac Neesh, and he answered brokenly, while with difficulty he suppressed the climbing grief: " O my Queen, demand aught else that is in thy power to ask, or in mine to grant, but against Cuculain, who has my heart's love, demand not that I lift up my spear. Sooner against myself would I draw the hard sword and spill my own life."

CHAPTER XXXVII.

PLOT.

" And with weak hands but mighty heart."

SHELLEY.

BUT Queen Meave, resolute in her mind as a merchant who, sailing from the Iccian Port or Tor Brogan of Espâna, with purpose to vend his wares, wine or silks, or variegated beautiful armour and trinkets, at the great fair of Cahirmän, though oft beat back by storms, and though oppressed at once with broken oars and mutinous mariners, nevertheless stems northward with fixed heart, so the great queen steeled herself to the thought that by the hands of Lewy Mac Neesh should be slain the champion of Ulla—tenacious and unweariable as the weasel that through many fields and through the deep earth pursues always the same quarry, till she seize it, and shrill screams of pain and terror pierce the heart of the still evening. Then to her, plotting, this stratagem seemed the best.

There was in the camp a young chieftain whose ancestral Dûn was where the Avon Lua broadens into beautiful lakes below that deep glen where the saint, Fion-barra, retiring, built his cell on a green island in the gloomy mere, and a narrow causeway connects it with the land. From this source springing, the Lua foams along between ragged rocks till it reaches the lowlands, where it broadens into lakes. Thence came Fireaba Larna ; but ere this his daily pastimes had been to snare trout in the Lua, setting lines and damming the tributaries, or in shooting arrows from his red-yew bow, and rapid and very straight was his cunning archery. Moreover, exceeding skilful was he to play on the tiompan, and to sing many and bright songs which himself had made, and he brought laughter and lightness of heart into any company that he entered, for very frolicsome and gay was Fireaba Larna. Now between him and Lewy Mac Neesh was there a bond of bardic brotherhood, for many a cunningly woven rann with rhymes and alliterations and the subtle charm of assonance had they put together, and joined to a fitting music ; but Lewy Mac Neesh was bound by his gæsa to avenge the death of his friend, and this the great queen knew. Him, then, the queen summoned to her pavilion, but in her presence his laughter and gay speech forsook him, and he spoke brokenly. But she placed him on a couch by her side, and caressed and flattered him, and related how she had

come to the verge of extreme disaster through the great
prowess of Cuculain, for that on account of him the
narrow stream of the Oun Dia was like the lofty rampart
of some great cathair, enclosing the lands of Ulla, and
much she spake of his skill in archery, and she pro-
mised him her youngest daughter, Fionavar, in marriage, with a great dowry, and the chieftainship of a
wide territory around Loch Oribsen, where Mananan
Mac Lear was worshipped by the Gæil, if by any means
he should pierce the strong heart of Cuculain with one
of his arrows.

But Fireaba Larna was astonished, and he said that
on the morrow he would meet Cuculain with his weapons. After this he left the royal pavilion, and rejoined
his comrades, stalking proudly, and he spake little, but
loftily, though before very garrulous, and they sought to
divert him from the combat, but in vain, and there was
great wrath against the High Queen. Then after that
he went in to sup with Queen Meave; and now, for the
wine had made a glad riot in his veins, and Fionvar was
there sitting beside her mother, he boasted of his skill,
and said that no thicker would be the fall of heavy snow
driven by a strong south wind than would be the flight
of his feathered arrows against Cuculain. "Not easily,
I think," said Fireaba, "shall he escape that deadly
shower, and I am meditating whether I shall smite him
to the heart through his shield and breast, or whether
I pierce the bone of his forehead between the bright
eyes." But Fionavar sat grave and tender beside her
mother, and spake not at all throughout the feast, nor
looked at him, though she heard all his words.

CHAPTER XXXVIII.

COUNTER-PLOT.

Τ΄ις δ΄ ούτω κατὰ νῆας ἀνὰ στράτον ἔρχεαι οῖος
Νύκτα δι' 'ορφνάιην ότε θ' εὕδουσι βροτοὶ ἄλλοι.

HOMER.

BUT when Lewy Mac Neesh was aware of the cunning
plot that had been laid against him, he called Angus
Lamderg, his faithful friend and attendant, and one who
was prepared to give his life for the prince of Cliu Mæl.
For when Lamderg was yet a stripling, he had gone to
the great fair at Cahirmān, expecting that he would win
renown there as a poet, and he brought thither, inscribed
on tablets of the pear tree, a poem on the slaying of
Eterskel by Nuada Nect, who had been King of Erin,
and regulated the Feis of Temair, until he was himself
slain by Conairey the Beautiful.   There, in a great
booth, hard by the Ossorian chariot course, he recited
his poem before many of the young nobles who were his
coevals.   Now of these, one, a bastard-brother of Connor
the red-browed Tanist of a Mōr-tuath of Lahan, ridi-
culed his poetic pretensions, exciting much laughter
amongst the youths.   But, sitting awhile silent, he ran
suddenly on the other and stabbed him with his colg in
the neck, for pride and folly had taken away his mind,
and the other fell, and his life-blood poured forth upon
the rush-strewn floor.   Then the young princes seized
and bound Lamderg, and were for leading him before
the king, to whom, at that time, was the regulation of

the great fair. But certain amongst them pleaded hard
for him on account of his youth and his wild contrition ;
moreover, the slain man, too, was not loved, for he was
accustomed to be overbearing in his discourse, and besides, no eric was permitted to be accepted for any deed
of violence done at that fair, but the use of a weapon
was punished by instant death. Therefore, it was resolved that he should be given a chance to save his life,
and they provided him with a chariot and swift horses,
and permitted him to pass secretly from the fair before
word was given to those who orderedthe fair. Then Angus, who was thenceforward called Lamderg, went away
westward, swiftly, flying for his life, and he travelled day
and night, for he hoped to pass into the country of the
Fir-bolgs, north of the Shannon, whither extended not
the authority of the great Ænech of Cahirmán. But he
was overtaken by the avengers hard by the well-built
cathair of Lewy Mac Neesh in Cliu Mæl, and he was
then only a flaut in his tuath. Now, Lewy was returning from the chase in the evening, and he saw one flying
towards his palace with tired horses that stumbled and
swerved in their course, and others pursuing with fresh
steeds, and the fugitive was overtaken on the lawn of
the Dûn, and was seized. Then Lewy went thither
with his people, and when he heard all, he had compassion upon the boy, and he claimed for him the right of
sanctuary. But the officers denied the right, saying he
was taken outside the limit, and there was much wrangling. But in the end the authority of the King and the
Ard-ollav of the tuath was invoked, and before witnesses
Lewy Mac Neesh took in his hands the canairsa, by
asting which the sanctuary was determined, and the
wretched homicide stood by while the generous youth

o

exerted himself to save his young life. Then Lewy took off all his raiment, except the lena, and, standing at his door, took the hammer in his hands, twelve palms was its length from the brass to the haft-ferrule, and, wheeling, cast it far beyond the foss, upon the green lawn, tearing up the dark sod upon the dew-sprinkled glittering grass, for it was early morning, and he went thither and cast again, and went on until he had exhausted the throws which were permitted him by the Cain Cairda of Southern Erin, viz., sixteen casts, for he was an airey-tweesa of the tuath, though in later times the sanctuary was determined by a fixed measurement, and hardly, and in the last cast did he enclose the spot at which Lamderg had been overtaken and seized.

Then Lewy led the homicide into his house, and he became one of his household, and faithful and devoted beyond all to the son of Neesh, but thenceforward he did not bear arms, and ceased to practise the subtle art of the poets, and Lewy Mac Neesh rendered to the King of Cahirmān the huge diera which had been incurred by the fugitive.

Him then he called as he entered the booth; but Lamderg ran when he heard his voice, for he was at the other side daubing with wind-excluding clay the chinks between the wattles, and inside he had suspended rugs all round the walls. And Lewy Mac Neesh told him all that had taken place, and desired him to go to Cuculain and enjoin him that he should not slay Fireaba Larna on the morrow. " But come now with me," said he, "to the house of Fergus Mac Roy, and he will teach thee how to find Cuculain."

Then they wrapped round them their brattas with cowls to cover the head, for it was cold; the skies too

were dark, and the wind high, and went down the main
street of the camp past the market-place, and past the
royal pavilion, where Fireaba Larna was being feasted
to his destruction, and they reached the large four-sided
tent of Fergus Mac Roy. Now before the entrance on
the right side as one might leave the tent, was there a
tall staff fixed, bearing the banner of Fergus Mac Roy,
and armed warriors guarded the way. But from within
the yellow light streamed forth both through the entrance and by many a chink in the rudely woven walls,
and there was a sound of abundant festivity, the noise of
many voices, the laughter of young men, and the music
of the harp and the reed.

But when Lewy spake to the guards concerning
Fergus, they said that he was in the tent of Cormac Conlingas, his fellow-exile. Then as they turned to leave,
there came forth the sons of Fergus, Ciar first, and after
him Corc and Conmac, and also Mainey Maherail, son
of Aileel and Meave, and very dear to his mother, whence
also his surname ; but they came out with a clamorous
hospitality, that they might bring in Lewy Mac Neesh
and his charioteer to the feast, for they recognised the
voice of Lewy. Now these three sons of Fergus were
very noble and warlike, and though youthful and exiles,
their authority was great over the western tribes, for
they had inherited their father's unconquerable soul.
But they were born to him in his palace at Rath Fergus
on the eastern sea, while he was yet Tanist of the Province of Ulla, and they were boys at the time of the rebellion. But now they were supplanting the Rie-damnas
of the Olnemacta, the sons of Aileel and the sons of
Magách, yet not designedly or from ambition, but their
own greatness drew men's hearts after them.

Moreover in the end they ruled over many tribes, and
their posterity spread and multiplied, so that the names
of Ciar and Conmac are upon wide territories in the west
of Erin to this day. But as yet they were only brave
youths, foster-sons of the High Queen, and this night
they feasted their many friends who had been their foster-brothers.

But when Lewy Mac Neesh informed them wherefore
he had come they desisted, for they themselves loved
Cuculain.

Then Lewy Mac Neesh and Angus Lamderg returned
and went to the tent of Cormac Conlingas, and it stood
round, clean-built and lofty in a place by itself, but it
was ever the handsomest in the camp of Meave. And
when they went in they found Cormac Conlingas and
Fergus Mac Roy sitting at a table drinking, and the
head of Fergus was stooped between his hands. Then
Cormac arose and received them hospitably, and ordered
his men to bring couches and drinking cups, and to
hang the spears and shields upon the rack; but in the
middle of the booth blazed a bright fire, hard by the
roof-tree, and a leathern flue ending with a broad and
bell-shaped band of brass, received the smoke.

Then Lewy Mac Neesh related wherefore they had
come, and Cormac Conlingas laughed, and, having a
lively mind, made a picture in words of the scene en-
acted between the queen and Fireaba Larna, and he
said that poets were dangerous associates, and that they
had made his father mad, and he related how he had
seen the chief Kerd of the Kerd-ree repairing the broken
cath-barr. But Fergus Mac Roy restrained him as he
jested concerning the queen. Then Fergus took Lamderg
apart, and explained to him carefully the way to Cucu-

lain's dell and the partings of the passages in the labyrinth, and Angus wrapped his thick bratta around him
and went out. But Lewy Mac Neesh said to Cormac:

" I hear a sound as of a blacksmith's iron hissing in
the trough, and I know that it is the spear of Lu
Lamfada which thou tookest out of the Dûn of Kelkar,
the son of Uther, in the great war concerning the children of Usna. But if it is allowable I would desire very
much to see it, for many times have I heard of this
marvel, both by common rumour and in the tales of the
poets."

Then Cormac led him to where was a long-handled
black spear, of which the haft was fixed in a frame
against the wall, and the head plunged deep in an urn
containing a liquid, dark, save where the bubbles rose
to the surface, but the spear shivered and writhed like a
live thing. Now the urn was filled with the juices of
lethean and soporific herbs which dulled its fury, but for
which it would of its own accord rush against men flesh-
devouring, a marvel amongst the ancient Gæil, for a fell
principle of destruction dwelt within it, an emanation of
the war-demons, but in after-days, with the advent of the
Talkend, it expired. But Cormac took it from the frame,
and its head out of the urn, and held it strongly in both
hands, holding it before him like a fishing-rod, and the
divine spear writhed and strained in his hands like a serpent stiffened out but not subdued by the charm of the
enchanter, and it struggled fiercely to get away, as a kite
strains strongly against the hands of him who holds the
cord. Then he plunged it again into the urn, and made
the haft fast in the frame, and its fury was allayed ; but
the face of Lewy Mac Neesh was distorted with pale fear,
and after that he sat down at the table trembling.

Now thus, according to the ancient historians, was the marvellous spear brought into Erin. At the Fairy Brugh upon the Boyne, the Tuatha De Danan assembled according to their custom, and Lu of the long arms, the slayer of Balor, was not amongst them. But to them assembled the next day, out of the north came Lu Lamfada, his sun-like countenance overcast, and he sat beside the Dûda, and shed a cloud over the divine people. For the three sons of Toorān, Brian, Iuchar, and Iucharba, meeting his sire alone, had fallen upon him, and had not drawn against him the bright, clear bronze, but his beauteous body they had foully mangled with stones and ragged rocks. Six times they sought to conceal him in the earth, and six times the earth, indignant, had cast forth the sacred body, but the seventh time they piled above it a mighty cairn of great stones, and departed.

Thereafter from Mananán's Isle, came Lu Lamfada to Erin, to wage war against the Fomoroh. In the currach of Mananán Mac Lear he came, which needs nor oar nor sail, but skims along the sea, obedient to the thought of the mariner, a marvel amongst the ancient Gæil—Skoove thoyna the ocean-sweeper, Mananán's sacred bark. With the arms of the son of Lear, too, he came, his helmet and impenetrable breast-plate, his irresistible sword the Fraygarta, and his steed Anvarr, fleet as the naked cold winds of March, whose hoofs bent not the grass, nor indented the soft floor of the sea. But as he, full of high thoughts and joyful anticipation of battle, crossed the fertile plains of Murthemney, with its orchards and nut-groves, he heard a dolorous cry sounding from a new-made cairn, and he recognized the voice of his father, and learned the fell deed.

Therefore, with countenance overcast, and full of

wrath and sorrow, he harangued the Tuatha De Danan. Then the divine people resolved that an eric should indeed be accepted by Lu, but that he might demand what eric he chose, and Lu, with a fell purpose, imposed upon them the procuring of the greatest and most strictly guarded treasures of the world, and amongst them the fiery, living spear of Pisärr. But the three sons of Toorán, with vast labour and suffering, toiling many years over the world, brought together the mighty eric. But as they ascended the Boyne, bringing back the last of the eric, their spirits went out of their bodies, for they were worn and wasted with toil, and hunger, and wounds.

But Lamderg, in the meantime, had escaped the guards of the camp, and gone up the river about four miles till he came to where was a ford. There he waded the river, and then descended the thither bank till he reached the Ford of the Combats, after which he struck north-westward to the hills, keeping in mind the injunctions of Fergus Mac Roy; but the wolves howled around him in the forest. Then, at last, he came to the dell where was Cuculain, and Cuculain heard him, for he slept not at all, but wept, for his mind was troubled and confused, and he said that the Red Branch loved him not, and that it would be pleasing to them if he perished at the hands of the Southerns. Then he arose, and he stood at the entrance of the bower against the red fire, and Lamderg, when he saw him there, gaunt and terrible, and heard his untuned accents of fierce interrogation, was afraid, and he stood still, as one who in the woods suddenly meets a man whose disordered mind impels him to wild places, where he strips off his clothes and feeds on berries, and confronts horribly the wayfarer. So trembled he when he beheld Cuculain. But soon recovering his heart, he told wherefore he had come, and Cuculain answered him gently, and led him in, and spread a rug for him before the fire, and he cooked for him a portion of deer's flesh, and gave him mead to drink, and much he inquired after his friends who were in the camp of Meave. But Sualtam did not awake. Then Angus departed, and Cuculain came back, and wrapped his rug around him, and lay down beside the red fire, wolf-scaring.

CHAPTER XXXIX.

DEATH OF FIREABA LARNA.

" Dared the unpastured dragon."

SHELLEY.

Now the next morning, at the appointed hour, Fireaba Larna advanced to the ford, stepping lightly over the dew. On his sloping shoulders, unwarlike, hung an oblong shield, bright with gold-leaf, and rivets of white findruiney; in one hand he carried two spears, and in the other his bow of red yew, inscribed with oghamic verses, and tipped with carved walrus tooth which he had procured from the fishermen of Dûnamarc. This the ancient kerd, whose house was beside the Avon Garf, at the ford of the old chariot, had carved and fitted to the bow; at one end, the likeness of the head and shoulders of a trout with open mouth, and it he had stained deftly, and dotted with crimson spots, and at the other, of a swallow with partly expanded wings, and the forked tail ran in upon the polished wood. But when he came to the ford he dashed the rattling spears upon the ground, and the shield with its strap, and stringing his bow, plucked at the sweetly-sounding string. Then, fitting to it an arrow, he awaited the approach of Cuculain, nought-fearing.

But on the other side came down Cuculain, with long strides through the stunted willows, soiled from the spring floods, to which adhered many bands of dried grass moving knee after white knee, but his eyes were fixed on the ground, and his left hand held the shield low, exposing his breast, and behind, he trailed the hafts of his spears. Then, indeed, had Fireaba Larna obeyed the voice of Meave, and Bras Mac Firb standing near him, he had slain the hound of Ulla; but as he bent to aim, he shouted a clear cry of challenge. As when one travelling swiftly in the dawn meets on lonely roads a car piled up aloft with merchandize, securely fastened with ropes and canvas, but on the top lies the driver, outstretched and asleep, overworn with much journeying; but the horse unguided draws the car awry upon the narrow road. Him, then, the other awakes with a shout, and he starting swiftly from slumber, snatches at the reins. So cried Fireaba Larna, and so started Cuculain, lifting rapidly both head and shield, and forthwith the singing arrow stuck fast in the brass plating and the tough leather of the light shield, nor penetrated to the hero's breast. Then ran Cuculain forward, and reached the stepping stones, springing with long strides to every third stone, but for every stride flew an arrow from the light hands of Fireaba Larna, and regular and unintermitted as is the sound of two threshers advancing and receding towards and from one another was the

sound of Fireaba's arrows as they entered the shield of
Cuculain, and they stood there thick as pins in the pin-
cushion of a girl, conspicuous with their white feathers.
But of these one penetrated the right side of the shield,
and, passing through, fixed itself in Cuculain's hand,
between the root-bones of the fore and middle fingers,
and another entered the fleshy part of the left thigh on
the left side of the bone. Nay-the-less, though limping,
Cuculain came up to Fireaba. Then he, Fireaba Larna,
snatched at the handle of his sword, but ere he could
draw it, Cuculain dropped his spears, and smote him
with the palm of his hand upon the ear, on the left
side of his head, and a cloud came over his mind. Then
Cuculain brake his bow, and poured his arrows into the
river. After that Cuculain shook him and bruised till he
cried out like a boy chastised by his master. Then Cuculain drew his short colg from his side, and cut into
the flesh, and took out the arrows from his leg and from
his hand, and he flung behind him his shield, and in
spite of pain strode indignant to his retreat, disappearing among the trees, and with difficulty did he return
to his place, and a darkness came over him.

But his companions came around Fireaba Larna, and
he lay on the grass gulping, and the red blood poured
out of his mouth. But, as a trout vainly gasps in the
fisherman's basket after its first struggles are o'er, so
gasped the unhappy Fireaba, pouring the blood from
lips whence only songs and laughter and happy breath
came before. Nevertheless, he died not, but lived, yet
ever after he was afflicted with pains in his bones, nor
even went to his bed without groaning, nor left it without woe. His singing, too, and gay music were ended.
For, like a song-bird with bright plumage and glittering

eyes which a boy captures, spreading lime upon a rail, and confines in a narrow cage, so did he droop, and his beauty left him, and his sunny soul was overcast. Instead of songs, henceforward he composed satiric ranns and heart-vexing lampoons, and in the end he was slain by Brasal, second son of Banat, founder of the Bantree, in single combat, on the sandy shore of the harbour of Bera, hard by Dûnamarc.

CHAPTER XL.

LŌK MAC FAVASH.

" Alone in defence of the Ultonians—
Solitary, keeping ward over the province—
Lōk, the fierce King of Lath Moah,
He has slain my two black-birds,
Myself too, he severely wounded
When I was entangled by the eel. "

SIC CECINIT CUCULAIN.

THEN amongst the men of Meave arose Lōk Mac Favash, the king of a mixed people in the south, for the Irian colonists, to whom Rury Mōr had given lands in Des-Mooan, had mingled there with the Clanna Nemeth, who derived their origin from the ancient race of the giants, from whom, too, sprang the Tuatha De Danan, immortal and all powerful on the one hand, and many of the nations of Erin on the other.

But amongst his friends he said, " Sufficient is now the renown of Cuculain to render him a quarry worthy of my spear. To-morrow, the host of Meave, released from this check, will cross the Oun Dia, invading the lands of Ulla, and in my armoury the brains of Cuculain mingled with clay, shall be an ornament of my Dûn, and a boast to my posterity." But in the morning his squires arrayed him in his battle-dress, his helmet and neck-piece, and capacious leathern coat clasped round his breast and mighty waist, and over that bound his strong breast-plate. But he advanced to the ford like a moving tower, on legs like the trunks of trees, and though corpulent, and past the prime of his youth, nor very quick upon his feet, yet was his strength and power irresistible, which, indeed, all men knew; for, in the previous year, at the feast of Lunosa, held annually in honour of Lu Lamfada, on the plain of Tailteen, on that day which men in later times named the Kalends of August, he had broken in the skull of a strong bull with a single blow of his heavy hand. Seven folds of tanned ox-hide stitched close together, o'er-ran the firm osier work of his shield, and above that was plating of brass two inches thick, and no man in the host of Meave, save Fergus only, could wield it, but on his arm it was lighter than the bratta which in sudden quarrel a man winds round his left arm, a defence against a knife. It three brothers of the city of Limenick had made for him, and there was a painted device in the middle.

But, on the other side, came down Cuculain unarmoured, his linen tunic and crimson bratta soiled, and his brooch dulled with rust, his gold tresses tangled, and his countenance hollow and overcast; but harder than steel was his heart in his breast, and the men of Meave were astonished and said, " Is this, indeed, he who played at goal with us ?" for mighty seemed his stature, and terrible his advance, striding through the stunted willows to meet his enemy. Then his feet pashed in

the shallow water of the ford, but suddenly he shrieked,
and his spears fell from his hand; for, above the head
of Mac Favash he beheld the horrid ghoul that had
accompanied him unseen from the south, resting a
bearded chin upon skinny knuckles, and it smiled upon
Cuculain; but he (Cuculain) stood like one petrified,
his eyes starting from their sockets, and his yellow curls
unwound themselves, and stood out from his head.
Then advanced Lōk Mac Favash, and poising, cast his
heavy spear at Cuculain's bare breast, but it erring,
went lower towards the left, and passed through the
shield at the upper rim, and entered the fleshy part of
Cuculain's upper arm. Then dire agony took possession of Cuculain, which was his safety, for it restored
him to himself; but Lōk Mac Favash drew to him the
thong of the spear, drawing the head out of Cuculain's
flesh, but the shoulders held fast in the shield, wherefore he dragged Cuculain forward, struggling and stum-
bling in the water, as the fisherman draws to land some
noble fish, and the blood spurted out and reddened his
white tunic and his knees down to the calves, and the
men of Meave raised a shout, and that shout was heard
in Emain Macha, and Læg sprang from his lethargy,
and listened, with wild eyes, like a hound listening
with head erect, and after that, he heard Cuculain cry
out in his agony. Then forthwith all his mind came
back to him, and in the royal stables he heard the
steeds of Cuculain whinnying, and stamping, and pulling madly at their halters, and in the chariot-house the
growling and mutterings of the war-demons, with short
snarls, and long wolf-like howls, and in the Tayta Brac
Concobar's shield groaning, and far away the Tonn
Rury moaning in the north. But he rushed to the

stables, and led forth the steeds, and drew out the war-
car, and ran to the Tayta Brac, and returned with all
Cuculain's arms and warlike equipment, moving unseen
beneath the mighty load, and quickly he fixed them in
their places in the war-car, and he yoked the horses,
and seized his scourge, and like grinding thunder were
the brazen wheels sounding through the block-paved
streets of Emain Macha, and so drave Læg, as when in
a city in the night there is a cry of fire, and straightway
with the sound of the horn, and thunder of wheels, and
steel-shod hoofs, the rushing steeds bear onward through
dark streets the fire-subduers, and sparks fly out on
every side from the smitten flint. So Læg, the son of
Riangowra, drave through the city of Emain Macha,
and the cloud of war-demons shouted, pursuing him on
his swift way.

But meantime Lōk Mac Favash was dragging Cuculain
through the ford, and he insulted the noble Cuculain :
" Verily ere now, O men of Meave, have I had good
sport in fishing. For in the sea below Limenick and in
the harbour of Oileen Arda Nemeth have I drawn into
my boat fish, many and great that strongly resisted, increasing the sport, and when I brought them into the
boat, if troublesome, I struck them on the head with a
short stick. But never till now have I drawn in a fish
so vigorous, or that yielded such good play. Nevertheless, him too will I mollify, stroking him down with my
little stick." Therewith holding the spear thong in his
left hand, he drew his war-mace with his right, the
head alone weighing seventy pounds, and it was of
brass, with spikes standing out upon it like the sea ur-
chin, and he shook it towards the men of Meave.

Then was there a respite for Cuculain, and very

quickly, and ike the crooked track of the lightning, he drew his sword and smote the spear of Mac Favash just in front of the shield, and struck in twain the strong ashen tree. Then he drew up to him by the thongs the spears which had fallen from his hands, and with a cry he leaped from the ford, strong and vigorous as a salmon springing over a cataract in early summer when he seeks the upper pools, and poising, was on the point of casting one of his spears at Lōk when again the spectre, breathing in his face an icy breath, confronted him more hellish than before. Yet this time he shrieked not, nor was afraid, despair and wrath had made him mad. Wherefore altering the direction he hurled at herself the long spear, and it seemed as though it passed through a hollow eye socket, and the thong of that spear snapped, but a horrid cry penetrated the host, whereat the warsteeds and the beasts of burden ran together alarmed, and the whole host shuddered, and men saw some formless thing fall heavily into the ford. Then, ere Cuculain could clutch his second spear, Mac Favash bare down upon him like a great ship that throws her billows on both sides from her broad prow, and beat him back into the ford, using both shield and club, and twice in succession he smote with his mighty club the shield of Cuculain, and shattered all the middle of that light shield; but Cuculain stepped back nimbly, and again lifted his spear. But once more Cuculain cried out with mingled rage and fear, and he stood a moment as if glued to the spot, with his legs close together and working frightfully with his bloody knees, and a great compassion swept like the wind through the host of Meave. Then as Lōk Mac Favash was advancing to slay him, Cuculain sprang high out of the water, and around his

ankles and below the calves of his legs was there coiled
three times lapped, the twine of a great eel, blue, with
glittering eyes and close-clapped tail; but as he sprang
high in air, Cuculain smote at it with his spear, using
it like a staff, striking on the left side, and with a croak
like a raven the horrid thing unwound, and fell into the
bloody water. Then Cuculain poised once more his
spear, and cast it at Lōk Mac Favash, but the other held
his round shield at an angle, and the spear screeched
against the thick brass, grooving it as the ollav grooves
the sand with his pen, teaching children to write, and
once again Cuculain cried out, trampling wildly with his
feet, and the spray went up and concealed the combat
from the fierce trampling of the son of Sualtam, and the
torn fragments of a tough-fibred water-weed floated down
the stream from where Cuculain trampled, subduing the
third transformation of the deadly spectre, and in that
agony he lost the thong of the spear which he had discharged against his foe.

But while he was powerless Lōk Mac Favash struck
him on the left breast with his club. Now all the
middle of Cuculain's shield was broken away, and there
was a ragged border all around, and with this border,
the weakest part of the shield, he intercepted the blow,
but the heavy mace brake through it and fell full upon
his breast, and the spikes tore his flesh. Then Cuculain
staggered. Nevertheless he drew his brazen sword and
smote at Lōk, but the other caught it on the very boss
of the shield where the brass was four inches thick, and
the sword brake and showered about the stream.

Then Cuculain looked a moment to the wide heaven
and the sun, for it was blazing noon, and his lips moved,
and, swerving swiftly to the right, he stooped. Now a

row of great pebbles crossed the ford, the work of some
ancient king, and in a crescent-shaped line traversed
the water and the dry land on each side, in order that,
even in times of flood, there might be a passage for travellers, and below this was the chariot-ford where the
heroes fought; but Cuculain dropping the fragments of
his shield, laid his great hands on the largest of these,
smooth and white on the top, worn by many feet, but
black and mossy upon the sides, and it two strong
navvies, such as men are now, could with difficulty roll
to the shore, using crow-bars, but Cuculain raised it
without difficulty, as a boy, eager to get at the sweet
kernel, with ease lifts the strong-shelled fruit of the
palm-tree, and smashes it against the flagged basement,
so Cuculain raised on high above his head the mighty
pebble, standing with legs apart in the ford, and dashed
it on the centre of the huge shield of Lōk Mac Favash.
But, as the trained rider breaks through the paper hoops
held up before her, and the fragments flutter around,
and some of them adhere to her gauzy raiment, so the
great stone smashed through the broad shield of Lōk
Mac Favash, and smote him below the breast in the
wind, and bore him to the ground, falling upon him as
one who wrestles with his enemy and falls with him to
the ground, and it crushed him down under the water;
but it wanted not water to suffocate him, for his body
was broken from the impulse of the heavy missile. Then
Cuculain seized the spear-tree of Lōk's spear which was
edying around the place and leant upon it, panting, red
all over as though he had ascended out of a bath of
blood. Then he drew himself together and sat down on
one of the great pebbles, bowing his head between his
hands, and vomited much blood into the stream. After

P

that, he rose upon his feet and walked to the other shore, staggering as he went, and steadying his steps with the spear, and he passed in between the willows; and the whole host of Meave was silent, and every eye watched him, warriors craning forward with raised hands, watching eagerly if he would fall. As when a sportsman and his beaters watch eagerly the flight of a bird which they deem is wounded, and one says he will fall, and another not, so the great host of Meave, in silent expectation, watched Cuculain as he went back till the trees concealed him, and then there broke out an universal clamour; but beyond the trees, amid nettles and night-shade, Cuculain lay outstretched in a deadly swoon.

CHAPTER XLI.

THE TEMPTATION OF FARDIA.

> " And dear the helpless creature we defend
>   Against the world, and dear the schoolboy spot,
>   We ne'er forget, though there we are forgot."
>
> BYRON.

THEN it was resolved by Queen Meave and the saba of her kings, that Fardia of the Fir-bolgs should go out against Cuculain on the morrow, and those who knew Fardia, the son of Daman, marvelled with one another how the queen would fare in that undertaking. Now Fardia was not of the blood of Milith, nor equal in rank to the race that now ruled over Erin, but in the ancient days his people had the sovereignty of the isle. Out of the east, beyond Slieve Alpa, and the country of the

Franks and the Lochlannah, had they come into Erin, whence, too, their fathers, the Clanna Nemeth, had been driven out by the Fomoroh, and they made peace with the Fomoroh, and dwelt there, and their sovereignty was over all the land, and some say that they first erected a Muir at Tara, but the wiser ollavs have denied this. Moy Tura was their capital city, and here they held their games and solemn assemblies, and here they interred their kings; but from Tailteen they ruled all Erin, putting their will upon subject tribes, and gathering in their tributes, for here in a mighty cairn they concealed the ashes of Taylta, bride of Yeoha Mac Erc, and daughter of Mah-Mōr, a king of Espâna, and ever after held solemn games and assemblies every third year on the Kalends of August; but their power was great in the land, and not without many battles did they yield before the might of the Tuatha De Danan, extending their sovereignty westward from the Boyne. Now, indeed, they tilled the soil, and tended cattle, paying tribute to the children of Milith throughout Banba, but of them too, there were many warrior tribes, and they went out to war with kings of the race of Milith, fighting battles not their own. Such were the Ernai of Moon and the Clan Dia of Iar-Oluemacta, the Gamaradians of Inver Scena, the Fir-Gaileen on the banks of the Blaney, the Fir-bolgs of Eyrus also, and Inver Downan, and the Western Isles, and of the Clan Dega, the son of Daman, son of Dary, was by far the bravest.

But, thinking upon these things, and seeing the indignities put upon his nation, he loved not the warfare of Erin, and his youth he had spent in foreign lands where no disgrace attached to his people, and he bore

himself proudly to the lords of the race of Milith, but
his own people loved him.

Then Queen Meave called to her Brasal Bawn the
herald, and he came humbly, bearing the white staff, and
adorned with insignia more gaudy than was customary
in his office, for he was of a great and swelling presence,
and she ordered him to bid to the feast that night in the
royal pavilion, Fardia, son of Daman of the Fir-bolgs;
and Bassal Bawn bowed himself very low before the
queen, and went out, and passed through the camp
glancing sideways as he went, bearing the herald's white
staff. But when he came to the quarter of the Fir-
bolgs he passed between the spear-men at the entrance,
and passed the armourer's quarter, loud with a noise
of files, and he found the Fir-bolgs amusing themselves casting great stones, with much clamour and
loud laughter; mighty of bone and thew were those
champions, only not so comely to look upon as the warriors of the race of Milith. But he passed roughly
through the crowd that encircled those who competed,
and they gave way before the envoy of the High Queen.
Then said Brasal Bawn :

" Such are ever the rude pastimes of the Fir-bolgs,
therefore it is well that ye should be segregated from
the rest, but cease now your rock-throwing, and tell
me if ye know one Fardia, the son of Daman, for I bear
to him a command from the High Queen."

But a cloud passed over the faces of the warriors, for
they deemed that the fame of Fardia was greater than
was implied in the words of the herald; nevertheless
they led him to where was Fardia, for he lay on the
grassy side of a mound gazing southwards, to where in
the rear of the host among the camp-followers, was the

pavilion of the queen's people, and it was there that
Fionavar was accustomed to be, and Æd Shievra, a
young prince of the Fomorians, lay near him. Then
Brasal approached and touched him roughly with the
end of the herald's staff, as those who rouse a hound
from his place upon the hearth, and, at the same time,
he delivered his message,

But Fardia turned quickly, and sat up, shaking his
yellow locks, drawing down his heavy brows, and forthwith he stood upon his feet, and seized the staff from
the herald, and strook him back-handed across the right
side of the head above the ear, and the staff brake, and
Brasal Bawn fell to the ground heavily, as an ox falls
when his forehead yields inwards before the brazen axe.
Then the rough warriors smiled, rubbing their hands
between their knees, but anon they feared at the insult
put upon the herald of the High Queen ; but Fardia
cried aloud, " Take beyond the lines this fool and jester,
let him not come again amongst the Fir-bolgs with his
tricks." So saying, he flung from him the end of the
staff that remained in his hand ; but Brasal arose from
the ground trembling and dazed, and him Æd Shievra
led outside the lines whimpering, and he went by a
secret way to where was his own booth, avoiding the
young nobles, and he sent a messenger to Meave. Him
then his servants washed, and they dressed the wound,
and set before him hog's flesh with onions, and the red
root of the macan, curds in a wooden bowl, and ruddy
ale, and his heart revived in him. Then he sent for
Far-camal, the son of Rechta, who lived under the shadow of the king's Dûn at Ath-an-Rie, one cunning in the
laws, but not held in great honour amongst the discerning, and with others of his craft he followed the host of

Meave. But straightway he appeared, and with him a
boy bearing the notched tablets, in which were set down
the enechlān of every rank in Erin, and the diera and
the eraic, and he explained with precision to Brasal
Bawn the ancient laws of the Fenechas, as they dealt
with insult and injury, and Brasal Bawn was well
pleased, and his greatness returned to him again, and
many times he pledged Far-camal in the red ale, and
reviled Fardia, the son of Daman.

Then Lewy Mac Conroy, whose Dûn Cuculain had
dismantled, and whose sire he had slain, and Mainey
Lamgarf, son of Aileel, and Cormac Conlíngas, son of
the King of Ulla, for they were the most honourable of
the knights of Meave, were sent by the saba of the kings
to bring Fardia to the feast; and Fardia saw them afar
off passing between the tents in their glittering equipment and bravery, and he heard their light laughter and
merriment, and this displeased him, for haughty and
melancholy was he in mind, and he arose and went as
though he saw them not, though now very near him,
and went and stood among his own people where they
hurled the great stones, and he differed not at all in raiment from the chiefs of his nation, but went roughly like
themselves, though in Gaul and Espâna, and in the
Northern Isles, with the Picts and the Albanah, no
chieftain or king excelled him in his equipment. Only
in stature and behaviour did he differ from them at all,
and the warriors stood aside when he approached.

Then came the envoys of the queen before him, and
saluted him, and Cormac Conlíngas delivered the message from the queen. But Fardia answered that it was
one of his gæsa, and a silly one, that he should not feast
in Erin with the children of Milith, but only with his

own people; and when Cormac Conlíngas began to
reason with him, he answered imperiously that it was
not the custom of the Fir-bolgs to infringe upon their
gæsa, and he nodded to Æd Shievra that he should
bring forth ale. Then wrath collected in the heart of
Mainey Lamgarf, and he moved uneasily on his feet,
but the son of Concobar drew down his brows upon him
and caused him to withhold his speech. Then Cormac
Conlíngas went to where were the Fir-bolgs, and he
poised the stone in his hand, great enough to be the
top stone of a cromlech, and returned to where was Fardia, and said that no champions in Erin were so mighty
as the Fir-bolgs, and that if such warriors were around
him in the great war concerning the children of Usna
he would never have been expelled out of the north by
the Ultonians. Then, in spite of shame, a light beamed
in the face of the son of Daman, and the bright tear
started into his eyes, and the great flagon trembled in
his hand.

There, then, before a table of red yew, in front of Fardia's booth, they drank the ruddy ale, and Fardia forgot his haughtiness, and told many stories of the wars
between the Africans and the nations of Espâu. But
when they rose to depart, Mainey Lamgarf, son of Aileel
and Meave, brake forth and said, "O Fardia Mic Daman, methinks that thou art the noblest and bravest
in all this great host. Well indeed can I believe the
rumours concerning thee, seeing thee with my eyes to
be so great and fair. Wherefore, no man shall hereafter, I being by, disparage, in my hearing, the race of
the Fir-bolgs. And I love not stratagem or conceal-
ment, therefore know that the High Queen desires that
thou shalt slay for us the son of Sualtam, and deliver

us from the toils of the pernicious contract, and a great
reward is prepared for thee in land, and in cattle, and
in gold."

Then Fardia felt sick at heart, and a pallor overspread his face, and he said:

"Not if the saba of the kings should give to me the
whole of the level plain of Ai, which is the public land
of the Olnemacta; not if to this were added all the
treasures laid up in Moy Tura, both that of the Fomorians, and that where my own people are interred, or all
that are contained in Tlatga, Wisna, and Taylteen, nor
all that the sacred territory of Tara holds within its
border at the Feis Temrah what time its king is undis-
puted lord of all Erin; not for this would I look in anger
upon Cuculain, the son of Sualtam, nor slay him, nor
dishonour him; though this, too, I know full well, that
I alone, of all that Erin contains within its sea-swept
bounds, am able to subdue the Hound of battle of Murthemney. And tempt me not again, O son of the High
Queen, for not a gentle answer shalt thou receive. Well
ye knew the ancient friendship between me and Cuculain. Our sovereignty we have long since lost, and our
lands, and our honours, and ye, the children of Milith,
desire that we should still further dishonour the vows
of our order, and expel our heart's love at your pleasure.
Verily, O son of the High Queen, the Fir-bolgs, in their
degradation, are more kingly."

Then returned the envoys in silence to the queen, and
the saba of her kings, and they told what had happened,
and said, "Prouder than the King of Tara, when all
Erin admits his sovereignty, is this haught champion
of the Fir-bolgs." And Cormac Conlíngas said, "Thyself, O queen, or thy fair daughter, alone can bend his

stubborn soul," for very subtle-minded and discerning
was he.

Then the queen sent for Fionavar, and Fionavar came
into the camp, and she obeyed the orders of the queen,
and Fardia came forth to meet her, and the noblest of
the Fir-bolgs with him, for he saw her when she came
into the camp, and Fionavar wondered at their stature,
for they were very great, majestic, with unshorn beards.
And Fardia bowed himself very low before the daughter
of the High Queen, but she raised him with her hand,
and said :

" Shame fills me, O son of Daman, and sorrow, when-
e'er I come into the presence of thy nation, knowing
whose are the Dûns in which we dwell, and who reclaimed from forest the territories whose tributes and
sovereignty we enjoy ; and not by our own prowess, too,
did we come to this, but through the contrivance of the
Tuatha of Erin who brought down thy race, for their
power is over all. And verily, often ere this have I been
sad, seeing the nobleness of thy nation, and their kingly
bearing, and their might. But now the queen hath
sent me, for she greatly desires that that thou shouldest
feast with her to-night in the royal pavilion, and because
of thy gæsa there shall not be bidden to this banquet
any of the children of Milith, and truly this vow was
most right, for they, the haught princes, revere not
always those whom the Tuatha have cast down, when
ale hath loosed their tongues. But thou and thy comrades, Aileel, and Meave, and myself, will be present at
this feast."

Then Fardia answered very humbly, saying that he
would go, and protested much concerning the ancient
boyish vow, and after that Fionovar talked with Fardia

and the Fir-bolgs, turning sweetly from warrior to rough warrior.   Then an attendant poured forth metheglin into a silver cup, and presented it to Fionavar, and she drank it, and spake of the making of the drink, for she herself was accustomed to make mead, and at Cruhane her bees were hived in a sunny field, eastward from the great Dûn, beneath a warm hedge, and that field was called Gort Fionavar; but further to the east, not many roods, was there a sacred well-head, whence flowed a bright stream, and to this stream Fionavar and her maidens were accustomed to bring garments, and to wash.   Moreover, this was the sacred well-head where Patrick and his disciples baptized the two princesses, meeting them there in the dawn, while the dew was still on the ground, and the maidens deemed that they were fairies, seeing their white garments and tonsured crowns.   But when she left with the queens that were her company, Fardia sent a battalion of spear-men, and they attended her and her retinue to the royal pavilion, and came back and dispersed each man to his tent.

CHAPTER XLII.

AN ANCIENT TOILET.

"And all went merry as a marriage bell."

BYRON.

THEN went Fardia into his booth, bending his lofty head in the door-way, for the Fir-bolgs had made for him a great booth, by the meeting of tall, straight firs set on end, with interlacing rods and lissom twigs of the

willow gathered along the banks of the Avon Dia, and
they covered it above and on the sides with water-flags,
securing them from the wind with ropes of twisted hay,
crossing and recrossing like a trellis-work, and with
wicker windows in the sides, to be opened and closed
as the wind blew from this point or from that. Yet
though high the angled door-way, still bowed Fardia,
his yellow head entering the booth. Now, within were
three large boxes of pine-wood ranged against the wall,
and these he unlocked, and took from thence many
garments bright with corcur, and rue, and glaisheen,
and short colgs of glittering bronze, with handles of
ivory riveted with silver studs, and long shapely swords,
straight throughout, and tapering or broadening towards
the middle, but ending in a point, keen as a needle,
most like the beautiful blade of the water-flag growing
luxuriant in the spring-time in the wet inches of the
river, and trembling with its golden flower. Thence
make boys their mimic boats with feathery sails, and
launch upon the running stream. These all he took
and laid upon rugs upon the ground, and Æd Shievra
assisted him.

After this he despatched his attendant to the chiefs
of the Fir-bolgs, selecting by name such as were noblest
and most princely, and most worthy to sit at meat with
the great queen and the gentle maiden, twenty five in
all; and when they came to him, he distributed to each
man raiment and bright weapons, brooches and torcs,
and minds, and shining shields, out of the great diara,
which he had obtained. For, Fraysh, the son of Bay-
veen, who was a lord in the tuath which adjoined his,
after that, through the bounty of his divine ancestress,
he had become rich, began to keep a numerous and

well-armed retinue, senclaytas innumerable, and an
ambus worthy of a king, though he was but a flaut in
the tuath, and he trespassed upon Fardia; for he
bribed his ceileys to desert, and his fudirs, his free
tenants, and his base tenants, and they passed over to
Fraysh with their utensils, their ploughs, and mattocks,
and caldrons, and the abundant taurcrah, which, with
their lands, he had given them—for he was ever generous—and his estate was wasted.   Therefore, when he
returned from the wars in Espân, and thought to have
had instant vengeance upon Fraysh, his people suffered
him not, for the Olnemacta were bound together beneath Ailill, since the wars in which Yeoha Faydleeah
and himself had broken the power of the kings west of
the Shannon; and now tuath warred not upon tuath,
and they knew that violence would recoil upon themselves, and that the levied fine would be their destruction.   Therefore, they laid a complaint before the king,
and the saba of Fraysh's tuath, and the brehon awarded
them naught, for the power of Fraysh was great, and
there was a coward feeling against the Fir-bolgs.   Now,
amongst the Olnemacta at that time, each territory contained four tuaths, and the High King of the territory,
with his sub-kings, adjusted all differences between
tuath and tuath.   Therefore, when the host of Meave
was assembling in the four plains of Mayh Ai, Fraysh
appealed for justice to the king of the territory and his
saba, against the crooked verdict of the tribal brehon.
Then the brehon of the mōr-tuath awarded to Fardia a
mighty diera, for the wrong which had been done unto
him, for the abduction or seduction of every bodach and
fudir, and every sær ceiley and dær ceiley, and for the
abundant taurcrah which had been carried away, and

for the waste to the estate by reason of so much land, now a long time ungrazed and untilled. For Fraysh had made them all his own immediate vassals, and by no public election had they become incorporated with the tuath; therefore, they were as the fudirs and senclaytas of Fraysh, and he was liable for all that they had done. And this was the diera which the just brehon awarded :—thirty-five brattas of fine wool dyed, and ten of silk, and forty inars of dyed flax; forty belts of stained leather, with buckles of carved findruiney, and three score swords, each two of them with handles, worth a cumal; all these things to be the best of their kind. Moreover, twenty-three boys fit to manage steeds, and twenty girls taught to sew and to cook, active and comely, no slatterns, and besides all this, one hundred cumals. Now all the great fine had been levied upon Fraysh, only instead of the cattle, he had given brooches and minds, and twisted torcs, apples of gold for the hair, colgs, and shining shields, and the huge diera was levied to the last thread, and the last ounce of wrought metal. Yet, too, was the diera light, for Fraysh was youthful, loving ostentation, and not so much for injustice as from wanton bravery, and pride of blood, and sudden wealth, had he wronged so heinously the blameless Firbolg.

Out of this then Fardia made distribution amongst his comrades; to every man a brat and an inar and a lena, bright ocrat for the legs, and shoes glittering with silver thread and findruiney; and to his singing men and harpers, his jugglers and chanters of noble tales, he gave an equipment in like manner. But he urged them all to prepare for the feast, and to wrong not the Fir-bolgs before the great queen and the gracious princess Fionavar, of the delicate eyebrows. She was the youngest child of Aileel and Meave, having three sisters and seven brothers, but to Aileel there were born other children also, whom his concubines bore to him amongst the Olnemacta.

But meantime, Æd Shievra had borne water from without the camp, and filled the hero's keeve, and he himself, Fardia, the son of Daman, bathed his mighty limbs, pouring many times the cold water over his head, and he stood forth out of the bath while the steam ascended from his sides. But after this, carefully choosing, he put around him a lena of fine linen, three-fold, and it descended to his knotted knees, with loose collar, and stripes, black and white and red, running from the waist to the hem. Then he combed his yellow hair, lustrous like a sheaf of gold thread in the house of a kerd, falling in dense curls on his mighty shoulders. He who next touched that hair was Cuculain, raising tress after yellow tress, while the hot tears fell. But he, Fardia, exulting, put upon him an inar, also linen, dyed saffron, with loose sleeves, slashed and lined with fine, soft white skin brought from over-seas by the merchant. It, Ugainey More, Ard Rie Erenn Uli, had presented as a gift to the father of Dary, when in his royal circuit he was entertained by the Gamaradians of Iar Senann. Then from beneath the inar he drew forth the collar of the lena, decorated with gold thread and crimson, and it surrounded his neck and shoulders, and with many gold clasps he fastened the inar in front and at the throat with a fibula of gold, six ounces in weight. But after this he took out a belt made of innumerable tiny silver rings linked together, a span was its breadth, and in front where the ends joined was there the likeness of two serpents interlaced. This he himself had brought back from Espân, receiving it as a ransom, having taken prisoner a stripling, son of a noble African, for they were superior in the arts to the kinsmen of the Gæil, the children of Gædil still abiding in Espân. This then he clasped around his waist, confining the loose inar which descended not below his hips, covering the upper ends of the variegated stripes of the lena. Then upon his shining feet he bound his sandals, lined with soft doe-skin, winding over ankle and instep the pliant strap, and he turned down the ends carefully under the loop. Then into its place in the belt he passed his colg, gold-handled, a cubit in length, such as men wore then, and gems glittered in the gold. Last of all, over his right shoulder he flung his vast bratta of crimson silk, bright as the clouds of sunrise, glittering with strange hues that came and went, and like the sun, a great brooch of gold, round as a wheel, glittered upon the spaces of his mighty breast, the long delg traversing the folds of the gorgeous fuan.

Then Fardia sprang forth from his tent, and the Firbolgs shouted, and the young nobles ran round him jesting, yet they too were astonished, for no mortal man did he resemble, and they said such too was Angus-an Vroga, the son of the Dâda, for he seemed like a fairy prince of the Tuatha of Erin, emerging from a sacred dell in one of the mountains of the Shee. But along with Fardia came forth his attendant, bearing his sword and belt, his spears and a banqueting shield, pure white, inscribed with a cunning device wrought for him by a kerd of the Olnemacta.

CHAPTER XLIII.

FARDIA YIELDS.

"For sideways would she lean and sing
A fairy song."

KEATS.

THEN went forth Fardia and his comrades, and the armour bearers went before them, but in the main street, hard by the entrance of the quarter of the Firbolgs, stood Firænah, a sooth-sayer, very skilful in auguries and the notes of birds; and he came before Fardia, shedding tears, and cast himself upon the ground, and clasped his feet. Through nine generations his ancestors had served the ancestors of Fardia, but he was himself free, having been born in the tenth. But Fardia laughed, and raised him with his hand, for he cared not at all for auguries, and it was a grief to the Fir-bolgs when they heard him scoffing, for much travel and passing to and fro had made him unwise. But for Firænah they had erected a hut in a remote part of the camp, where there was a quiet hollow and a pond, and many wrens and ravens hopped around the hut or rested upon the roof, and there was a ceaseless clamour; but Firænah understood all their voices, ever listening with attentive ear, and the people honoured him greatly. Then with many tears he implored of Fardia not to go to that banquet, for an evil fate was impending upon him, for sinister and evil were the notes of all the birds; but Fardia laughed lightly, releasing himself, and so fared forward

with his comrades; but the old man returned to his hut
weeping, and the Fir-bolgs came around him, inquiring
eagerly. Then a dark rumour went through the camp,
and there arose a lamentation, as in a house of the dead
when the traveller sees the lights and hears the voice
of the mourners, so wept and lamented the blameless
Fir-bolgs over their champion, as though he were already
dead.

But Fardia and his companions were drawing near
the royal pavilion full of exultation and glory, and the
old king welcomed them according to the ancient custom, with a feeble clapping of his aged hands, a thin,
weak noise, not such as when, in the ancient days, he
had welcomed to Cruhane the many kings whom over
tuath and mōr-tuath he had appointed, having quelled
the lawless tribes of the Olnemacta, a bridegroom worthy
of the daughter of the High King. But she, Meave,
the daughter of Yeoha Faydleeah, rose with unfaded
majesty to receive the might of the Fir-bolgs, and along
with her the gentle princess. And Fardia marked where
his shield was hanged upon the wall, for the armour-
bearers were the first to enter the feasting-chambers;
and Aileel was upon his left hand, and Fionavar upon
the right.

There, then, they feasted under the light of waxen
tapers, tall as a warrior's spear, not permitted in the
houses of the nobles, and to the music of many an
angled harp.

Then, when the night was advanced, and Fionavar
and the princesses that were her company had withdrawn to the pavilion of the queen's people without the
camp, and when the red ale had made riot in men's
veins, Queen Meave unfolded to him the resolution of

Q

the saba of her kings, namely, that Fardia should be
selected to fight with Cuculain on the morrow, and that
if the hound of Ulla should fall by his hand, or be driven
from the ford, he should receive twenty ploughlands of
the level plains of Ai, paying nothing in cattle, gold, or
weapons, nor yet by military service, save voluntarily,
and also cattle and farm implements, and the youngest
daughter of the High Queen, the sweet-voiced princess,
in marriage, with an abundant dowry, which she very
minutely related ; and that if he refused, he should suffer
a proclamation of disgrace and outlawry, to be determined on at the council of the kings, and announced
before the whole people, with the opprobrious chanting
of satirists and druids, so that shame and disgrace
would cling to him and his nation to the end of time.
Then Fardia consented to meet Cuculain on the morrow, but not through fear of the druids and their hill-
top satires, nor from avarice ; but he concealed his mind
in his breast, and demanded security, for he feared lest
that upon which his mind was set might yet escape him.
For Fionavar he had marked, while she was yet a young
child, for she was accustomed to accompany Aileel and
Meave in the royal circuits which they made each year,
and, though warring in far lands, that gentle countenance was ever before his mind, star-like and pure.
Then the queen sent for six out of the nine kings of
territories which were kings under her, and a solemn
pledge was given before the airey-forawl of the province,
he who was president of the high court of the whole
nation of the Olnemacta, and in the presence of witnesses, according to the ancient law ; and besides all
this, Queen Meave invoked the sacred manes of Buan,

and Morann, and Coirpry Kinkæth, and the contract was ratified.

Then the High Queen took the royal brooch from her breast and gave it to Fardia, and Fardia gave his brooch to the queen. After that they devoted themselves again to merriment and festivity, and at midnight Fardia and his comrades returned to their quarters with much clamour, and dispersed among their booths.

Through the night there was silence in the wide host of Meave ; but at day-dawn Æd Shievra stood beside the couch of his lord with a cup of cold water from the spring, keen with frost, and Fardia drank it from the hand of his attendant, and sat up. But the inebriation had gone out of him, and he remembered all, and cried out, and tore his yellow hair, swaying to and fro, and Æd Shievra stood silent beside him. Then came the warriors of his tribe, and Fardia started forth from his couch, and arrayed himself in his battle-dress ; but he removed not the royal brooch from off his breast. Then harnessed Æd Shievra the war-steeds, and yoked the chariot, and Fardia came forth and sprang into the chariot, and Æd Shievra seized the scourge and urged forward the willing steeds.

But in like manner, from the rest of the camp, came forth the kings and warriors of the four provinces of Erin, and poured forth after the son of Daman to the ford, eastward. But on all the eminences and rising-ground rearward gathered the women and provision-bringers, even the innumerable camp-followers that followed the course of the men of war ; and the whole land, even to the verge of the plain where they darkened against the sky, was filled with the great multitude. But on the other side of the stream, lo, the silent woods

and the grey road, and beyond that the plains of Ulla,
all waste and silent, for there was no man there, neither
oxen, nor horses, nor any living thing that might be
seen, only empty fields and deserted homesteads.

CHAPTER XLIV.

THE AFFLICTION OF CUCULAIN.

> " And shapeless sights come wandering by,
> The ghastly people of the realm of dream
> Mocking me."
>
> SHELLEY.

Now, it was evening and chilly with frost, when Cuculain awoke out of the swoon, and his limbs were stiff, so
that he could not walk, and he lay down again and wept,
not for the pain, but for loneliness and sorrow.   But
after that, he essayed to move once more, and as he
arose, lo, an aged woman milking a very lean cow, and
she sat with her back to Cuculain, and a garment drawn
over her head, and Cuculain marvelled when he saw
her, for he deemed that all had fled out of that land.
Then he approached her, and begged that she would give
him of the milk to drink, for he was very faint.   But
she answered that she would not give him to drink
unless he blessed her.   Then Cuculain smiled in spite
of his faintness, and did what she desired.   Thereupon
she turned round and looked upon Cuculain, and Cuculain uttered a cry, for there was the face of a ghoul
within the hood, and he recognised the thing that had
plagued him at the ford.   But with a foul noise of victory and success the spectre vanished from his sight,

and the hero leaned trembling against one of the trees
in the forest.

Then he hurried through the forest fear-stricken, and
he came to his place, and the horses whinnied when
they heard him.

But, all that night, Cuculain's mind was clouded and
disturbed, and he said that his clan had conspired
against him, seeing that he was abandoned and alone,
warring now for many days against the whole host of
Meave, keeping ward over the gates of the province.
And now too, he knew that he should die, for the thought
of flight, and of the surrender of Murthemney to the
waster came not at all into his noble mind.   But he
called upon all the Red Branch by name, lamenting loud
Leairey the Victorious, and Kelkar the son of Uther,
Fergus Mac Leda, Factna Mac Mahoon, and his foster-
brethren, sons of the High King, and Konal Karna,
dearest of all, and his voice penetrated the starry night,
for he cried out as a woman cries when him she loves
has forsaken her; so in his agony Cuculain, the son
of Sualtam, lifted up his voice, and the men of Meave
heard him, for he said that he was forsaken, and all
men leagued against him.   Moreover, as the moon set,
he saw faces that moved amongst the trees mocking
him, and horrid things, formless and cold, estrays out
of the fold of hell, wandering blots of the everlasting
darkness, and there was laughter in the hollow chambers of the forest, and again the Ban-Shee of Lok Mac
Favash smiled at him and beckoned, and the cold
water-serpent clung around his feet, and all the sweet
chords of his mind were torn or unstrung, and the
Shee delivered him over to great affliction.   For,
like an army of devastators that waste and burn and

drive away, leaving behind them blackened homes and
streams made thick with blood, so wasted they all the
pleasant tracts of his noble spirit.   Now, the horses affrighted pulled madly at their tethers, but anon when he
sank down like a stone they approached him wondering,
and he felt their warm breath upon his face.   Then the
demons that affrighted him gave back, and he arose
and put an arm around the neck of either steed,
and stood between them trembling.   With their fleet
limbs, swifter than the naked winds of March, had he
borne away the daughter of Manach out of Bregia,
Munfada and Rayleen Gall were their names; they
were pale yellow in hue, save on the breast of one, where
the wind-pipe enters the lungs, a spot of purest white.
For two hundred cumals he had purchased them, and he
gave them to Emer.   But with her own hands each day
she fed them with barley and white curds and sweet
whey; very gentle were they, and they knew the thoughts
of those that loved them.

Then a milder mood came over the mind of Cuculain, and he remembered his friends who were with
Meave, and how they had received him coming, and he
recalled the firm friendship of Lewy Mac Neesh, and
especially he thought of Fardia, the son of Daman,
now warring among the Clanna Gædil in Espân, and, as
he thought on these things, lo, the dawn trembling
through the forest, and the hoar-frost glittering on the
grass.

Then started forth Cuculain, and he drew from the
chariot the venison which he had cooked, and ate
thereof, and drank his last draught of ale, making a
gurgle in his strong bare throat, and his strength revived in him.   Nevertheless his countenance was hollow

and wan, dull were his splendid eyes, and there was a wound in his hand and in his leg and in his left side, and his noble breast was mangled, and all his body black with dried gore.

Then he tore away the iron-work from his chariot, and filled the broken centre and upper rim of his shield, strapping it tightly with the leathern reins, and with the colg that was by his side he hewed down a young fir-tree, and shore away the crackling branches, and cut off the top. After this he brake off the steel peak of the chariot, and sunk it into the rough spear-tree, and bound it firmly to the wood. Then arose Cuculain, the unconquerable, striding through the forest, and he wondered which of the great champions of Meave should be brought against him that day; and when he came out into the open, he beheld the whole south country filled with a vast multitude, as it had been the Ænech of Taylteen or the great Feis of Tara when the authority of the Ard-Rio is supreme, and all the tribes of Erin gather together with their kings. But he saw not at first who was the champion that had come out against him, and he advanced through the willows, and came to the edge of the ford, and looked across, and he saw Fardia, son of Daman, of the Fir-bolgs, and Fardia looked upon Cuculain, and Cuculain looked upon Fardia.

CHAPTER XLV.

IN VAIN.

"Ἔρως ἀνίκατε."

SOPHOCLES.

THEN Cuculain blushed, and his neck and face above, and his temples waxed fiery red, and then again, paler than the white flower of the thorn, and his under jaw fell, and he stood like one stupefied; but Fardia held his shield unmoved, with his spears resting on the ground, and beneath the heavy cath-barr his brows stronger than brass.

But Cuculain sent forth a voice hoarse and untuned, and said:

"Is it Fardia Mic Daman of the Fir-bolgs, for there is a mist before my eyes?"

But Fardia answered not.

Then said Cuculain:

"Art thou come out to meet me in arms to-day seeking to slay me?"

And Fardia answered sternly:

"Go back, O Cuculain, to thy own people, and cease to bar the gates of the north against our host, and I shall not slay thee or dishonour thee, but if thou remainest, I shall slay thee here at the ford. Therefore, I bid thee go back into the province."

But Cuculain answered him, and his voice became like the voice of a young girl, or the accents of one seeking an alms.

"And is it thou alone of all this great host that has come out against thy friend, seeking to slay me or dishonour me. There are the battle-standards of all the warrior-tribes of Erin, save only the Ultonians, the banners of the children of Ith and Heber, all the far-spreading clans of Herēmon, the children of Amargin and Brega of Donn and Biela, and the Desie of Temair; there are the warlike clans of the Fomoroh, and the remnant of the people of Partholân, the Clanna Nemedh from the great harbour southwards, the children of Orba, the Ernai, and the Osree, the Gamaradians, and the Clan Dega. Could no champion be sought out of this great host that covers the green plains of Conaul Murthemney to the limits of the furthest hills to come out against me, but that thou alone shouldest stand forth against thy friend. Persist not, O son of Daman, but retire, and I will meet three champions instead of one from this day forward. We parted with mutual gifts and with tears, why does thy spear now thirst after my blood, and why dost thou seek to dishonour me?"

And Fardia made answer:

"Other champions, by their prowess, bear away many gifts, why should I ever have my hands empty? Bright as the sun is the brooch of Meave, which she has given me, the Royal Brooch of Cruhane, emblem of sovereignty among the Gæil. Gems glitter along the rim. Like a level sunbeam in the forest is the shining delg of it. I shall have honour while I live, and my clan after me shall be glorious to the end of time. Therefore, prepare for battle, O son of Sualtam; I remember thee not at all, or as one whom years since I met, and straight again forgot. Therefore, prepare thyself for battle, or I shall slay thee off thy guard."

And Cuculain said :

" O Fardia, I believe thee not. Full well dost thou remember. Beneath the same rug we slept, and sat together at the feast, and side by side we went into the red battle. Together we consumed cities, and drave away captives. Together we practised feats of arms before the warrior-queen, grieving when either got any hurt. Together we kept back the streaming foe in the day of disaster, when the battle-torrent roared over us, either guarding the other more than himself."

Then beneath his lowering brows the hot tears burst forth from the eyes of the son of Daman, and fell continuously from his beard, and he answered with a voice most stern, but that held within it a piteous tone like a vessel in which the careless eye sees not the hidden flaw, but at a touch, lo, it is broken. So sounded the stern voice of the warrior.

" Go back now, O Cuculain, to thy pleasant Dûn— Dûn Dalgan upon the sea. Go back now, for I would not slay thee, and rule over Murthemney and the rough headland of thy sires, and Meave will not waste thy territory or injure aught that is thine. And care no more for the Red Branch, for they have forsaken thee, and given thee over to destruction, who have conspired against thee, trusting in thy great heart that thou wouldst be slain on the marches of the province, holding the gates of the north against their foes, for Hound is thy name and Royal Hound thy nature. Therefore go back, O Cuculain, and save thy young life ; return now to thy infant son and thy sweet bride. Go back, O Cuculain, for sweet is life, the life of the warrior, and very dark and sorrowful and empty is the grave."

" I will not go back, O Fardia Mic Daman, but here

on the marches, while there is blood in my veins, and while reason like a king rebelled against but unsubdued, holds the sovereignty of my mind, shall I contest the borders of my nation, though forsaken and alone. My people have indeed abandoned me and conspired for my destruction; but there is no power in Erin to dissolve my knightship to the son of Nessa and my kinship with the Crave Rue. Though they hate me, yet cannot I eject this love out of my heart. And not the kings alone and the might of the Crave Rue, but the women and the young children of Ulla are under my protection, and all the unwarlike tribes, and this the sacred soil of Ulla upon which I stand. And this too well I know that no power in the earth or in the air can keep the Red Branch my foe for ever, and that loud and deep will be their sorrow when the red pyre flames beneath me. And seek not to terrify me with death, O son of Daman, for of yore too our minds did not agree, for dark and sorrowful death is not but a passage to the land of the ever young, the Tiernanōg. There shall I see the Tuatha face to face, and there the heroic sons of Milith and himself, a mighty shade, and there all the noblest of the earth. There hatred and scorn are not known, nor the rupturing of friendships, but sweet love rules over all."

"Go back, O Cuculain, go back now again, for I would not slay thee. Think no more of the son of Nessa and the Red Branch, than whom the race of Milith hath produced naught fiercer or more baleful. Rooted out and cast down shall be the Red Branch in this foray, whether thou, O Cuculain, survivest or art slain. Go back, O son of Sualtam, return to thy own Dûn. Once indeed thou wast obedient to me and served me, and polished my armour, and tied up my spears

submissive to my commands.   Therefore go back; add
not thy blood to the bloody stream."

"Revilest thou my nation, O son of Daman.   Talk
no more now, but prepare thyself for battle and for
death.   I will not obey thee or retire before thee, nor
shalt thou at all dishonour me as thou hast most foully
dishonoured thyself.   This indeed I well know, that I
shall be slain at the ford when my strengh has passed
away, or my mind is overthrown; but by thee, O son of
Daman, I shall not meet my death.   Once indeed I was
subservient to thee, because I was younger than thee.
Therefore was I then as a servant unto thee, but not
now; and which of us twain shall die I know, and it is
thou, O Fardia, son of Daman."

Therewith then they fought, and Cuculain had no
weapon save only his colg, for the Gæ Bulg, the rude
spear which he had fashioned, he dropped upon the
shore, and Fardia discharged his javelins at the same
time, for he was ambidexter, and quick as lightning,
Cuculain avoided them, and they stuck trembling in the
thither bank, and quick to right and left Cuculain severed
the leathern thongs rushing forward.   Then drew Fardia
his mighty sword that made a flaming crescent as it
flashed most bright and terrible, and rushed headlong
upon Cuculain, and they met in the midst of the ford.
But straightway there arose a spray and a mist from the
trampling of the heroes, and through the mist their
forms moved hugely, like two giants of the Fomoroh
contending in a storm.   But the war-demons too contended around them fighting, the Bocanahs and Bananahs, the wild people of the glens and the demons of
the air, and the fiercer and more blood-thirsty of the
Tuatha De Daman, and screeched in the clamour of the

warriors, the clash of the shields and the clatter of land
and meeting colg. But the warriors of Meave turned
pale, and the war-steeds brake loose, and flew through
the plain with the war-cars, and the women and camp-
followers brake forth and fled, and the upper water of
the divine stream gathered together for fear, and reared
itself aloft like a steed that has seen a spectre, with jags
of torn water and tossing foam. But Cuculain was red
all over, like a garment raised out of the dying-vat, and
Fardia's great sword made havoc in his unarmoured
flesh. Three times Cuculain closed with the Fir-bolg,
seeking to get within the ponderous shield, and three
times the son of Daman cast him off, as the cliffs of
Eyrus cast off a foaming billow of the great sea; but
when the fourth time he was rushing on like a storm, he
heard as it were the voice of Læg, the son of Riangowra,
taunting and insulting him, and himself he saw, standing in the river ford on the left, for he was accustomed
to revile Cuculain. Yet this time too the Fir-bolg
cast him off, and advanced upon Cuculain to slay him.
Then stepped back Cuculain quickly, and the men of
Meave shouted, for Cuculain's shield was falling to
pieces. But again rushed forward the hound of Ulla,
stooping, with the Gæ Bulg in his hand, using it like a
spearman in the battle, and he drave Fardia through the
ford and upon the hither bank, pressing against the
shield, but Fardia himself too retreated back. But when
the Fir-bolgs saw what was done they feared mightily for
their champion, and they raised a sudden howl of lamentation and rage, and rushed forward, breaking through the
guards. Which when Fergus Mac Roy beheld, he sprang
down from his chariot, shouting dreadfully, and put his
hand into the hollow of his shield, and took out his

battle-stone, and smote Imchall, the son of Dega, with the battle-stone upon the head, and he fell rushing forward amongst the first. But Cormac Conlíngas and Mainey Lamgarf ran thither with the queen's spearmen restraining the Fir-bolgs.

But, meantime, Cuculain lifted suddenly the Gæ Bulg above his head, and plunged it into Fardia; but it passed through the upper rim of the brazen shield, and through the strong bones of his breast beneath his beard, and he fell backward with a crash, and grasped with outstretched hands at the ground, and his spirit went out of him, and he died.

But Cuculain plucked out the spear, and stood above him, panting, as a hound pants returning from the chase, and the war-demons passed out of him, and he looked upon Fardia, and a great sorrow overwhelmed him, and he lamented and moaned over Fardia, joining his voice to the howl of the people of Fardia, the great-hearted children of Mac Erc, and he took off the cath-barr from the head of Fardia, and unwound his yellow hair, tress after bright tress, most beautiful, shedding many tears, and he opened the battle-dress and took out the queen's brooch—that for which his friend had come to slay him —and he cursed the lifeless metal, and cast it from him into the air, southwards over the host, and men saw it no more.

CHAPTER XLVI.

A SWIFT SUCCOUR.

" On the brink of the night and the morning
My coursers are wont to respire ;
But the earth has just whispered a warning,
That their flight must be swifter than fire."

SHELLEY.

Now Læg drave forth out of Emain Macha Cuculain's chariot and war-steeds, and the noble steeds themselves flew along, nor needed the scourge of the charioteer, which, nevertheless, the son of Riangowra laid furiously upon their foaming sides, leaning forward in the war-car, animating them with his cries.   And so drave Læg, as though upon the smooth plains of Taylteen he contended with the youths of Erin about a prize in the chariot-race.   But not now for brazen cauldrons contended Læg, or for bright weapons, or for gold, but for the life of his master and dear friend, the blameless Cuculain.

Over every territory through which he flew, far and wide penetrated the brazen din, for around him there arose a warlike noise of shaken shields and rattling spears, and javelins, swords, and battle-hammers, and defensive armour, even the whole martial equipment of Cuculain, and the wheels brayed upon the block-paved roads, and the clamour of the war-sprites increased, endlessly shouting around the son of Riangowra ; but Læg thought only of his master, and of that most precious life somewhere in jeopardy, and the cry of Cuculain ever sounded in his ear.

Thus all that day the chariot brayed along the stony way, or raced across the smooth plain. For where the land was tilled and enclosed, and the homesteads of men abounded, and their labours, there indeed were roads; but oftentimes he traversed wide plains where was no chariot-track or sign-post, save the distant hills, nor fences, nor tillers of the soil, only great herds of cattle feeding, and slaves on horseback that guarded them, and drave them this way or that. These indeed, with their dumb care, looked up astonished when they heard the distant din, for like the ringing of many swathes of iron rods, car-borne on lonely ways in the still night, was the ringing of Cuculain's warlike equipment about Læg as he sped over the smooth plains.

Across the Oun Calànn he rushed, while the foaming spray flew high above the trampling steeds, and along the reedy shores of Muckno, where, in the oak-groves, herds of many swine, under their keepers, battened on the root of the wild parsnip; but as the sun went down he came to the fertile tuath of which Brasal Glunduff was king, and he was uncle by marriage of the great Kelkar, the son of Uther, in the north.

Now as he crossed the frontier, he saw chariots and horses, and many spearmen advancing quickly in the direction of Emain Macha, but he recognised amongst them Brasal Duff Mac Fiontann; but his cousin Mac Lucta followed with the spearmen, who was the airey-ecta of the tuath. He, Brassal, was the second of the Red Branch who awaked out of the stupor, and he had summoned straightway his council, and levied the rising-out of the tuath, seven hundred men in all, and he hastened to the hosting of the High King at Emain Macha.

Then Læg rejoiced exceedingly, and reined in his steeds, calling eagerly to the son of Fiontann to turn southwards to the rescue of Cuculain. Yet he would not, but held on straight to Emain Macha, and Læg, indignant, reproached him with fierce words, giving rein once more to the steeds. Yet, not long after that he had passed the rear-guard of the spear-men, he saw that Shanglan laboured as he went; and no longer, indeed, would anyone call him raven-black, for he was covered with white foam, and Læg himself and the chariot were bespattered all over with the innumerable flakes that flew from his eager lips like snow. But the Lia Macha led on untired, and no one observing would say that she touched the ground, with such swift ease did she move.

Then Læg sprang down out of the chariot, holding the scourge between his teeth, and eased the yoke-strap around his neck, and the chin-strap of the head-stall, and sprang in again, bounding lightly over the rim, and gave them rein once more.

But now, again the son of Riangowra groaned aloud, and wrung his unavailing hands, for no longer did Shanglan travel unhurt, but stooped at every swift step, for the fierce pace had injured his tender hooves, unshod, for war-steeds were the steeds of Cuculain, and in wide, smooth plains was their place. But again Læg groaned, for the chariot, too, was impaired, not designed by the builder for such an usage. Moreover, against many a rock and stone had Læg dashed the wheels that day in his wild career. Then restrained he the steeds, and it was evening and the gloaming of

R

the day. But as Læg looked round he rejoiced, for not many roods in front there stood, as he deemed, the house of a noble. As he drew nigh, he recognized the person of the master, Ayha Cœlshanig, an exile out of the country of the Albanah; but his father was a Croothnean. His life, at one time, had been saved out of compassion by Cuculain, and with him Læg designed to rest his wounded steed, and to repair the shaken war-car.

For, while Cuculain was yet a boy at Dûn Dalgan, an oared galley, which was accustomed to ply weekly across the Muirnict to Mæna Coning of the Britons, returned, towing behind at the stern a miserable wight, whom the crew had found in mid-channel, strapped down with strong ropes upon fir-trees joined together raft-wise, and they saw in him a wretch for whose offence the laws of the Gæil did not suffer an eric to be accepted; but he was cast forth to the mercy of the waves, as an evil and pernicious thing. Nevertheless, when Cuculain saw him, he had pity on him, because for three days he had tossed to and fro upon the currents of the Moyle and the Muirnict, and with his own hands he chafed his wasted limbs, and gave him restoring draughts, upon the rude pier where the ships were wont to discharge their lading.

Now, according to the Fenechas, he to whose land such sorry waifs might be borne in ships or by the sea, was permitted to receive them into slavery; but Dectera did not think good to receive amongst her people a wretch cast forth out of his own country for some great crime, and she ordered her servants to return him again to the waves of the Muirnict.

But Cuculain was enraged, and that night he with-

drew him from the place where he was, while Læg prepared a chariot and horses, and they travelled swiftly,
and bore him outside the tuath; but he was yet speechless, and the ropes had torn and discoloured his flesh.

Now, in the morning, they reached the tuath over
which Fiontann was king, and Æd, who was his son's
son, was a friend and school-fellow of Cuculain. But
Æd was then at Emain Macha, wherefore Cuculain conferred with his sister, Brigamba, who was very prudent
and discreet, and a judge and counsellor amongst the
women of all that region, though so young; and Cuculain committed to her care the miserable Croothnean.
But, after this, they returned to Dûn-Dalgan, and incurred the wrath of the daughter of Nessa; but Læg,
himself, the son of Riangowra, she caused to be beaten.

CHAPTER XLVII.

A PIONEER.

> "I can make what merchandize I will,
> I stand here for law."
>
> SHAKESPEARE.

THIS, then, was he to whose house Læg approached,
leading his wounded steed and shattered war-car; and
Læg marvelled when he saw the house, for it was well
built and compact, though not spacious, and other
houses were around it for cattle and sheep, and a strong
bawn of earth and stone enclosed the whole. Moreover,
he heard the sound of the quern, and the noise of ham-
mers, and he saw where upon the hedges they had
spread garments recently dyed, and he saw into the

dye-house itself on the left side of the road, but the main-house stood on the other. Also, there were trim fences and young fruit-trees in enclosed plots, and all around the plain was strewn with fudir-houses, and of bodács, but beyond was only untilled ground and forest.

But Læg saw the master where he stood upon a fence by the roadside, beyond the house, and overlooked those who laboured beneath him in the field, lifting up his voice when any slackened in his labour ; and Læg marvelled at this, seeing that it was already night.

Then Læg approached, and saluted him courteously, telling how he journeyed to the relief of Cuculain, the son of Sualtam, on the southern marches, and how he desired rest and food for his steeds and for himself, and the assistance of his metal-workers to repair the chariot ; but he recalled not the matter of the Muirnict.

But the Croothnean eyed Læg narrowly, and moved towards the house meditating. Then said he :

" Why comest thou to me, O youth ? I am not the bru-fir of the tuath, nor supplied with territory and tributes, with servants and house-room for the entertainment of travellers. This duty belongs to him, and not many miles to the south and east is his house where thou mayest freely demand entertainment, and the assistance of workers in metal. It was not by the lavish entertainment of those who passed by this way that I have become rich and great as thou now see'st me, but by prudence and attention to my several affairs. If I supply thee and thine with entertainment and the labour of my slaves, look to it, I shall require a suitable reward !"

Then was the generous heart of Læg greatly enraged, and he answered :

" A suitable reward thou shalt most assuredly receive,

but bid now straightway a keeve of water to be prepared,
that I may wash my steeds and my chariot, and see,
too, that there is provender in the stable. Also provide
a place for myself to rest in, and food, and, look you,
tarry not."

" Not yet, O son of Riangowra," answered the other,
" but first thou shalt leave with me a pledge out of the
abundant armour and weapons which thou hast with
thee in the chariot."

" The armour and the weapons are the warlike equipment of Cuculain, who is now in great jeopardy, and I
hasten to his assistance. I cannot give thee a pledge,
but this I surely promise, that an abundant reward
shall be given to thee for thy entertainment, if upon
this so keeenly hast thou set thy thoughts. Therefore,
tarry not any longer, but give instant orders to thy
people, for my horses chill in the frosty air."

" Not by trusting in promises, O youth, have I became
what thou now seest me, but by compelling the performance of bonds contracted rightfully, according to the
laws of the Fenechas. For when I reached this tuath,
having been deported out of thine as though I had been
smitten with the plague, I was first indeed the slave of
Brigamba, wise and subtle, well skilled in the Bretha of
Erin, both Cain law and Urdas, and those administered
by the bru-fir in his forus, and I ushered before her
those who sought counsel, and listened to her conversation, and became myself well skilled in these things.
But having served for many months with much humility
and carefulness, I at last prevailed upon her to give me
a portion of the forest land upon the borders of her
estate, and she is the first woman in all Erin who has
held land in her own right; for her two brothers died,

one shortly after his birth, and the other, a very insolent youth, the friend of Cuculain, was slain in a sudden quarrel; but the old man, at his death, gave all to Brigamba, contrary to the law. Now the male kindred of Farniave claimed the land against the disposition of the old man's, and Brigamba herself, being very wise, and of persuasive speech, pleaded on behalf of the women of Erin before Shancha, the Ard-Brehon of the court of the High King at Emain Macha, and she prevailed so far as to retain a third of the lands of her father, but two-thirds went to the male kindred, and this is now the law amongst the Gæil. Thus became Brigamba a lady of the soil, even a fair territory, extending from the forus of the bru-fir to the shores of the Oun-Glieda, southwards, and on the forest land of this she gave me taurcrah, land, and cows, and domestic utensils. Here, then, I built me a small sheeling, and fed two cows, paying yearly the stipulated tribute, sending curds and butter for the maintenance of the household. Moreover, I performed other tasks for the people that surrounded me, hewing timber, and preparing fuel, and feeding their cattle and their swine, and I gave loans for hire, and prospered.

" Now all this time I was the slave and fudir of Brigamba, nor was I suffered to appear before the brehon of the tuath with my own complaints, but was represented by the lady of the soil, according to the law, and many times justice failed me, for she desired her Maor not to prefer my complaints before the brehon; moreover, of all that I recovered a share went to the flaut, and I was baulked in my rights, and I had no part or lot in the public land of the tuath.

" Thereupon, with the consent of Brigamba, I took me

three other fudirs like myself, and we entered into a
contract, joining our lands and rights, so that, being
thus joined together, we became entitled to the privileges of a boairey, to elect the king, to enjoy participa-
tion in the public land, and to have full rights before
the brehon and the bru-fir, and I was chief of this
guild.

" But after not many years I purchased the rights of
my fellow-guildsmen, and became a boairey and free-
holder of the tuath in my own right, and prospered year
by year, rising from grade to grade, and Brigamba conferred upon me much land, for my tributes I regularly
paid; also it is within my power to become a lord in
the tuath were I so minded; but I care not for ostentation, nor do I delight in the companionship of the
haughty flauts of this tuath, but I attend to my affairs,
and give the honour which is their due to the blessed
Shee. And now thou seest me as I am, having
slaves, and artificers, and many bodács and fudirs
under me, whose houses and cultivated plots thou
mayest see scattered over the plain. But since I
entered into this tuath I have trusted in no promises
which the bretha of Erin do not hold to be good,
though made regularly before free men, according to
the law, nor will I trust in thy promise, O Læg, son of
Riangowra, for I know that though thou sittest at meat
amongst the kings, at the table of Concobar Mac Nessa,
yet art thou a slave according to the laws of Ulla, and
thy promise is useless, and may not be performed; and
in like manner have I spoken ere this to those who are
greater than thee. Therefore shalt thou give me a
pledge out of thy possessions, or thou shalt go on to the
house of the bru-fir, leading gently thy wounded steed,

for very furious and reckless I doubt not has been thy driving. Therefore hie thee on to the bru-fir."

"I am no slave, thou base churl, but a king's son, and the friend and attendant of the mightiest and noblest of the Gæil. Methinks broad Ulla doth not contain within her borders one viler than thyself. Verily now for the last time wilt thou practice avarice in this tuath, which thou hast dishonoured with thy exceeding vileness; for the noble Kelkar, the son of Uther, loving well the son of Sualtam, and myself also, and in whose stables was foaled and reared the generous steed Shanglan till what time he was sent a present to the High King, and whose tender hooves endure now no longer the stony ways, will straightway drive thee out of thy possessions; for, by marriage with the good and wise Brigamba, he is lord of this territory, and very soon, with stripes upon thy avaricious shoulders, wilt thou carry thy vileness and thy cunning to another place."

Then Ayha, the Croothnean, laughed lightly at the impetuous charioteer, and said:

"Methinks, O youth, that thou wast reared amongst the Fir-bolgs or the Fomoroh, and not amongst the people of Ulla, for whom the ollavs have long since broken the violence of the lords, and their cruel exactions and oppressions. Kelkar, the son of Uther, is indeed lord of the soil, and a flaut in this tuath, but he is not lord of mine, nor do I owe submission and servility to any, save only to Brasal Mac Fiontann, who is the king. I care not for Kelkar, the son of Uther, nor do I tremble before his wrath, though well I know that he loves me not, nor doth the wise Brigamba, though she has extended to me her protection and support. I am a boairey and freeman of this tuath, and no man shall hurt me or disturb me whose power does not extend to the destruction of the ancient laws and customs of the Gæil. I am no fudir or base tenant of the son of Uther. My tributes and services are prescribed by the Fenechas, and may not be increased. For every ballybo of the land that I possess there proceeds yearly to the lord the value of a cow, with a three-year-old ox and three in-calf heifers, with their feeding for a year, and not only may he not require more, but I myself am punishable by the law if I slavishly, or for any other reason, consent. My land is mine, and no lord shall hurt or remove me ; verily, ere this, have I seen the grasping lords of Ulla dispossessed of their lands on account of their oppressions, at Daul and Feis, when the kings meet in council with their brehons and wise ollavs. Therefore, I care not for the mighty king of Dûn Sovarchey, for over me he has no power, nor for his armed men, though he command in war thrice seven hundred warriors, the battalion of th'e Mōr-Tuath. Nor speak to me concerning Cuculain, who hath entangled himself with the foe. My levy of armed men, fifteen in all, I have despatched to the hosting at Emain Macha, fully equipped, and with food for twenty days. I will not receive into my house wandering warriors, save that I receive a reward, and increase and not diminish my substance. Therefore, O youth, hie thee on to the bru-fir, for with me thou shalt not abide unless I receive from thy hands a goodly pledge."

Then answered Læg in great wrath :

"An evil time, indeed, will it be for the Gæil if the ollavs and their wisdom concur to plant among us such shrubs of deadly poison as thyself, O vile and avaricious stranger, without gratitude or nobleness or love for

aught save thy miserable accumulation of sorry pelf.
But this time assuredly thou shalt not be base with exultation, for out of thy possessions thou shalt afford food
and shelter to the steeds of the noble Cuculain, and to
myself also, and receive a severe chastisement at my
hands."

Therewith, then, the son of Riangowra chastised him
fiercely with a knotted scourge, and he fled howling from
the highway, and passed through the bawn and the
courtyard, and out into the field in which his slaves
toiled, while Læg pursued with many a stripe upon his
bare limbs as he flew, but he cried to his people for assistance, and they came together, but they feared to approach the fierce charioteer of Cuculain, and, moreover,
they loved not the Croothnean. Then at length Læg
seized him, and bore him weeping and protesting to the
house. Now in the courtyard was a pile of ferns and
rushes, which bullocks had drawn thither with ropes,
and Læg took therefrom a strong rope, and led the
miserable Croothnean within his own house, and made
him fast to the roof-tree, nor treated him with much
gentleness. Then he hastened out and gave orders to
the slaves, and they obeyed him swiftly, for very wrathful was the son of Riangowra, and a bright colg of glittering bronze hung by his side.

After this, then, Læg led the steeds of Cuculain within
the bawn, and released them from the chariot, and
washed them carefully, but the slaves poured abundant
barley into the mangers, and Læg led in the noble
steeds. Now, meantime the artificers in metal came
about the chariot under the light of torches made of
splintered bog-wood, and a loud din arose from the labours of the skilful craftsmen. But when this was

finished, and the chariot was washed and dried and polished, they drew it within the chariot-house with all its warlike furniture, and Læg shut to the strong oaken doors and locked them, and returned to the house.

There, before a huge fire, the son of Riangowra feasted on the good things of the place, eating roast flesh, with boiled roots, and butter and the white curd of milk, and drinking much ale. But the miserable Croothnean looked on in silence, for he feared lest the fierce charioteer might slay him, being so impetuous. Nay-the-less he computed in his mind the corp diara, and the eraic, and the enechlán, for he was ever a slave to avaricious thoughts. All the heavy fine he computed very accurately, though there were pains in his bones, and dire agony, and his limbs were bloodied and torn where the fierce charioteer had cut him with the knotted scourge. But he grieved much that he was not a flaut of the tuath, for then would the enechlán be much more abundant, for the insult offered to a noble might not be wiped out without an honour-price far heavier than was customary in the case of a plain freeman of the tuath, though his wealth might be great. And this was the reason why he had not attained the rank of a noble, for no possessor of soil, how wealthy soe'er he might be, was entitled to be proclaimed a flaut of the tuath unless that he had amongst those that held land under him, ten tenants at least, boaireys, free citizens of the tuath, paying the tributes enjoined by the Fenechas, viz., for each portion of land capable of feeding twenty-one cows, the tributes which the Croothnean correctly enumerated as proceeding out of each ballybo of his land to the King of Dún Sovarchey. Therefore, Cœlshanig established around him only fudirs and bodács, whose tributes were voluntary and not under the protection of the law, by which means he became wealthy indeed, but continued ignoble, not having a generous mind, which thing, namely, that he had not taken out his flautship in the tuath, now grieved him in his computations. Moreover, in his churlishness he was not wise, for he knew not the usages of war, and the suspension of the strict law in the imminence of danger, and the necessities of brave warriors, by whose prowess alone might all law be sustained, therefore, even in his avaricious mind he was not wise.

Now Læg regarded him not at all, but lay down, stretching his mighty limbs on a couch beside the fire, for it was cold, and his great heart was somewhat appeased, only he was troubled and fretful concerning his dear master. But for this reason he could not sleep, and he tossed restlessly from side to side, and sometimes he sat up and then again lay down, being troubled in his affectionate heart, for besides thinking upon his master his mind also was irritated from the conversation of Cœlshanig, and from contact with that grinding and avaricious soul, which exhibited neither courtesy to himself nor reverence for Cuculain, of whom he ever was accustomed only to hear praise. Therefore he could not sleep, but turned restlessly from side to side. But as that noble Ithacan, unrecognised in his own house, aware of all the meaness and injury, and listening to the voices of the greedy suitors where they conversed lewdly with the women of his household, rolled sleeplessly upon his bed, devoured by his thoughts, so tossed to and fro the good Læg in the house of Cœlshanig. But in the end, after a long time, he rose and went out and aroused the slaves, and inquired concerning the bard, who in those days was always attached to a wealthy house.

Now Cœlshanig delighted not at all in the society of bards and harpers, and he was accustomed to revile that sacred order, saying that he would rather see a weed in his fields than a poet in his house. Therefore was there a bitter enemity between the Croothnean and the singing tribe, and they delighted to repeat satiric ranns concerning Cœlshanig, and to afford amusement to those who were not pleased at his great prosperity. Nevertheless he had in his service a druid who interpreted for him dreams and omens and the notes of wrens and ravens, and who taught him the observances which were due to the Shee that they might be favourable to him in hisaffairs, and this druid brought to his hearth annually the sacred fire which was kindled upon the hill of Fohla at Wisna of the great congregations, and he himself sent regularly thither the dues of the college of druids of Wisna, to wit, a fat swine and a sack of corn or their equivalents, according to the customs of the times, and he obeyed implicitly the advice of the druid, and to him alone he was generous, and he stood greatly in awe of his reproof, and he would gape around him in his druidic observances, though to his dependents and others he was accustomed to be overbearing and contemptuous.

Then Læg bade the slaves to summon to him that bard who dwelt nearest, bidding them tell the bard who it was that desired his society, even Læg, the son of Riangowra, the esquire and charioteer of Cuculain, and the slaves set forth joyfully upon that quest. But in the meantime Læg busied himself about the steeds, for their welfare was ever the nighest to his mind, and after that he returned to the house. But ere long the slaves returned, bringing with them Anabeen, a skilful harper, whose liss was by the roadside further to the south, and he was a descendent of Cir, who followed Heremōn out of Espân, and delighted the children of Milith and Brogan in the palace of Heremōn at Ariget-Ros, upon the Nore. But he came, having his harp strapped upon his shoulder, and he came to the liss, and from its place in the wall he took the door-staff and smote upon the door ; but the warrior opened it and stood huge in the narrow entrance, and received the sacred bard joyfully. Then he drew forth more ale in a great vessel, ashen, with a border of white findruiney, and distributed to the bard and himself.

But meantime the harper tuned his harp, and Læg sat down gazing into the red embers, holding his auburn head between his great hands ; but outside in the bawn the slaves pressed close against the wattled walls, listening to the heart-subduing lays. Then commenced the bard to chant tales of ancient heroes, of elopements and courtships, of battles and nocturnal assaults, and of conflagrations of noble Dûns, from time to time touching the harp as he chanted with a musical voice, well-modulated, for he was carefully trained, and he had studied his art for many years in the south, where they excelled in recitation and the management of the voice, and his own soul too was sweet and noble, so that he felt the power of the things concerning which he sang. But Læg nodded with his head, keeping time to the measure of the chant, for not until long ages after this were the tales of the great heroes of Eiré expressed in words, tuneless and unrhythmic, when the disciples of the Talkend brake down and dishonoured the singing men, for that they drew away the minds of the Gæil to that old heroic life, and caused them to reverence the Fianna

and the Shee. Therefore was there bitter war between
the disciples of the Talkend and the bards, and those
being the conquerors, the bardic art was dishonoured
and the singing men were brought low, and it is recorded of the great Talkend of Iona how he insulted
the bards, while the verses of the poets of the Ossianic
cycle are replete with bitterness against the followers of
Patrick.

Such things took place in after times, but now the
ollavs and shanachies of Erin were supreme, in so much
that the Ard-ollav of the tuath was of equal rank with
the king, which is attested by the equivalence of their
enechlán before the laws, and of each generation of men
those whose minds were inflamed with high thoughts, be-
took themselves to the profession of poetry ; and, besides
the bardic dignitaries of each tuath, those who preserved
and transmitted with such additions as their own age
enjoined, the laws, the history, and the ancient wisdom
of the Gæil; and, besides, the chanters of noble tales
held in honour at kings' courts, were many of lesser
note who dwelt throughout the isle, or travelled alone
or in companies from place to place, held in great
honour amongst the people. But of these was Anabeen
the descendant of Cir, who now chanted for the son of
Riangowra, and listening to whom the troubled mind of
the charioteer was appeased. But, amongst other tales,
he chanted certain also concerning Cuculain ; for he
sung of the courtship of Cuculain, and of the first meeting of Emer and the son of Sualtam, and how Emer sat
upon the bright lawn of her father's Dûn, surrounded
by young maidens, to whom she communicated the skill
in embroidery and other beautiful arts, which she herself had acquired at Temair, at the court of Conairey

Mōr the Beautiful, having been brought up with the daughters of the High Queen of all Erin there. So sang the bard; and he chanted also another tale concerning Cuculain. For, when the children of Usna were slain by Concobar, and along with them, Illan the Fair, the son of Fergus Mac Roy, Cuculain was at Dûn Dalgan with Læg. But a great wrath like a madness descended upon him when he heard of the slaughter of Illan and the others, for they had been dear comrades and school-fellows; and this wrath bore him onward like a dead leaf on a rushing torrent. Therefore, he levied the rising-out of his tuath, not delaying to send the arrow by the hand of the slow hireling, but hastening himself from place to place, and his people took into their breasts the generous wrath of the boy, and with one accord they came together. But with them he hastened straightway upon Emain Macha, vowing that he would burn Emain to the ground, and destroy all those who were concerned in the slaughter of Illan the Fair, and the sons of Usna; and his own wrath filled the minds of all around him. But a swift word went before him, and reached Emain first, and a sudden council was held in the night, and there was great dismay; for a panic pervaded the city, and many of the citizens fled thence into the fields, and there were mutinous faces in the permanent battalion of Emain Macha, and many warriors declared that they would not fight against Cuculain, nor lay a hand in anger upon the boy, and there was a great dissension and panic. For the friends of Fergus Mac Roy were already standing apart from Concobar Mac Nessa, and to rebel they only awaited a word from Fergus out of the north, which they expected each hour; and Dûvac Dæl Ulla, a mighty champion

of the Ultonians, went through the guards inflaming
them against the king, and Cormac Conlingas had refused to come into his father's presence. Therefore
was the council in alarm, and confused, for they knew
how it stood in the city, and that the entrance of Cuculain bearing war against his uncle, would be a signal
for revolt to the angry and mutinous warriors. But
when they found no escape, proposing many plans, and
then again rejecting them, Cathvah the seer rose, and
harangued them, proposing a subtle counsel, for he
knew the mind of Cuculain. But Concobar adopted the
counsel, and three noble women in the court of the
High Queen of Ulla, who was Einey, the daughter of
Cairbry Nia-far, King of Tara, consented to obey Cathvah, and work deliverance for the city. Then Læg
and Cuculain approached Emain, coming swiftly from
the south-west, and Cuculain himself guided the steeds,
and all that day no word had passed his lips, and his
brows were drawn down over his eyes, and Læg sat terrified beside him; but far behind clattered the cars of
his warriors.

But as they swept through the Glens of Faha, and
were now hard by the entering into the city, Cuculain,
leaning forward, saw in the midst of the road where was
a bridge that crossed a tributary of the Oun Calànn,
three women standing together naked upon the bridge
over which the chariot should pass, and their faces were
turned to the warriors. Then the reins dropped from
the hands of the boy, and red shame suffused his neck
and face; but as he was embarrassed and confused with
drooped head, Concobar Mac Nessa himself hastened
forward, and took Cuculain by the hand and led him
into the city to the Dûn; and after that Cuculain shed

s

many tears. So sang the bard; but there were certain
satiric ranns in the poem made concerning Læg himself, and these the wily bard omitted, resuming the thread
of the poem. But by his words concerning Cuculain,
he relaxed the mind of the charioteer, and the generous
charioteer himself wept and shed tears, the while drinking deep draughts of the red ale, while the miserable
Croothnean observed all silently from his place.

But while the bard still sang, the morning dawned,
stealing in through the narrow windows, and Læg took
from his arm a heavy bracelet of gold, many ounces in
weight, and he gave it to the bard.

CHAPTER XLVIII.

AH CU !

> " A love in desolation masked a Power
> Girt round with weakness."
>
> SHELLEY.

THEN Læg went forth quickly and harnessed his horses,
and yoked his chariot, and fared southwards. He passed
the house of the bru-fir and entered on a wide plain,
which was the public land of that tuath. Now, the
house of the bru-fir was on the edge of the plain, and
many houses surrounded it, and the authority of the
bru-fir was over these. His Forus, too, was opened,
and he sat and adjudicated, though the sun had but just
risen, for all matters relating to the public land were
brought before him, and all questions relating to tres-

pass, and the maintenance of fences, and roads, and small differences arising between man and man. Moreover, in his Forus was the king of the tuath inaugurated, and the tanist, and here was held the tocómrah of all the free citizens of the tuath to elect the officers of that small realm, and to adopt the laws decided on by the king and the saba of his lords and ollavs.

But the arbitrament of the wise bru-fir was not now a care to Læg, nor the hospitality of that house where preparation was made each day for the entertainment of strangers, and he fared forward swiftly across that plain, and dashed through the Oun Glieda, and never tarried ; and it was evening when he came in sight of the Avon Dia. But, ere he reached the ford, the Lia Macha pulled violently to the right, and with difficulty did Læg restrain her, and drave on to the ford. But when he came to the river he saw the splintered weapons and the trampled shores, and he saw blood upon the stones, and the great pebble that had been displaced by Cuculain, and he drave through the ford, and careered across the smooth plain—but afar he saw the camp of Meave, south-westward, and, smit with sudden fear, he wheeled round the steeds and returned to the ford. Now, about a stone's cast from the ford was there a woman weeping over a new-made grave, and Læg approached her, and inquired concerning the marks of combat at the ford. But she looked up between her tears and torn dishevelled hair, and said:

" There many brave warriors of the host of Meave have been slain by the invincible Cuculain, whose right hand that slew Far-Cu, would that the blessed Shee might grant that it were now between my teeth. To-day he hath slain Fardia Mic Daman of the Fir-bolgs, and men say that he will not survive until the morrow, but that like a wolf pierced with a deadly arrow he will perish alone in his bloody lair."

But Læg trembled when he heard the voice of the woman and saw her countenance disfigured with revenge and sorrow, for she was young, and not uncomely, and he gave the rein to the Lia Macha, endlessly straining forward, having a thought in her eager mind, and he crossed again the Oun Dia, and under the guidance of the divine steed he was borne through the dark alleys of the forest, by many winding and devious ways, bordered with trees and dense impenetrable scrub, a labyrinthine maze, and at length he heard the whinnying of the horses, to which the war-steeds responded, making an echo in the hollow forest, and, on a sudden, lo, a grassy glade open to the stars, and the yellow steeds of Emer Munfada and Rayleen Gall, and one standing between them, as it were a tall and noble warrior, but drooping down with his head.

Then sprang Læg from the chariot, and he ran towards him, for he recognised the form of Cuculain, calling him by his own name, Setanta; but there was no answer from Cuculain, and no smile upon his lips, and he was at first affrighted, but after that looked sorrowfully without recognition upon Læg with wild eyes full of suffering. But Læg uttered a loud and bitter cry, and fell upon the ground, and tore his auburn hair, and he remained at the feet of Cuculain weeping till a third part of the night was passed, grovelling low upon the ground—and the divine steeds, too, of Cuculain were distressed, bowing their splendid heads, and the long fair mane of the Lia

Macha flowed upon the ground, grieving for the noble Cuculain. But after that, Læg arose, still weeping, and he let down the war-car, spreading rugs and skins, and he washed the blood from Cuculain, and bound up his wounds, and took from the other chariot clean linen, and made a bed for Cuculain, and Cuculain obeyed him in all things like a young child, being very gentle and submissive, and Læg took the head of Cuculain and laid it in his breast, the head that all Erin could not abase or dishonour, and he wept anew over Cuculain.

But after this, like a torrent which has burst some compact barrier, the great host of Meave invaded Ulla, and they devastated all Murthemney, and every day there went westward to the Shannon herds of many cattle, and waggons loaded with the spoil of the Ultonians. But they came to the Dûn of Dary, and he only awaited them, for his sons and warriors had fled to Emain Macha, and he girt about him his battle-dress, and took his shield and sword, and stood before the house of the Donn Cooalney; and the noble old man was slain, guarding the trust of the Ultonians, for Mainey Lamgarf slew him, striking him in the neck with his javelin, and it passed quite through, and pinned him to the oaken door. There was the old king transfixed, and his feet were extended before him, and his hands, from which the shield and spear were rudely shaken, hung down limply by his side, and his head drooped beside the murderous javelin, and the blood issued from his mouth—a sight most piteous.

But when the door was opened the Donn Cooalney rushed forth with rage and precipitation, and trampled and gored many of the host of Meave, but in the end he was sent away westward, enclosed in a ring of spearmen, who guarded him, restraining his fury with levelled spears, and many strange tales are told by the bards concerning that bull.

Now, the impetuous Kethern, half-armed, with half-armed warriors, was the first to arrive to the relief of Murthemney, for he awoke dazed out of the deadly swoon, and finding no weapons, he seized a great spit, on which an ox was accustomed to be roasted whole, [and his companions armed themselves in like manner with aught that came to their hand, and they waited not for the hosting at Emain Macha, but came on straight to Murthemney, and flung themselves on the host of Meave. Nevertheless they were repulsed, and many of them slain, yet Kethern himself escaped but in woeful plight, and how he slew the physicians who told him that he would die, or discoursed with too much learning concerning their art, and how he fraternised with Fineen, the wise and hopeful physician from Slieve Few, has been related by the ancient bards and historians of Erin.

But now all the warlike clans of the north were aroused, and wide Ulla roused herself from the fatal stupor, and from every tuath the armed battalions of the Crave Rue came together to their king, to Emain Macha. Came Leairey Bewda, tall and courtly, with deep brows, revolving princely thoughts, the tanist of all Ulla; yet he came not into the sovereignty of the Crave Rue, for his own generous heart destroyed him what time he sprang indignant out of his Dûn to save the life of Æd, an erring bard, and smote his forehead against the brazen lintel. Came Factna Mac Mahoon, deep-hearted, with his stern warriors from Slieve

Few; they glittered not amongst the glittering knights, but it was not easy to escape from them in the day of battle. At night men heard them chanting songs in honour of the Dâda Mōr, and of Macha. But darker browed and more stern, came the battalions of Murthemney, enraged for the slaying of Cuculain—for men said that he had been overtaken by the men of Meave, and slain. They came under the leadership of Fiechna, the brother of Sualtam; but Sualtam was no longer alive, for when the second time he came to Concobar Mac Nessa, and he answered him after the same fashion, no longer able to contain himself with wrath, Sualtam ran from the house; but at the threshold he tripped, and falling, his neck came against the sharp edge of his shield—made razor-sharp to be a weapon as well as a defence—and it cut his neck half through. Thus foolishly died the father of Cuculain. Came Conn Mac Morna, glorious as the dawn, with his brilliant battalions, and Fergus Mac Leda, destined to rule over all the Ultonians. Came Glass and Mainey, and Conairey, pillars of the sovereignty of Concobar over the wild western nations, not yet weaned from the chiefs of Nemedian race, whose capital was Aula Neid, and cemetery the Isle of Towers, in the northern sea, and all the other kings and captains whom Concobar the son of Nessa had established throughout Ulla, to the hosting of their High King at Emain Macha.

After this commenced the great wars of the Tan-bo-Cooalney, aimed at the subjugation of the Red Branch, wide-wasting wars, that lasted many years, bright with battles and many heroic deeds; but bright beyond all shines the name of Cuculain, the son of Sualtam, for his

fame grew until it filled Erin and Alba, and crossed the
Muirnict, and was known to the Clanna Gædil in Espân.
For that high heart the Shee suffered not to be for ever
cast down. Three days and three nights wept Læg beside
his couch, hearing afar the noise of Meave's host wasting
Murthemney; and ever between his tears he spake to
Cuculain of old boyish days, when they were together at
Dûn Dalgan, and of that raid upon the Bregians, when
they carried off Emer, the daughter of Manah, the
haughty bru-fir, and of the honour in which he was
held by the Red Branch, soothing in every way his
troubled spirit, hoping that somewhere through the
clouds of suffering that surrounded the mind of Cuculain, some ray of light and hope might penetrate, to
warm and illumine his dark spirit; but on the third
day, at even, Cuculain sat up, and looked at Læg, and
put his two hands upon his shoulders, and kissed him;
and the Lia Macha came near, and Cuculain put his
hand upon her face. And the same evening Læg heard
voices, and felt strange presences around the son of
Sualtam, and he retired into the shadows of the forest,
cowering amongst the trees. For a swift word had
traversed all Erin, coming upon the cold blasts of the
wind to every fairy rath and glen and sacred hill,
and the ancient plains of tomb and temple, and
with one accord the happy Shee came forth out of
Fairy Land, out of Tiernanōg, where they live in bliss,
consuming the "feast of age." From Wisna, and
Tlatga, and Taylteen; from Cruhane, and Tara, and
Awlin; from Gowra, Knock Ainey, Dûnamarc, and
Bru Liah, Adair, and Lahran, and Oileen Arda Nemed;
from Brugh-na-Boyna, and Tu Inver, and Fionaháh, of

Slieve Few, Slieve Blahma of the Layhees, and Slieve-
na-man Fion of the Osree ; came the Shee of the ancient
Fomoroh out of the west, and the Shee of the Fir-bolgs ;
came Kasár, the hoary queen, paling, melting into the air,
before the growing glory of the Tuatha De Danan ; even
she, though smit to death, wan and faded as the moon
struck by the beams of the rising sun, came with her
waning sovereignty to comfort the guileless Cuculain.

From the Shannon, where the hills are dark above
the waters of the Red Lake, came Bove Derg, endlessly
grieving for his grand-children, the cruelly transformed.
They indeed came not, for the cold waters of the Moyle
detained them, where they wandered swanlike—Æd
and Fiechra and comely Conn, and Finoola, their sister
maternal, though so young. They themselves came
not, but from the north out of the sea, proceeded slow,
sweet fairy music, most heart-piercing, most beautiful.
Came Lear of the Shee Fionaháh, on Slieve Few, whose
were the sweet children. His dominion was over the sea,
and he lorded it over the lawless sea. Came Mananán,
the son of Lear, from his isle, eastward in Muirnict,
traversing the soft waves in his chariot, drawn by fairy
steeds that brake not a bubble nor severed the wave-
crest. Came the warrior queens of the Gæil Bauv, and
Macha, and Moreega, relaxing their stern brows above
the couch of Cuculain, and the three sweet sisters Eire
and Fohla and Banba, whose gentle names are upon Inis
Fail. They met and welcomed the children of Milith,
what time having consumed their ships they marched
inland to subdue the island. Came Brihid, adored by
the singing tribe, and Angus-an-Vroga, dazzling bright,
round whom flew singing-birds, purple-plumed, and no

eye sees them, for they sing in the hearts of youths and maidens. Came Goibnen, the father of craftsmen, and Yeoha Mac -Erc, surnamed Ollav Fohla, and the Dâda Mōr, who ruled over all the Tuatha De Danan, from his green throne above the waters of the Boyne. Came Ogma, the inventor of letters, and Coirpry Kin Kæth, surnamed also Crom and Cruag, "the stooping one" and "the stern," whose altar was upon Mah Slact when the Talkend, cross-bearing, with his clerics, came to Inis Fail, and many more of the Tuatha De Danan came to visit Cuculain that night; but there also came the Fianna of ancient Erin, the most ancient of all before the Fomoroh and the Clanna Nemed, before the paling queen, Kasár, they viewless possessed Inis Fail, honoured widely by the Gæil, and their fame is among the tribute-paying peoples this day. Came Fion, the son of Cool, the serpent-slayer, whose hair was like silver, huge Oscar of the gentle heart, Kaylta Mac Ronan, Diarmait, dusky-haired, pearl-toothed, with light laughter and fearless heart, bald Conan, corpulent, laughter-moving, and Ossian, the warrior-bard. All the blessed Shee throughout Erin came that night to honour the Hound of Murthemney, and Cuculain saw them all plainly, face to face, as a man speaking with his friend, benign countenances and venerable, high hearts made pure and noble by death, out of Fairy Land, where they dwell in bliss, controlling and correcting the minds of the Gæil. And as when to a child weeping in the night, his parents appear with soothing hands and words, so above the mighty Cuculain appeared the blessed Shee, speaking words of comfort and of praise, and Cuculain conversed with the Tuatha De Danan, being noble of heart like themselves. And Læg saw them not, but he felt the awful presence, and crouched back among the shadows, veiling his eyes with his hands, for he feared lest he should he smitten with blindness or struck suddenly dead, seeing with his eyes the blessed Shee. But after this, Cuculain fell into a deep sleep, without a dream, that lasted for the space of a day and a night.